The Rejected Body

FEMINIST PHILOSOPHICAL
REFLECTIONS ON DISABILITY

Susan Wendell

ROUTLEDGE

New York ✦ London

Published in 1996 by

Routledge
29 West 35th Street
New York, NY 10001

Published in Great Britain by

Routledge
11 New Fetter Lane
London EC4P 4EE

Printed in the United States of America

Poem by Barbara Ruth reprinted from *Past, Present and Future Passions* (1987). Collection to be sold to and shared with women only. Available from HerBooks, P.O. Box 7467, Santa Cruz, California, 95061 U.S.A.

A version of chapter 7 appeared in 1993 as "Feminism, Disability and Transcendence of the Body" in *Canadian Woman Studies* 13(4):116–122.

Library of Congress Cataloging-in-Publication Data

Wendell, Susan.
    The rejected body : feminist philosophical reflections on disability / Susan Wendell.
      p.   cm.
    Includes bibliographical references.
    ISBN 0-415-91046-3 (cloth). — ISBN 0-415-91047-1 (pbk.)
    1. Sociology of disability.   2. Body, Human—Social aspects.
    3. Handicapped women.   4. Feminist ethics.   I. Title.
HV1568.W433   1996
362.4'082—dc20
                                          95-51391
                                            CIP

Contents

Acknowledgements

My deepest gratitude goes to my beloved partner, Bob Hadley, who nursed me, did everything for me that I could not do for myself, listened to my anger, depression, and despair in the middle of many nights, set up my computer and taught me to use it, gave me good advice, and, as always, encouraged my work. Anyone who thinks that men cannot nurture should talk to me.

My dear friend and counsellor Joyce Frazee helped me learn to live with long-term illness and preserve my creativity. I am also deeply grateful to Mary Barnes, William Barnes, Barbara Beach, Elliott Gose, Kathy Gose, Cynthia Renwick, and Gordon Renwick for their insights and encouragement, and to my father, Warren Wendell, my stepmother, Marjorie Wendell, and my sisters, Lynn Wendell Foy, Elizabeth Wendell, and Catherine Wendell for their unflagging moral support. Thank you also to Jennifer Menard, whose practical help enables me to work, and to Valerie Oglov, who assisted me with proofreading the manuscript.

I want to express my appreciation to Drs. Dorothy McWatters, Marie Gribble, and Anne Junker, who believed me, gave me a diagnosis, and supported my efforts to recover and then adjust in the early years of my illness. I am also very grateful to Drs. Ellen Coburn and Lai Na Ho, and Nurse-practitioner Donelle Clarke, who help me to live with illness now. I have learned the inestimable value of medical professionals who listen carefully to patients.

The Canadian Society for Women in Philosophy has always been a source of inspiration and strength to me, and my colleagues in CSWIP stood by me in sickness and in health. I particularly want to thank Susan Sherwin, the late Winnie Tomm, and Barbara Secker for their enthusiastic encouragement of my work on disability.

Many friends and acquaintances have discussed disability issues with me and supported this project, for which I am very grateful. Ron Amundson was especially generous with his own ideas and critical responses to my work. I also want to thank Karen van Biesen, Bonnie Burnside, Ellen Frank, Bonnie Klein, Joan Meister, Carolyn Porter, and Anita Silvers.

Colleagues and students in the Department of Women's Studies at Simon Fraser University have not merely tolerated my ventures into a new field of teaching and research—disability studies—but welcomed it. I give special thanks to Meredith Kimball, Sandy Shreve, and Mary Lynn Stewart for their personal support. I am also grateful to the department for the timing of my research leave in 1995, which enabled me to finish the manuscript on time, and to Simon Fraser University for a sabbatical year in 1992–93.

Introduction

This book is a feminist philosophical discussion of disability. It focusses on some of the issues concerning disability that interest me most. These issues are theoretical in the sense that they cannot be settled solely by discovering facts about the world, but they are also practical in that they have practical manifestations in the lives of people with and without disabilities. The book is not written primarily for an audience of professional philosophers (although I would like professional philosophers to read it); I have tried to make it accessible to any educated person interested in the issues it discusses.

I will begin with a short account of my own disability and my discovery of disability politics, which I hope will give the reader a sense of who I am and what my relevant experiences are, as well as some personal and social context for what follows. Then I will offer some warnings about the limitations of the book, and some explanations of choices I made in writing it, including choices about language. Finally, I will give a brief overview of the chapters which follow this introduction.

Personal Beginnings and Political Discoveries

In February of 1985, I was healthy. I was teaching philosophy and women's studies, coordinating the women's studies programme, working with graduate students, writing academic articles, and enjoying the company of my friends. I was also exercising regularly, eating reasonably well, and taking my vitamins. One weekend, I came down with what I thought was the worst flu I had ever experienced—high fever, coughing, nausea, light-sensitivity, perceptual distortions, and intense pain in my joints and muscles. I went to bed. A week later, the fever was down and I felt somewhat better, but the pain and perceptual distortions were still there, and—ominously—I was exhausted and getting weaker. A month later, I was virtually bedridden and could not walk a block; the effort of a telephone call soaked my nightgown with sweat. Six months later, on a good day, I could write a letter, shower, and wash my hair; I spent my days on the couch or in bed and still could not walk a block. A year after I fell ill, I had managed, by a tremendous effort of will and gentle, gradual exercise, to condition myself to walking five blocks on a good day. In January of 1987, almost two years after falling ill, I returned to teaching half-time at the university. Reaching that point was the most difficult thing I have ever done.

I was very lucky in my doctors. My primary-care physician recognized at once that something was seriously wrong. Blood tests suggested a viral infection. When she could not make a more specific diagnosis, she sent me to a specialist in infectious diseases. She never trivialized my illness and never indulged in speculative psychoanalysis. The specialist in infectious diseases, and the immunologist to whom *she* sent me, found abnormalities in my blood. At first I was diagnosed with acute infectious mononucleosis, then, when I was still very ill after six months, with chronic Epstein-Barr virus syndrome (a diagnosis which is now believed to be wrong, since the EB virus is not the culprit, although there are very high levels of antibodies to it in many people with my disease), and finally with myalgic encephalomyelitis (as it is called in England, Canada, and the other Commonwealth countries), or chronic fatigue immune dysfunction syndrome (as it is called in the United States).

At the time I became ill, ME was virtually unknown in North America, although some English doctors had been familiar with it since the 1950s, when there was an epidemic of it at the Royal Free Hospital (discussed in chapter 5). The history of my own illness has coincided with the gradual discovery of ME/CFIDS by the rest of the world. Among researchers who work on ME, it is generally believed that there was an epidemic in the U.S. in the late 1970s to early 1980s, and in Canada around 1984–86. It is now recognized as a disease syndrome by the Centers for Disease Control and as a neurological disorder by the World Health Organization. Some people with ME seem to recover completely from it, after months or even years of illness. Some adults and children of both sexes remain bedridden indefinitely. Many, like myself, recover partially from a devastating early stage of illness but continue to have significantly disabling symptoms.

I still have constant muscle pain, muscle weakness (especially in my arms), periods of profound fatigue (much more total and exhausting than any fatigue I experienced when healthy), overlapping periods of dizziness and/or nausea and/or depression, headaches lasting for several days, and intermittent problems with short-term memory, especially verbal recall. To function well, I need to sleep ten hours every night and spend several hours lying down every day. I use a luggage cart to carry my books and briefcase. I now work three-quarter time at all the usual duties and pursuits of a professor, but otherwise live a quiet, rather careful life.

My struggles now are not primarily with the disease. After ten years it has become a given, a somewhat unpredictable limitation around which I must plan as best I can. I try to commit myself to doing only as much on any given day as I could do if I were going through a bad period of illness, since on any given day I might be in an ME valley, but I make long-term commitments based on what I can manage on an average day. I adhere faithfully to routines of acupuncture, Chinese herbal medicine, and therapeutic touch, and I take pain medications and rest breaks, but my life does not revolve around the disease as it once did.

My struggles now are primarily social and psycho-ethical. I live in the world of the healthy (or fairly healthy). I do not 'look sick' or 'sound sick,' as people tell me all the time, and I think only those who know me well can see when I am having a hard time with fatigue, nausea, or pain. It is probably sometimes obvious that I am having difficulty finding words or remembering names, and my colleagues and students are good at supplying the missing pieces, but this is a weakness to which many of us who are over forty-five are susceptible. In short, the disability caused by my chronic illness is not readily apparent to most of the people around me. Moreover I love my work, and I am usually fairly cheerful and easily excited by ideas.

A person with a disability (or illness) that is not readily apparent, who has a social position with some prestige and power, who earns a good income, who is creative and productive, happily partnered, and obviously enjoying life, violates just about every stereotype about people with disabilities (or illnesses). It is hard for others to accept that anything is really wrong, and, in a sense, nothing is, because a disability or illness is like any other difficulty with which, or around which, a person can live a good life. But illness must be accommodated, by me and sometimes by others. I need other people to accept my physical limitations, to take my word for it that I cannot do more than I am already committed to, or that when I say I need to rest, I do, or that I had to spend the previous day in bed. Some people offer such acceptance readily, others greet every statement of limitation with scepticism, and most need to be reminded from time to time. How can I convince or remind them without seeming to complain or to ask for sympathy, without embarrassing myself and them, without risking the accusation that I simply do not want to carry my share of the load (to which I could only reply with more of the same information about my limitations)? Adding to the difficulty, the subculture of feminists of my generation is one of self-sacrifice. Good feminists, like good women everywhere, are supposed to give 'til it hurts; everyone is supposed to feel exhausted and overworked, so why should I be the exception? 'We' don't have time to be ill, to coddle ourselves.

It is not surprising that my greatest psycho-ethical struggle is with guilt. Sometimes I feel guilty towards everyone—my students and colleagues for not being able to do more work, the community of women activists with disabilities for not being able to contribute more time, my friends for hardly ever having the energy to do things with them, my family for not writing or visiting more, my partner for being tired or in pain during so much of our time together.

Social analysis helps a lot. I have learned from other people with disabilities that most non-disabled people cannot wrap their minds around the possibility that someone can be disabled or ill and also work productively, have intimate relationships, or be happy. People without disabilities tend to assume that a person with a disability is unable to participate in most of the life activities they consider important. Thus they infer that someone who can work at all cannot be significantly disabled. Overcoming the common assumptions about disability is a long-term project in which I have found many brilliant women and men engaged. Their struggle is now my struggle.

The story of my experience of illness and disability is told throughout this book, wherever my own experience contributed importantly to my thinking about a subject, and often where it is relevant to illustrating a point. My story has been very much affected by other people's stories. After about nine months of illness, the specialist I saw regularly told me there was nothing more she could do for me; I was still very ill. I was by turns frightened and despairing. Some weeks later, I had the first hopeful inkling that I might be able to live well, even if I never recovered, when I saw a woman interviewed on television who had had severe arthritis for more than twenty years. I remember that she said, "The disease is not the problem; living is the problem."[1] At that moment I realized that people with disabilities already knew what I needed to learn, and I began to read what they had written.

I have worked for more than twenty years in the area of feminist social and political theory. The more I learned about other people's experiences of disability and reflected upon my own, the more connections I saw between feminist analyses of gender as socially constructed from biological differences between females and males, and my emerging understanding of disability as socially constructed from biological differences between the disabled and the non-disabled. In addition, I was increasingly impressed by the knowledge people with disabilities have about living with bodily suffering and limitation and about how their cultures treat rejected aspects of bodily life. It was clear to me that this knowledge did not inform theorizing about the body by non-disabled feminists and that feminist theory of the body was consequently both incomplete and skewed toward healthy, non-disabled experience. I began to do some feminist theorizing about disability.

In 1990 I developed an undergraduate course on women and disability, which I have since taught several times. The students in that course, many of whom have disabilities, have taught me a great deal more. I am personally and intellectually interested in the lives of women with disabilities, and in gender differences in both the experience of disability and the treatment of people with disabilities. Nevertheless, this is not a book about women and disability. There are several excellent anthologies on that topic, including: Rooney and Israel 1985; Browne, Connors and Stern 1985; Saxton and Howe 1987; Fine and Asch 1988; Driedger and Gray 1992; and Stewart, Percival and Epperly 1992. This book is, however, very much informed by the writings and conversation of women with disabilities. It is also informed by the writings of non-disabled feminist women and the writings of men who have perspectives on disability or on the body that I find illuminating.

Some Limitations and Explanations

I focus on physical disability here, both because I know much more about physical disabilities than I do about mental disabilities, and because I am particularly interested in attitudes towards the body. I know that many people with disabilities have both physical and mental disabilities, and I am interested in mental disability, of which I have some personal experience; but since it raises some different, additional issues, I discuss mental disability specifically only a few times in the book. I have tried, however, not to make any unqualified generalizations about disability without questioning whether they apply to mental disabilities.

It should go without saying, but I want to emphasize that I do not speak for people with disabilities, or women with disabilities, or feminist philosophers with disabilities, or fifty-year-old Anglo-German-American-Canadian disabled feminist philosophers born in Brooklyn (well, maybe). In my opinion, no one speaks for anyone else unless s/he is explicitly authorized to do so by those being represented. However, I recognize that the claim to speak only for myself does not relieve me of responsibility not to overgeneralize on the basis of my experience and not to construe issues narrowly in the interest of promoting my own viewpoint. I have tried to present and consider a wide diversity of experiences of disability in the text, as well as many points of actual and possible disagreement among those of us who think about the issues it addresses. In addition, I believe that speaking only for myself does not reduce my responsibility for the effect of my words on people who read them or on people who might be touched by them indirectly. These are early days in the development of philosophy of disability. Since relatively few voices have been heard on the subjects I raise, I feel a particular responsibility to invite further conversation about them, rather than trying to have the last word. Thus, although I hope I have made my own views, and my reasons for them, apparent throughout the text, I have tried to raise questions and open the subjects to further thought and discussion, rather than closing them with my own opinions.

It is in the nature of philosophy (and philosophers) to generalize—to try to discern and describe a significant pattern in the details. Philosophy about human beings and human lives always carries the danger of overgeneralizing. Refusing to generalize avoids that danger only at the cost of limiting one's thought to meditation on an individual, usually oneself. I have attempted to steer a course between false universalizing on the one hand and unjust exclusion through over-particularity on the other. I doubt that I have always succeeded. If we are to philosophize at all, we must take some risks and hope that others will correct our mistakes.

I have not solved the problems of using "I," "we," and "they" to my satisfaction. "I" seems to personalize too much in some contexts, as though "I" take possession of shared experience that has been described by others as well. "We" seems to speak for everyone included in the "we." Sometimes it is ambiguous who is included, and sometimes it may be presumptuous to include either myself or others. For example, would other people with disabilities include themselves in my "we," or me in theirs? Yet sometimes I do not want to exclude myself or others, and sometimes I want to express my identification with a particular group of people. At other times I want to use "we" persuasively, to invite the reader, disabled or non-disabled, to include her/himself, or just to think along with me. Of course, using "we" can be an abrogation of the author's responsibility for what s/he is saying, or a glossing over of possible disagreement, and I have tried to guard against these. "They" presents other problems—problems of tone and attitude. It seems to objectify or at least to separate those written about from the writer, increasing their 'Otherness' in relation to the writer. The best solution I could find is to use all three, attempting to create a balance in tone while trying to avoid the appropriation of "I," the presumption of "we," and the distancing of "they."

I have quoted extensively from academic books and articles, but also from popular books, newspapers, magazines, and newsletters. Much, probably most, of the truth about disability is not to be found in academic writing, so I take fruitful ideas and informative descriptions of experience seriously wherever I find them. When I know that someone has already said something as well as, or better than, I could say it, I have quoted rather than paraphrasing it; for me, this is a way of respecting other people's voices.

Throughout the text, I use single quotation marks as scare quotes, that is, to draw the reader's attention to concepts I question or to uses of language about which I have reservations. For example, I use scare quotes around 'the Other' (a concept discussed in chapter 3) to indicate that, while the concept is a recognized way of thinking about people who are different from oneself, 'the Other' is not a way of referring to people which I accept or take for granted. I reserve double quotation marks for simple quotation of things people have said or written. I use "[sic]" in quoted passages when I notice the person I am quoting using language that is not inclusive or not respectful of the people to whom it refers.

A Brief Overview of the Book

I begin in chapter 1 by asking who is disabled, which is not as easily answered as it might seem. I consider definitions of disability, including the highly influential United Nations definitions of "impairment," "disability," and "handicap," arguing that neither impairment nor disability can be defined purely in biomedical terms, because the biological and the social are interactive in creating (or preventing) both. I also examine the controversial question whether people with illnesses and people experiencing the frailties and limitations of old age should be considered disabled. I then discuss who defines disability and for what purposes, and how their purposes may affect the definitions. Finally I turn to issues of identification—who identifies her/himself as disabled, who is identified by other people as disabled, and how these may be in conflict—and some political issues of disability identity, including whether "people with disabilities" is a meaningful category.

Chapter 2 is focussed upon the social and cultural factors that, in interaction with biological differences, create disability. These factors include social conditions that cause or fail to prevent damage to people's bodies, social expectations of performance, the physical and social organization of societies on the basis of a young, non-disabled, 'ideally shaped,' healthy adult male paradigm of citizens, the failure or unwillingness to create ability among people who do not fit the paradigm, cultural representations and failures of representation, and the cultural meanings of disability. I discuss how disability could be socially deconstructed and consider some obstacles to its deconstruction.

In chapter 3 I examine the stigma of disability and illness, beginning with Goffman's famous study of stigma. I consider the concept of 'the Other,' developed in feminist theorizing, as a way of understanding the social position of people with disabilities, look at some of the symbolic meanings of disabilities and illnesses, and describe some consequences of being 'the Other' in this particular way. I then turn to the possibility of regarding disability as a neutral or valuable form of difference that is, among other things, a source of knowledge. I discuss the standpoint-epistemology question in relation to people with disabilities—whether having a disability gives a person access to a less distorted and more complete perspective on certain issues—in the light of recent criticisms of feminist standpoint epistemologies. I also discuss some political issues among people with disabilities centring around the question whether to emphasize similarities to the non-disabled or differences from them, and some disputes about language—what to call ourselves and what changes in linguistic usage to promote. Finally, I consider the question: If we value the differences of people with disabilities (as I do), what implications does that have for efforts to prevent or cure disabilities?

Chapter 4 is concerned with the idealization and objectification of the body in the commercial-media-soaked societies of North America. These create demands that we control and attempt to perfect our bodies, which in turn create rejection, shame, and fear concerning both failures to control the body and deviations from body ideals, which in turn contribute to the stigmatization and 'Otherness' of people with disabilities. Refusal to come to terms with the full reality of bodily life, including those aspects of it that are rejected culturally, leads people to embrace the myth of control, whose essence is the belief that it is possible, by means of human actions, to have the bodies we want and to avoid illness, disability, and death. I examine various contemporary versions of the myth of control, including those of scientific Western medicine, those of some alternative therapeutic practices, various versions of mind-over-body, and some theories about how people 'make themselves' ill or disabled by mismanaging their lives, their psyches, or their spirits. I discuss the burdens of blame and guilt that are fostered by these versions of the myth and the widespread, profound reluctance to admit that bad things happen to people who do not deserve them, or seek them, or risk them, or fail to take care of themselves. I do not advocate giving up all attempts to control the body or abandoning all aspects of the myth of control, but I do discuss how they might be changed to the benefit of people with and without disabilities.

In chapter 5 I discuss some of the consequences of the cognitive and social authority of scientific Western medicine to describe our bodies in the societies where it holds sway. This authority affects how we experience our bodies, contributing its objectifying perspective to the alienation already fostered by other aspects of commercial cultures. It affects how a society describes our experiences and validates or invalidates them, adding the burden of epistemic invalidation to many people's experiences of illness and disability. It also affects how a society supports or fails to support our bodily suffering and struggles, for people who are ill or disabled without a medical diagnosis are not eligible for social programmes and are frequently abandoned by friends and family. The authority of medicine shapes and limits, through its effects on the flow of communication about bodily experience, what our culture knows about the human body. It also profoundly affects the relationship of medical practitioners to patients and the quality of medical care. Those medical practitioners with the most authority tend to measure their success by the 'objective' state of the patient's body and to regard death as their greatest failure, while patients are more likely to measure a healer's success by the quality of their subjective experiences and to consider medicine's greatest failures to be unrecognized, unsupported, meaningless, or hopeless suffering. I conclude by pointing out that philosophers of biomedical ethics have tended not to question the authority of medicine and to adopt medicine's preoccupation with life-and-death issues. I give reasons for hoping that the emerging field of feminist medical ethics will produce a critique of medicine that speaks to the concerns of people with disabilities and people with unrecognized or incurable illnesses.

In chapter 6 I argue that the experiences and interests of both people with disabilities and those who care for people with disabilities are vitally relevant to the projects and issues of feminist ethics, including the attempt to develop an ethic of care and to balance it with a morality of justice, the critical re-examination of the ethical ideals of autonomy and independence, and feminist ethical approaches to abortion, euthanasia, and health care reform. By discussing the analyses and concerns of people who have some experience with disability, especially those with feminist perspectives, I attempt to show how they must be included in any adequate treatment of these projects and issues. I maintain that feminist ethics needs the insights of people with disabilities, that people with disabilities need feminist ethics, that some people involved in disability ethics and politics are already practicing feminist ethics, and that more feminist ethicists should be practicing disability ethics.

Chapter 7 is devoted to what might seem like an esoteric subject—transcendence of the body. In fact, for many people with disabilities, it is a practical matter of immediate daily concern. Ideas of transcending the body have generally been rejected by feminists, partly in reaction to philosophies and religions that derogate the body (especially women's bodies) and partly because feminist theorizing about the body has not fully confronted the experience of bodily suffering. I describe some strategies for living with pain, sickness, and physical limitation gathered from my own experience and the writings of other people with disabilities, and argue that a more complete feminist understanding of the body might include some concept of transcendence.

1

Who Is Disabled?
Defining Disability

The question of how we should define disability is not merely the beginning of an analytic exercise. We encounter the problem of definition as soon as we take an interest in disability. For example, how many people have disabilities? Estimates of the incidence of disability worldwide and within countries vary greatly among the estimators, because not only methods of gathering information about disabilities, but also understandings of what constitutes disability, vary greatly among those gathering the information. Questions of definition arise in countless practical situations, influence social policies, and determine outcomes that profoundly affect the lives of people with disabilities.

Definitions of disability officially accepted by government bureaucracies and social service agencies determine people's legal and practical entitlement to many forms of assistance, where assistance is available. This may include economic help for such purposes as: education, training, and retraining; obtaining equipment, such as wheelchairs for basic mobility or computers for basic communication; modifying a home or a vehicle to enable a person with a disability to use it; hiring assistants to help with bodily maintenance and household tasks; even obtaining medical supplies such as medications and bandages. For people with disabilities who are unemployed, it includes the basic support to buy food and shelter. It also includes eligibility for accessible housing and special forms of transportation, and even for such seemingly minor (but actually major) means of access as a disabled parking sticker.

Socially accepted definitions of disability determine the recognition of disability by friends, family members, and co-workers. Recognition of a person's disability by the people s/he is closest to is important not only for receiving their help and understanding when it is needed, but for receiving the acknowledgement and confirmation of her/his reality, so essential for keeping a person socially and psychologically anchored in a community. It is not uncommon for friends and even family members to desert a person who has debilitating symptoms that remain undiagnosed. They may insist that the ill person is faking, or mentally ill and unwilling to get appropriate treatment. People whose disability is unrecognized are frequently pressured to keep up a pretense of normality, to continue to work as if nothing were wrong, and/or to undergo unnecessary psychiatric treatment.

Definitions of disability are important to those who are organizing people with disabilities for political purposes, for example, to press for fuller recognition of their rights, for increased accessibility to public places, or for better opportunities to work. There have been struggles within political groups of people with disabilities, especially in recent years, to include more categories of people. For example, people with AIDS and with debilitating chronic illnesses like ME fought within disability groups for the recognition that they too are disabled, share similar needs and struggles, and suffer similar forms of insult, discrimination, distrust, and exclusion.

Definitions of disability affect people's self-identity. Recognizing yourself as disabled and identifying with other people who are disabled and learning about their experiences can all contribute to understanding and interpreting your own experiences, and to knowing that you are not alone with problems that you may have believed were unique to you. But being identified as disabled also carries a significant stigma in most societies and usually forces the person so identified to deal with stereotypes and unrealistic attitudes and expectations that are projected on to her/him as a member of this stigmatized group.[1]

A careful effort to define disability can clarify our conceptions of disability and reveal misconceptions and false stereotypes. For example, for many people the paradigmatic disabled person is a young, healthy, paraplegic man who has been injured in an accident but continues to be athletic, or a young, healthy, professionally successful blind woman who has 'overcome' her handicap with education. In fact, arthritis, rheumatism, heart and respiratory disease, stroke, Parkinsonism, hypertension, and epilepsy are major causes of disability in Canada, the United States, and Great Britain, and many people with disabilities in these countries are also ill and/or old (Health and Welfare Canada and Statistics Canada 1981; Statistics Canada 1986 and 1991; Pope and Tarlov 1991; LaPlante 1991; Bury 1978).

The United Nations Definitions

The United Nations definition of disability (UN 1983: I.c. 6–7) is widely used and tends to be favoured by disability activists and other advocates of greater opportunities for people with disabilities (Wright 1983, 10–12; Fine and Asch 1988, 5–6). It offers the following definitions of and distinctions among impairment, disability, and handicap:

> "Impairment: Any loss or abnormality of psychological, physiological, or anatomical structure or function. Disability: Any restriction or lack (resulting from an impairment) of ability to perform an activity in the manner or within the range considered normal for a human being. Handicap: A disadvantage for a given individual, resulting from an impairment or disability, that limits or prevents the fulfillment of a role that is normal, depending on age, sex, social and cultural factors, for that individual."
>
> Handicap is therefore a function of the relationship between disabled persons and their environment. It occurs when they encounter cultural, physical or social barriers which prevent their access to the various systems of society that are available to other citizens. Thus, handicap is the loss or limitation of opportunities to take part in the life of the community on an equal level with others. (UN 1983: I.c. 6–7)

There are two things I like about the UN definitions. First, they are general enough to include many conditions that are not always recognized by the general public as disabling, for example, debilitating chronic illnesses, such as Crohn's disease, which limit people's activities but do not necessarily cause any immediately observable disability. I shall return to this aspect of the definitions later in this chapter. Second, the definition of handicap explicitly recognizes the possibility that the primary causes of a disabled person's inability to do certain things may be social; they may be lack of opportunities, lack of accessibility, lack of services, poverty or discrimination, and they often are. It is this latter aspect of the definitions that makes them appealing to advocates for people with disabilities.

Nevertheless, there are several criticisms I have of the UN definitions that may throw some light on the nature of disability and the problems associated with defining it. First, the definitions of "impairment" and "disability" seem to imply that there is some universal, biologically or medically describable standard of structure, function, and human physical ability. As we shall see, there would be important advantages to employing some universal standards, should we be able to agree on them. Yet surely what are "normal" structure, function, and ability to perform an activity all depend to some degree on the society in which the standards of normality are generated. For example, I, who can walk about half a mile several times a week but not more, am not significantly disabled with respect to walking in my society, where most people are not expected to walk further than that in the course of their daily activities. But in some societies, in Eastern Africa for example, where women normally walk several miles twice a day to obtain water for the household, I would be much more severely disabled. It is not just that I would be considered more disabled in those societies but that I would in fact need constant assistance to carry on the most basic life activities. What is normal ability in urban Western Canada is neither normal nor adequate ability in rural Kenya.

Failure to recognize that standards of structure, function, and ability are socially relative could be dangerous to people with disabilities. If the standards employed are generated by people in highly industrialized societies, many people in less industrialized societies and in rural areas where there are fewer technological resources will be considered non-disabled when they are in fact in need of special assistance to survive and participate in life where they are.

On the other hand, definitions of impairment and disability could be relativized too much to some societies. If most people in a particular society are chronically undernourished, that society's standards of "normal" functioning might become so low as to mask the widespread disability among its citizens that starvation is causing. Another particularly disturbing example is the genital mutilation of girls. In societies where the majority of people approves of the practice and the vast majority of girls has been mutilated, the girl who has a clitoris (and other external sexual organs, depending on the form of mutilation practiced) is considered abnormal. Yet because genital mutilation often causes severe infections, shock, hemorrhage, and chronic physical and mental health problems, in addition to reducing or destroying some women's capacities for sexual pleasure, I cannot believe that the rest of the world should accept uncritically those societies' standards of normal structure and function for women. To do so seems a betrayal of the girls and women whose lives, health, and sexuality are endangered by mutilation.[2]

Iris Marion Young's statement that "women in sexist society are physically handicapped,"[3] and her arguments in support of it present another strong challenge to the idea that culturally relative standards of physical structure, function, and ability should be accepted. Young argues that lack of opportunities and encouragement to develop bodily abilities, rigid standards of feminine bodily comportment, and constant objectification and threat of invasion of their bodies combine to deprive most women in sexist societies of their full physical potential. In these societies, a "normal" woman is expected to lack strength, skills, and the range of movement that "normal" men are expected to possess and that she might have developed had she grown up in a less sexist society. If we accept these standards uncritically, we will tend to overlook the ways that those societies create physical disadvantages for women.

Thus there seem to be problems both in denying the social and cultural relativity of impairment and disability (as used in the UN definitions) and in accepting it. The UN definitions seem to recognize the relativity of standards of ability while attempting to universalize them by using the phrase "in the manner or within the range considered normal for a human being." Unfortunately, that does not amount to a practical recognition of the relativity of disability. A woman in Kenya who can walk only as much as I can will still not be considered disabled with respect to walking, because her ability falls within the worldwide *range* considered normal. Nor does it universalize standards enough to create the basis for criticizing societies whose standards of health and good functioning fall too low for some or all of their members. The standards of such societies could still be seen to fall, by definition, in the "range considered normal for a human being."

Philosopher Ron Amundson suggests that we define disabilities as "the absences of basic personal abilities." (Amundson 1992, 108) "Basic personal abilities" enable us to perform such actions as "moving one's arms, standing, seeing and hearing things in the environment," and also to remain alert for several hours a day and to remain active without unreasonable fatigue. The actions they enable us to perform are "biomedically typical of the human species (suitably relativized to age and perhaps sex)." This is an attractive attempt to universalize the concept of disability via an appeal to common sense (with some additional appeal to biomedical standards). Yet the idea of a basic personal ability seems less clear when we ask,

"How well?" or "How much?" How well must one see or hear in order to have the basic personal ability? How long must one be able to stand or how fast must one be able to walk? Is running a basic personal ability? I find myself unable to answer these questions without first asking about the circumstances of the person whose abilities are being discussed. How much ability is basic, like how much ability is normal, seems to depend on how much is necessary to perform the most common tasks of daily living in a particular physical and social environment. For example, far more strength and stamina are necessary to live where there is no water on tap, where it gets cold and there is no central heating, where a fire has to be built every time a meal is cooked, and all the clothes are washed by hand. In such an environment I would be considered a helpless invalid, and indeed I would lack most of the personal abilities I would need.

Appeal to what is biomedically typical of the human species would not seem to help settle the question, since people who are biomedically identical have different personal abilities, and people who have the same personal abilities are biomedically different. Eyeglasses, hearing aids, good prostheses, and other products of medical technology optimize the abilities of some people, while others, who have identical physical conditions but do not have access to the technology, lack the same abilities. People who use strong but completely effective corrective lenses may have the same personal ability to see as people with uncorrected good eyesight; do we want to call them or their seeing biomedically identical? Of course, in asking whether a person is disabled we could consider only whether a person's biology is typical of the human species, but Amundson would not like that, since, as he points out, atypical and even pathological biology is not necessarily disabling, that is, it does not necessarily affect a person's abilities adversely. I think we are stuck with the problem that the question of what abilities are basic, like that of what abilities are normal, is to a significant extent relative to the environment in which the abilities are exercised.

This is not the same point as claiming that a person's physical structure, function, or ability may or may not be *disadvantageous* in a given environment. Like the authors of the UN definitions and others (e.g., see Wright 1983), Amundson distinguishes "disability" from "handicap." He defines "handicap" as "an opportunity loss sustained by an individual resulting from the interaction between that individual's (biomedical) disability and the specific environment in which the individual's opportunities exist" (Amundson 1992, 111). So, applying this to my most recent example, I might lack most of the basic personal abilities required in my environment, but I still might live quite well, participate actively in my community, and have many valuable opportunities if I could buy the services most people perform for themselves. For reasons I will explain shortly, I like Amundson's definition of "handicap" better than that offered by the United Nations.

Nevertheless, we still need some recognition of the relativity of standards of structure, function, and ability to the customs and conditions of different societies so that what the UN calls "impairment" and "disability" will be concepts that are useful and accurate in identifying those individuals who may need adjustments in their environment or direct assistance in order to survive and participate in their societies. On the other hand, we also need some cross-cultural comparisons and criticism of societies' standards of structure, function, and ability to perform activities. Such comparisons could contribute to raising the standards and, eventually, the levels of health in a society and help to protect people whose ill health or disability might serve the interests of others within their society.

My other criticisms of the UN definitions concern how they define "handicap." Because that definition refers to "a role that is normal, depending on age, sex, social and cultural factors, for that individual," the definitions imply that women can be disabled, but not handicapped, by being unable to do things which are not part of the "normal" roles of women in their societies. Thus, for example, if it is not considered essential to a woman's role in a given society that she be able to read, then a blind woman who is not provided with education in Braille or good alternatives to printed material is not handicapped by that lack of assistance, according to these definitions. In general, where the expectations for women's participation in social and cultural life are considerably lower than they are for men, disabled women's opportunities will be severely constrained, and the UN has, through its own definitions, robbed itself of the ability to criticize the circumstances in which many disabled women live.

Moreover, disability in women often goes unrecognized and rehabilitation of women is often minimal because of the expectation that women need only be able to function well enough to perform household duties (Fine and Asch 1988; Russo and Jansen 1988; Driedger and Gray 1992). On the other hand, because women's unpaid work in the home (and in volunteer activities) is not publicly valued, and because disability is still defined in many places as the inability to earn wages, women's inabilities to perform their traditional unpaid labour often go unrecognized as disability (Reisine and Fifield 1988).

In addition, the UN definitions suggest that we can be disabled, but not handicapped, by the normal process of aging, since although we may lose some ability, we are not "handicapped" unless we cannot fulfill roles that are normal for our age. Yet the fates of old people and of people with disabilities tend to be linked in a society because aging is disabling. A society that provides few resources to allow disabled people to participate in its activities will be likely to marginalize all people with disabilities, including the old, and to define the appropriate roles of old people as very limited, thus disadvantaging them. I think the UN should recognize that old people can be handicapped unnecessarily by their societies, but its definitions seem to prevent that recognition.

Realizing that aging is disabling helps non-disabled people to see that people with disabilities are not 'Other,' that they are really themselves at a later time. Unless we die suddenly, we are all disabled eventually. Most of us will live part of our lives with bodies that hurt, that move with difficulty or not at all, that deprive us of activities we once took for granted, or that others take for granted—bodies that make daily life a physical struggle. We need understandings of disability and handicap that do not support a paradigm of humanity as young and healthy. Encouraging everyone to acknowledge, accommodate, and identify with a wide range of physical conditions is ultimately the road to self-acceptance as well as the road to increasing the opportunities of those who are disabled now.

Ron Amundson objects to Norman Daniels's classifying the disabled with the group Daniels calls the "frail elderly," that is, those who, according to Daniels, are experiencing a normal reduction in biomedical functioning associated with aging. Amundson says of this: "To the extent that frailty and opportunity reduction is a natural consequence of aging, classifying disability with age-frailty again falsely depicts handicaps as a natural and expected part of human existence" (Amundson 1992, 115).

I appreciate Amundson's concern that grouping the "frail elderly" together with nonelderly people with disabilities will lead most people to assume that the opportunities of the latter are reduced by nature and not by the failures of society. But I prefer challenging the underlying assumption about what is natural to pressing the distinction between the two groups. It is not obvious to me that the reduction of opportunities experienced by the elderly are any more attributable to nature than the reduction of opportunities experienced by nonelderly people with disabilities.[4] True, there may be many physical feats they will never accomplish again, but this is also true of nonelderly people with disabilities, and it does not imply for either group that their opportunities to do other things must be diminished. In fact, many elderly people who used to take too many limitations on their activities for granted now take advantage of improvements in accessibility, such as ramps and lowered curbs, that were made with nonelderly people with disabilities in mind. I imagine that if we did not construct our environment to fit a young adult, non-disabled, male paradigm of humanity, many obstacles to nonelderly people with disabilities would not exist.[5]

When disability is carefully distinguished from the expected frailties of old age, we lose the main benefit of the insight that aging is disabling. That insight enables non-disabled people to realize that they are temporarily non-disabled, and that in turn enables them to see that it is in their own direct interest to structure society so that people with disabilities have good opportunities to participate in every aspect of social life. Therefore, I do not think that for most social and political purposes it is a good idea to make distinctions among disabilities according to whether they were brought on by aging.[6] It is partly for this reason, and partly because it does not relativize handicaps to sex roles, that I prefer Amundson's less qualified definition of "handicap" to the UN definition.

Is Illness Disability?

Amundson proposes that we make a strong distinction between illness and disability. Although he defines "disabilities" as "absences of basic personal abilities," which would seem to apply to the conditions of many people who are ill, he says : "In paradigm cases of disability, a blind man or a paraplegic woman require nothing special in the way of medical care," and "Unlike ill people, disabled people are not (typically) globally incapacitated *except insofar as the environment helps to make them so*" (Amundson 1992, 21, 22). Amundson has two purposes in distinguishing illness and disability. First, he wants to correct a common mistaken impression, sometimes encountered in the literature of medical ethics, that people with disabilities require extraordinary medical care. His second and major concern is to change the widespread false belief that people with disabilities are "globally incapacitated" by their physical conditions. He believes that "the social devaluation of people with disabilities derives in large part from the image of the globally incapacitated disabled person" (Amundson 1992, 22).

How concerned should we be to distinguish disability from chronic illness? From life-threatening illness (such as AIDS or cancer)?[7] Of course, even when chronic or life-threatening, illness need not always be disabling, and it may be useful to distinguish those who have some disability due to illness from those who do not, such as people with epilepsy whose seizures are completely controlled by medication or people with multiple sclerosis (MS) whose disease is in remission and therefore presents no disabling symptoms during a given period of time (always keeping in mind that they may nevertheless share in the handicapping social stigma of other people with 'imperfect' or devalued bodies).

It is also true that many people with disabilities are healthy. Nevertheless, I think Amundson's paradigm cases of disability may lead him to underestimate the proportion of people with disabilities who are either disabled by what we would all recognize as illness or ill as a consequence of disability. If we consider that many more people in North America are disabled by arthritis, heart or respiratory disease, or diabetes[8] than by blindness or paraplegia, we are compelled to adopt very different paradigms of disability. In addition, some disabilities not caused by disease, such as paraplegia and quadriplegia due to spinal cord injury, have significant tendencies to cause health problems, including chronic pain, circulatory difficulties leading to skin breakdown, and recurring bladder infections (Morris 1989; Murphy 1990, 178).

Perhaps most important, we must recognize that, like healthy people with disabilities, most people who have disabilities due to chronic or even life-threatening illnesses are not "globally incapacitated." The inclination to keep those who are more than temporarily ill out of the stream of work and social activity is based as much on ignorance and prejudice as is the inclination to keep other people with disabilities hidden in the private realm. Thus there are issues of access for people with chronic and life-threatening illnesses that need to be addressed.

For people with chronic illnesses, access to the workplace often includes the ability to work part-time, with some flexibility to accommodate periods of greater or lesser illness. Disability leave and insurance schemes frequently make the assumption that workers are either fully disabled from working or able to work full-time, leaving people with chronic illnesses, or people with progressive life-threatening illnesses, in impossible positions. Either they must push themselves beyond endurance to appear to be capable of working full-time or dishonestly declare themselves unable to work at all, often when they want very much to continue working. The desire of their co-workers to avoid the realities of illness, especially potentially fatal illness, often contributes to their difficulties in finding a way to work. Some of these problems have been made more visible recently by people with AIDS who have had to fight for their right to continue to work as much as they are able. I will discuss these problems at more length in the next chapter. Here it is important to note that although issues of time flexibility may not be important to that group we might call the "healthy disabled," so many people with disabilities also have health problems, and so many people with illnesses are disabled by their illnesses, that it seems to make sense to make common cause on these issues by recognizing them as aspects of access to opportunities for people with disabilities.

Some of the initial opposition in disability rights groups to including people with illnesses in the category of people with disabilities may have come from an understandable desire to avoid the additional stigma of illness (see Gill 1994, 7), especially such heavily stigmatized ones as AIDS and cancer. People with physical disabilities often insist that they are not mentally disabled, because of the additional stigma of psychological or developmental disabilities in most societies. Of course, in both cases there is the valuable point to be made that a person with a disability is not disabled in all respects, that a deaf person or someone with paraplegia may be otherwise healthy, and that someone with cerebral palsy may not be developmentally disabled. Nevertheless, many people with disabilities are also ill, and many people with physical disabilities also have developmental or psychological disabilities.

Perhaps having ME makes me sensitive to the limitations of these distinctions. I am chronically ill, partially "globally" disabled in that the amount of any activity I can engage in is much more restricted than it is for a healthy person, and specifically disabled sometimes and in some contexts (for example, some days my arms are too weak and painful to write on the blackboard, open heavy doors, or carry anything). I have also experienced some psychological disability in that my disease causes profound mental as well as physical fatigue and has caused depression (primarily in the first two years), inability to concentrate, and short-term memory problems, including trouble finding the right words in conversation and remembering the names of even close friends. The psychological symptoms occasionally reappear in less severe form during periods of increased illness. Some people with ME, many of whom share these recurring symptoms, emphasize that they have a physical rather than a psychiatric cause. This is not (or not just) to avoid the stigma of psychiatric disability, but to avoid psychiatric diagnoses, which are no help to us, since attempts to cure our symptoms by psychotherapy are ineffective and may prevent us from receiving the care we need. Nevertheless, ME does combine physical and psychological disability, and experiencing that complex combination has led me to believe that what matters most in identifying disability is identifying the difficulties people face in surviving and contributing to their societies.

How Should Disability Be Defined?

I am not going to recommend specific definitions that I would like to see adopted by the United Nations. The definitions they use have to serve specific political purposes of the World Health Organization and other agencies, and they have to be arrived at by a complex process of political compromise, of which I know virtually nothing. My purpose in criticizing the UN definitions is to bring to light issues that may be glossed over or missed altogether if we accept them too readily and try to apply them in all contexts.

Nevertheless, I think that on the basis of the discussion so far, I can summarize some characteristics that good definitions, for both educational and practical purposes, should have: Good definitions of impairment and disability should recognize that normal (i.e., unimpaired) physical structure and function, as well as normal (i.e., non-disabled) ability to perform activities, depend to some extent on the physical, social, and cultural environment in which a person is living, and are influenced by such factors as what activities are necessary to survival in an environment and what abilities a culture considers most essential to a participant. However, they should also take into account the possibility that some members of a society may have a vested interest in defining 'normal' structure, function, and ability for other members in ways that disadvantage those other members and/or mask ill treatment of them. Thus it is important before accepting a society's standards of normality to compare them to those of other societies; if they are lower than, or markedly different from, many others, or if they are different for different groups (e.g., sexes, races, classes, or castes), the possibility that disability is more widespread in that society than its standards would recognize should be carefully examined.

In addition, some terms, such as *handicap*, may be useful to refer specifically to any loss of opportunities to participate in major aspects of the life of a society that results from the interaction of a disability with the physical, social, and cultural environment of the person who has it. The fact that a society does not consider an opportunity necessary or appropriate for a person belonging to some particular group (e.g., age, sex, class) may[9] be irrelevant to whether the person is handicapped, since it is not unusual for a society to handicap large groups of its own people. On the other hand, not every loss of opportunity is a handicap, despite the fact that one often hears or reads the observation that everyone is disabled or handicapped in some way (for example, see Murphy 1990, 66). I will not go into detail here about how much loss of opportunity constitutes a handicap but will discuss this as an aspect of the social creation of disability in the next chapter.

In general usage, the distinction between "disability" and "handicap" is not usually maintained. Introducing it does have an educational function, reminding people that many of the obstacles faced by people with disabilities are not necessary consequences of their physical conditions. On the other hand, it also tends to create the mistaken impression that disability is purely biological and handicap is social, when in fact both are products of biological and social factors. In this book, I will most often use the term "disability" to refer to any lack of ability to perform activities to an extent or in a way that is either necessary for survival in an environment or necessary to participate in some major aspect of life in a given society. I will assume that disability has biological, social, and experiential components.

Who Defines Disability and for What Purposes?

I believe that discussion of how disability *should* be defined is essential for clarifying our understanding of disability and, ultimately, for formulating policies. But defining disability and identifying individuals as disabled are also social practices that involve the unequal exercise of power and have major economic, social, and psychological consequences in some people's lives. To ignore these practices would leave us with an idealized picture of the problems of definition. To understand how the power of definition is exercised and experienced, we have to ask who does the defining in practice, for what purposes and with what consequences for those who are deemed to fit the definitions.

On the subject of defining race, Evelyn Brooks Higginbotham says:

> Like gender and class, then, race must be seen as a social construction predicated upon the recognition of difference and signifying the simulta-

neous distinguishing and positioning of groups vis-à-vis one another. More than this, race is a highly contested representation of relations of power between social categories by which individuals are identified and identify themselves. The recognition of racial distinctions emanates from and adapts to multiple uses of power in society. Perceived as "natural" and "appropriate," such racial categories are strategically necessary for the functioning of power in countless institutional and ideological forms, both explicit and subtle. (Higginbotham 1992, 253–54)

Much of what Higginbotham says about race is also true for disability, although the positioning of groups (disabled versus non-disabled, those with acceptable bodies versus those with rejected bodies) and the contesting of representations (e.g., pitiful cripple, inspiring example) are, I think, in earlier stages of development in disability politics than they are in racial politics. Despite the fact that there is sometimes more biological reality underlying distinctions between the non-disabled and the disabled than there is underlying distinctions between races, the belief that 'the disabled' is a biological category is like the belief that 'Black' is a biological category, in that it masks the social functions and injustices that underlie the assignment of people to these groups.

Charlotte Muller (1979, 43) points out that the providers of health care and of benefits and services to people with disabilities generally define who needs their help. This is an important reminder that the power to define is not necessarily in the hands of those who are most affected by the definitions. Later in this book, I will discuss more fully the cognitive authority (Addelson 1983) of medical professionals and bureaucrats to describe us to ourselves and others, and the practical consequences of that authority. Here perhaps it is sufficient to note that there may be important differences between the definitions of disability employed by so-called 'providers' and the definitions of disability employed by people with disabilities. It is in the interest of many providers to define disability narrowly, so that fewer people are seen to be entitled to the benefits they are supposed to provide than if disability were defined more broadly. Many examples of this can be seen when insurance companies are involved as providers; clearly it is in their direct financial interest to define disability as narrowly as they can without risking costly litigation.[10] The multiplicity of providers can create confusion about who is disabled; it is not uncommon for people with disabilities to find themselves fitting some bureaucracies' definitions of disability and not others.[11]

Who Identifies Herself/Himself as Disabled?

It is important to keep in mind that some people who consider themselves disabled are not identified as disabled by everyone else, and that not everyone who is identified by other people as disabled (either for purposes of entitlement, purposes of discrimination, or others) considers herself or himself disabled.

On the one hand, many people who identify themselves as disabled because their bodies cause them great physical, psychological, and economic struggles are not considered disabled by others because the public and/or the medical profession do not recognize their disabling conditions. These people often long to be perceived as disabled, because society stubbornly continues to expect them to perform as healthy non-disabled people when they cannot, and refuses to acknowledge and support their struggles. For example, pelvic inflammatory disease (PID) causes severe prolonged disability in some women. Women with PID are often given psychiatric diagnoses and have to endure the skepticism of families and friends, in addition to living with intense and unrelenting abdominal pain (Moore 1985).

Of course, no one wants the social stigma associated with disability, but, as I have already pointed out, social recognition of disability determines the practical help a person receives from doctors, government agencies, insurance companies, charity organizations, and often from families and friends. Moreover, if you are correctly identified by others as disabled, your experience of your own body is (at least to some extent) recognized by your society and the people who surround you; denial of their experience is a major source of loneliness, alienation, and despair in people with unrecognized disabilities (Jeffreys 1982). In addition, for many people with disabilities, identity as a person with a disability has a vital political meaning; they are members of a group of people who share the social oppressions of disability and struggle together against them.

On the other hand, there are many reasons for not identifying yourself as disabled, even when other people consider you disabled. First, disability carries a stigma that many people want to avoid, if at all possible. For newly disabled people, and for children with disabilities who have been shielded from knowledge of how most non-disabled people regard people with disabilities, it takes time to absorb the idea that they are members of a stigmatized group. Newly disabled adults may still have the stereotypes of disability that are common among non-disabled people. They may be in the habit of thinking of disability as total, believing that people who are disabled are disabled in all respects. Since they know that they are not themselves disabled in all respects, they may resist identifying themselves as people with disabilities. They may fear, with good reason, that if they identify themselves as disabled, others will see them as wholly disabled and fail to recognize their remaining abilities or, perhaps worse, see their every ability and achievement as 'extraordinary' or 'courageous' (Wright 1983).

For some people, having hoped or expected to recover from accident or injury, or having hoped for a 'cure' since childhood, identifying themselves as disabled may mean giving up on being healthy, or being able to walk, see, or hear (for example, deaf children often expect to grow up into hearing adults), and accepting the prospect of the rest of one's life with the body and abilities one currently has (Wright 1983). Canadian filmmaker Bonnie Klein describes how, sixteen months after a debilitating stroke, she did not accept herself as disabled. Even though she used a wheelchair, she chose "a glamorous cinema with inaccessible bathrooms" for the premier of one of her films (Klein 1992).

For people who identify themselves strongly with their work and fear (or know) that they cannot continue the same work with their new bodies, accepting disability means making a deep change of identity. Barbara Rosenblum, who became ill with cancer in midlife, wrote:

> My work identity runs through my very cellular structure. For me, work is like a religion. I have devoted my life to it. Being a sociologist has been central to my identity and now I am giving that up. I was frightened when I thought of going on disability. Would they write "disabled professor" on my records at the hospital? (Butler and Rosenblum 1991, 63)

Recognizing myself as disabled certainly required that I change my self-identity and adopt a radically new way of thinking about myself. This included accepting the reality (though not the justice) of the stigma of being chronically ill,[12] especially the shame of being unable to do many things that people still expected me to do. It also required reimagining my life with a new, much more limited, and perpetually uncomfortable body, and then reorganizing my work, home, and relationships to make this different life possible. All of this was difficult, but another very important part of changing my identity helped me through the rest. I found that I could make sense of what was happening to me by talking with other people with disabilities and reading books and articles by them. They already knew how the stigma of disability works, and how to live well with illness and physical limitations. In the process of learning what I needed to know from them, I recognized myself as one of them. When I identified myself as a person with a disability, I no longer felt I was struggling alone.

It was easier to identify myself as disabled to myself than it was to identify myself as disabled to others. For me, this was not primarily because I was afraid of the stigma; I had already encountered the most profound ways that the stigma of chronic illness would affect me. The problem was that when I had recovered enough strength to return to work part-time, I no longer *looked* very ill although I still fought a daily battle with exhaustion, pain, nausea, and dizziness, and I used a cane to keep my balance. I was struggling, and since people could not see that I was struggling, I was constantly explaining to them that I was struggling, that I could no longer do things that I had done before, and that I did not know when or even if I would ever be able to do them again. I simply wanted my friends and the people I worked with to recognize my limitations and to accept, as I had, that they might be permanent, but it is hard to describe the invisible reality of disability to others without feeling that you are constantly complaining and asking for sympathy. Then too, others resisted believing that I might never regain my previous health and ability. They tried to talk me out of attitudes and actions that they saw as "giving up hope" and that I saw as acceptance and rebuilding my life.

In addition, there was another obstacle to identifying myself to others as disabled. Although I felt that the struggles of people with disabilities, especially women with disabilities, were my struggles (and I still do), I also felt a kind of unworthiness to count myself among people with disabilities, because I was so much better off than they were.

I have heard other people with disabilities, some of them in terrible circumstances, say that they do not consider themselves disabled because "others are so much worse off than I am." I think it is sometimes a way of minimizing one's own difficulties in order not to feel frustration, grief, or shame. Or it can be a way of clinging to one's right to pity others, and therefore to feel stronger, healthier, and more 'normal' than them. I think it is sometimes based on the stereotype of disability that pictures people with disabilities as totally disabled, unable to do anything for themselves or others, and therefore in need of charity; as long as they can do anything, people who have this stereotype in mind refuse to think of themselves as disabled out of pride and to avoid charity.

27

Something else was also bothering me. My reluctance came partly from awe of people who lived with more disabling conditions than mine; after all, I had learned most of what I knew about how to cope from them. It also came from guilt and shame that while I was able-bodied I had barely noticed, and certainly had not begun to understand, the struggles of people with disabilities or the privileges I had because I was not disabled. I realized too how lucky I was to have built a professional life before I became ill that provided not only adequate disability insurance but also the possibility of continuing my work with my new limitations.

Bonnie Klein describes feelings similar to mine, which occurred the first time she attended a meeting of the DisAbled Women's Network, Canada:

> I feel apologetic, illegitimate, because I was not born disabled, and I am not as severely disabled as many other people. I feel guilty about my privileges of class, profession (including my disability pension), and family. I am a newcomer to the disability movement; I have not paid my dues. (Klein 1992, 73)

My own embarrassment and fear of rejection gave way to the reality of shared work, shared experiences, and mutual understanding. When I began teaching a course on women and disability and meeting a lot of women with disabilities, I found that they treated me as one of them, welcomed my contribution to disability movement, and taught me about their lives with great generosity, regardless of the severity of their own disabilities and disadvantages. Although I am still very aware of my privileges, I no longer feel unworthy to call myself a disabled woman.

Some Politics of Disability Identity

Whether to identify oneself as disabled can be a contentious political issue. For example, there is a lively debate among the Deaf[13] about whether to include themselves in disability rights groups, since many Deaf people do not consider themselves disabled. Because the Deaf have sign language and a rich culture separate from hearing people, it is very clear that the Deaf are not disabled in *all contexts*. As Roger J. Carver puts it:

> Indeed, as one enters into the world of the Deaf, disability as a factor in their lives ceases to exist. A hearing person unfamiliar with the lan-

guage and customs of the Deaf community will instantly find himself handicapped in such a context, arising from his disability in the area of communication. In the same vein, a Deaf person will feel the same way when he [sic] is among speaking hearing persons. This handicap is no different from that incurred by visiting a foreign country in which a different language is spoken. It explains in large part why the Deaf do not feel at home among other disabled persons; they do not share the same communications system. Put "wheelies" together into a group; they are still confronted by the reality of their disability. The same is true for the blind or even the hard of hearing. (Carver 1992)

From medical and rehabilitative practitioners' point of view (which is also the point of view of most hearing people), a deaf child is disabled by her inability to hear, and so the child becomes the focus of efforts to 'normalize' her as far as possible within the hearing community. But from another, equally valid point of view, the same child is handicapped by hearing people's (often including her parents') ignorance of Sign. In a Deaf, signing community, she is already normal, assuming that she has signing ability appropriate for her age. The validity of this second point of view is weakened or even forsaken when the Deaf identify themselves as people with disabilities and join disability rights groups to work for their own welfare.

On the other hand, since most medical and rehabilitative authorities, as well as the hearing majority, consider the Deaf disabled, the Deaf must often identify themselves as people with disabilities in order to obtain the equipment and services they need. Carver says, "In the eyes of the Hearing, our technical devices are medical devices or 'assistive living aids;' in the eyes of the Deaf, they are mundane, everyday instruments in much the same way the Hearing regard their telephones, TV sets, alarm clocks, and doorbells" (Carver 1992).

Moreover, since the Deaf are widely regarded as disabled, they are treated in some of the same ways as (other) people with disabilities, and therefore they have some common causes with (other) people with disabilities, including the goal of being accepted as different rather than rejected as defective (Vlug 1992). For this reason, some of the Deaf identify themselves as people with disabilities and/or want to work within organizations of people with disabilities.

Many of the same things Carver says about the Deaf are true of most people with disabilities: We are disabled in some, but not all, contexts; the

disability in a given situation is often created by the inability or unwillingness of others to adapt themselves or the environment to the physical or
psychological reality of the person designated as 'disabled'; and people
with disabilities often regard the accommodations they make to their physical conditions as ordinary living arrangements and their lives as ordinary
lives, despite their medicalization by professionals and most people's insistence that they are unusually helpless or dependent. These facts are more
obvious in the case of the Deaf, because the contexts in which the Deaf are
not disabled are more readily available, more total, and more public than
for most people with disabilities. Thus Carver says that other people with
disabilities are still confronted with their disabilities when they are in each
other's company; but that is not entirely true. It is true that people who use
wheelchairs still have the same difficulty walking when they are in the
exclusive company of other people who use wheelchairs, but walking is
out of the question for the whole group, and so it is not an issue or an
obstacle to participating fully in the group's activities. Disability is contex-
tual for everyone, not only for the Deaf.[14]

Nevertheless, many of the concerns raised by the Deaf are important
general concerns for political organizations of people with disabilities.
What, if anything, do people with disabilities have in common? Do those
with similar disabilities have more in common, or do other factors such as
gender, class, race, age, or sexual identity have a more profound effect on
the experience of disability? Does identifying ourselves as disabled rein-
force the very perception of us as radically 'different,' which is a source of
stereotypes and assumptions that stand in our way? Does it perpetuate the
practice of regarding our different bodies, rather than the inaccessible and
unaccommodating environment, as the source of our problems? Should we
emphasize our similarities to non-disabled people or our differences from
them, including our different strengths and abilities? Should our political
goals emphasize full integration of people with disabilities among people
without disabilities, or should people with disabilities maintain some separate organizations and perhaps nurture separate cultures based on our
different experiences and knowledge?

These concerns in turn raise questions about the meaningfulness of the
category, "people with disabilities," the subject of this chapter. Is that category a product of false universalization, as some feminist writers claim is
true of the category "women?"[15] Is it not likely that living with disabilities
is very different for people with different disabilities, and different for
males and females, people of different ages, races, classes, occupations—

perhaps so different that to lump them all together in a single category serves no useful purpose? Does the category obscure the differences and perhaps even swallow up the diversity of experiences, absorbing them into the experiences of articulate, relatively privileged white males with certain disabilities?

Researchers working on disability have, as Fine and Asch put it, "focused on disability as a unitary concept and have taken it to be not merely the 'master' status but apparently the exclusive status for disabled people"[16] (Fine and Asch 1988, 3). One consequence is that gender differences in the experience of disability have only recently been brought to light, primarily in the writings of women with disabilities. Nevertheless, there is already strong evidence that there are major gender differences in the experience of disability (Fine and Asch 1988, 1–4). This gives us reason to suspect that further research will reveal the importance of other factors, such as race and class, to the experience of disability. Does this mean that we should be suspicious of the category, "people with disabilities?" Yes. Does it mean we should discard it, or does it retain some meaning and usefulness? Fine and Asch suggest an answer when they consider similar questions about the category "women with disabilities," the subject of their book:

> It is ironic to note that the very category that integrates this text, "disabled girls and women," exists wholly as a social construct. Why should a limb-deficient girl, a teenager with mental retardation, or a blind girl have anything in common with each other, or with a woman with breast cancer or another woman who is recovering from a stroke? What they share is similar treatment by a sexist and disability-phobic society. This is what makes it likely that they will be thrown together in school, in the unemployment line, in segregated recreational programs, in rehabilitation centers, and in legislation. (Fine and Asch 1988, 6)

Widespread perceptions that people with disabilities are similar in very significant ways create the category, "people with disabilities." Thus it is various aspects of their treatment by their societies that people with disabilities are most likely to have in common; these will often be aspects of social oppression. In North America, they include: verbal, medical, and physical abuse; neglect of the most basic educational needs; sexual abuse and exploitation; enforced poverty; harassment by public and private sector bureaucracies; job discrimination; segregation in schools, housing, and workshops; inaccessibility of buildings, transportation, and other public facilities; social isolation due to prejudice and ignorant fear; erasure as a sexual being; and many more subtle manifestations of disability-phobia, experienced as daily stress and wounds to self-esteem. As in every oppressed group, not everyone will have experienced all aspects of the oppression, but the pattern of oppression produces overlapping patterns of experience among group members. This overlap, combined with the awareness that many things happened to them because they are identified by *others* as members of the group, can motivate people of diverse experiences to work together for their common welfare, to identify themselves willingly as members of the group, and to redefine for themselves what being one of the group means.[17]

I will discuss issues of diversity among people with disabilities and the dangers of false universalizing at length in chapter 3. For now, it is enough to say that I think "people with disabilities" is not a meaningless category as long as there is social oppression based on disability, even though the forms this oppression takes, and the ways it is experienced, may vary greatly among societies and according to other factors, such as age, gender, race, class, religion, caste, and sexual identity. What the category will mean (if anything) in the future will depend in part on what meanings people with disabilities give it through their cultural interpretations and their political actions. As Audre Lorde says of Black women and men: "[I]t is axiomatic that if we do not define ourselves for ourselves, we will be defined by others—for their use and to our detriment" (Lorde 1984, 45).

We have seen that disability is defined, and people are identified as disabled, for many purposes. How a society defines disability and whom it recognizes as disabled are of enormous psychological, social, economic, and political importance, both to people who identify themselves as disabled and to those who do not but are nevertheless given the label. How a society defines disability and whom it recognizes as disabled also reveal a great deal about that society's attitudes and expectations concerning the body, what it stigmatizes and what it considers 'normal' in physical appearance and performance, what activities it takes to be necessary and/or valuable and for whom, and its assumptions about gender, age, race, caste, and class.

In the ethically ideal situation, the only practical reason for defining disability would come from the need to identify people who should receive certain resources in order to have both the necessities of life and good opportunities to develop their potential and to participate in a given community. But this need would apply to everyone, not only to people with disabilities. Thus, if this need were a society's only concern with disability, the category "people with disabilities" would be useless—too specific to identify those in need of resources and too general to identify what kinds of resources are needed. In such an ideal circumstance, the category itself would probably disappear.

2

The Social Construction
of Disability

In chapter 1, I argued that neither impairment nor disability can be defined purely in biomedical terms, because social arrangements and expectations make essential contributions to impairment and disability, and to their absence. In this chapter, I develop that argument further. I maintain that the distinction between the biological reality of a disability and the social construction of a disability cannot be made sharply, because the biological and the social are interactive in creating disability. They are interactive not only in that complex interactions of social factors and our bodies affect health and functioning, but also in that social arrangements can make a biological condition more or less relevant to almost any situation. I call the interaction of the biological and the social to create (or prevent) disability "the social construction of disability."[1]

Disability activists and some scholars of disability have been asserting for at least two decades that disability is socially constructed.[2] Moreover, feminist scholars have already applied feminist analyses of the social construction of the experience of being female to their analyses of disability as socially constructed (Hannaford 1985). (Fine and Asch (1988, 6) were among the first to compare the two kinds of social construction explicitly.) Thus I am saying nothing new when I claim that disability, like gender, is socially constructed. Nevertheless, I understand that such an assertion may be new and even puzzling to many readers, and that not everyone who says that disability is socially constructed means the same thing by it. Therefore, I will explain what I mean in some detail.

I see disability as socially constructed in ways ranging from social conditions that straightforwardly create illnesses, injuries, and poor physical functioning, to subtle cultural factors that determine standards of normality and exclude those who do not meet them from full participation in their societies. I could not possibly discuss all the factors that enter into the social construction of disability here, and I feel sure that I am not aware of them all, but I will try to explain and illustrate the social construction of disability by discussing what I hope is a representative sample from a range of factors.

Social Factors That Construct Disability

First, it is easy to recognize that social conditions affect people's bodies by creating or failing to prevent sickness and injury. Although, since disability is relative to a person's physical, social, and cultural environment, none of the resulting physical conditions is necessarily disabling, many do in fact cause disability given the demands and lack of support in the environments of the people affected. In this direct sense of damaging people's bodies in ways that are disabling in their environments, much disability is created by the violence of invasions, wars, civil wars, and terrorism, which cause disabilities not only through direct injuries to combatants and noncombatants, but also through the spread of disease and the deprivations of basic needs that result from the chaos they create. In addition, although we more often hear about them when they cause death, violent crimes such as shootings, knifings, beatings, and rape all cause disabilities, so that a society's success or failure in protecting its citizens from injurious crimes has a significant effect on its rates of disability.[3]

The availability and distribution of basic resources such as water, food, clothing, and shelter have major effects on disability, since much disabling physical damage results directly from malnutrition and indirectly from diseases that attack and do more lasting harm to the malnourished and those weakened by exposure. Disabling diseases are also contracted from contaminated water when clean water is not available. Here too, we usually learn more about the deaths caused by lack of basic resources than the (often lifelong) disabilities of survivors.

Many other social factors can damage people's bodies in ways that are disabling in their environments, including (to mention just a few) tolerance of high-risk working conditions, abuse and neglect of children, low public safety standards, the degradation of the environment by contamination of air, water, and food, and the overwork, stress, and daily grinding deprivations of poverty. The social factors that can damage people's bodies almost always affect some groups in a society more than others because of racism, sexism, heterosexism, ageism, and advantages of class background, wealth, and education.[4]

Medical care and practices, traditional and Western-scientific, play an important role in both preventing and creating disabling physical damage. (They also play a role in defining disability, as described in chapter 1.) Lack of good prenatal care and dangerous or inadequate obstetrical practices cause disabilities in babies and in the women giving birth to them. Inoculations against diseases such as polio and measles prevent quite a lot of disability. Inadequate medical care of those who are already ill or injured results in unnecessary disablement. On the other hand, the rate of disability in a society increases with improved medical capacity to save the lives of people who are dangerously ill or injured in the absence of the capacity to prevent or cure all the physical damage they have incurred. Moreover, public health and sanitation measures that increase the average lifespan also increase the number of old people with disabilities in a society, since more people live long enough to become disabled.

The pace of life is a factor in the social construction of disability that particularly interests me, because it is usually taken for granted by non-disabled people, while many people with disabilities are acutely aware of how it marginalizes or threatens to marginalize us. I suspect that increases in the pace of life are important social causes of damage to people's bodies through rates of accident, drug and alcohol abuse, and illnesses that result from people's neglecting their needs for rest and good nutrition. But the pace of life also affects disability as a second form of social construction, the social construction of disability through expectations of performance.[5]

When the pace of life in a society increases, there is a tendency for more people to become disabled, not only because of physically damaging consequences of efforts to go faster, but also because fewer people can meet expectations of 'normal' performance; the physical (and mental) limitations of those who cannot meet the new pace become conspicuous and disabling, even though the same limitations were inconspicuous and irrelevant to full participation in the slower-paced society. Increases in the pace of life can be counterbalanced for some people by improvements in accessibility, such as better transportation and easier communication, but for those who must move or think slowly, and for those whose energy is severely limited, expectations of pace can make work, recreational, community, and social activities inaccessible.

Let me give a straightforward, personal illustration of the relationship between pace and disability. I am currently just able (by doing very little else) to work as a professor three-quarter time, on one-quarter disability leave. There has been much talk recently about possible increases in the teaching duties of professors at my university, which would not be accompanied by any reduction in expectations for the other two components of our jobs, research and administration. If there were to be such an increase in the pace of professors' work, say by one additional course per term, I would be unable to work more than half-time (by the new standards) and would have to request half-time disability leave, even though there had been no change in my physical condition. Compared to my colleagues, I would be more work-disabled than I am now. Some professors with less physical limitation than I have, who now work full-time, might be unable to work at the new full-time pace and be forced to go on part-time disability leave.[6] This sort of change could contribute to disabling anyone in any job.

Furthermore, even if a person is able to keep up with an increased pace of work, any increase in the pace of work will decrease the energy available for other life activities, which may upset the delicate balance of energy by which a person manages to participate in them and eventually exclude her/him from those activities. The pace of those other activities may also render them inaccessible. For example, the more the life of a society is conducted on the assumption of quick travel, the more disabling are those physical conditions that affect movement and travel, such as needing to use a wheelchair or having a kind of epilepsy that prevents one from driving a car, unless compensating help is provided. These disabling effects extend into people's family, social, and sexual lives and into their participation in recreation, religious life, and politics.

Pace is a major aspect of expectations of performance; non-disabled people often take pace so much for granted that they feel and express impatience with the slower pace at which some people with disabilities need to operate, and accommodations of pace are often crucial to making an activity accessible to people with a wide range of physical and mental abilities. Nevertheless, expectations of pace are not the only expectations of performance that contribute to disability. For example, expectations of individual productivity can eclipse the actual contributions of people who cannot meet them, making people unemployable when they can in fact do valuable work. There are often very definite expectations about how tasks will be performed (not the standards of performance, but the methods). For example, many women with disabilities are discouraged from having children because other people can only imagine caring for children in ways that are impossible for women with their disabilities, yet everything necessary could be done in other ways, often with minor accommodations (Matthews 1983; Shaul, Dowling and Laden 1985). Furthermore, the expectation that many tasks will be performed by individuals on their own can create or expand the disability of those who can perform the tasks only in cooperative groups or by instructing a helper.

Expectations of performance are reflected, because they are assumed, in the social organization and physical structure of a society, both of which create disability. Societies that are physically constructed and socially organized with the unacknowledged assumption that everyone is healthy, non-disabled, young but adult, shaped according to cultural ideals, and, often, male, create a great deal of disability through sheer neglect of what most people need in order to participate fully in them.

Feminists talk about how the world has been designed for the bodies and activities of men. In many industrialized countries, including Canada and the United States, life and work have been structured as though no one of any importance in the public world, and certainly no one who works outside the home for wages, has to breast-feed a baby or look after a sick child. Common colds can be acknowledged publicly, and allowances are made for them, but menstruation cannot be acknowledged and allowances are not made for it. Much of the public world is also structured as though everyone were physically strong, as though all bodies were shaped the same, as though everyone could walk, hear, and see well, as though everyone could work and play at a pace that is not compatible with any kind of illness or pain, as though no one were ever dizzy or incontinent or simply needed to sit or lie down. (For instance, where could you rest for a few minutes in a supermarket if you needed to?) Not only the architecture, but the entire physical and social organization of life tends to assume that we are either strong and healthy and able to do what the average young, non-disabled man can do or that we are completely unable to participate in public life.

A great deal of disability is caused by this physical structure and social organization of society. For instance, poor architectural planning creates physical obstacles for people who use wheelchairs, but also for people who can walk but cannot walk far or cannot climb stairs, for people who cannot open doors, and for people who can do all of these things but only at the cost of pain or an expenditure of energy they can ill afford. Some of the same architectural flaws cause problems for pregnant women, parents with strollers, and young children. This is no coincidence. Much architecture has been planned with a young adult, non-disabled male paradigm of humanity in mind. In addition, aspects of social organization that take for granted the social expectations of performance and productivity, such as inadequate public transportation (which I believe assumes that no one who is needed in the public world needs public transportation), communications systems that are inaccessible to people with visual or hearing impairments, and inflexible work arrangements that exclude part-time work or rest periods, create much disability.

When public and private worlds are split, women (and children) have often been relegated to the private, and so have the disabled, the sick, and the old. The public world is the world of strength, the positive (valued) body, performance and production, the non-disabled, and young adults. Weakness, illness, rest and recovery, pain, death, and the negative (devalued) body are private, generally hidden, and often neglected. Coming into the public world with illness, pain, or a devalued body, people encounter resistance to mixing the two worlds; the split is vividly revealed. Much of the experience of disability and illness goes underground, because there is no socially acceptable way of expressing it and having the physical and psychological experience acknowledged. Yet acknowledgement of this experience is exactly what is required for creating accessibility in the public world. The more a society regards disability as a private matter, and people with disabilities as belonging in the private sphere, the more disability it creates by failing to make the public sphere accessible to a wide range of people.

Disability is also socially constructed by the failure to give people the amount and kind of help they need to participate fully in all major aspects of life in the society, including making a significant contribution in the form of work. Two things are important to remember about the help that people with disabilities may need. One is that most industrialized societies give non-disabled people (in different degrees and kinds, depending on class, race, gender, and other factors) a lot of help in the form of education, training, social support, public communication and transportation facilities, public recreation, and other services. The help that non-disabled people receive tends to be taken for granted and not considered help but entitlement, because it is offered to citizens who fit the social paradigms, who by definition are not considered dependent on social help. It is only when people need a different kind or amount of help than that given to 'paradigm' citizens that it is considered help at all, and they are considered socially dependent. Second, much, though not all, of the help that people with disabilities need is required because their bodies were damaged by social conditions, or because they cannot meet social expectations of performance, or because the narrowly-conceived physical structure and social organization of society have placed them at a disadvantage; in other words, it is needed to overcome problems that were created socially.

Thus disability is socially constructed through the failure or unwillingness to create ability among people who do not fit the physical and mental profile of 'paradigm' citizens. Failures of social support for people with disabilities result in inadequate rehabilitation, unemployment, poverty, inadequate personal and medical care, poor communication services, inadequate training and education, poor protection from physical, sexual, and emotional abuse, minimal opportunities for social learning and interaction, and many other disabling situations that hurt people with disabilities and exclude them from participation in major aspects of life in their societies.

For example, Jongbloed and Crichton (1990, 35) point out that, in Canada and the United States, the belief that social assistance benefits should be less than can be earned in the work force, in order to provide an incentive for people to find and keep employment, has contributed to poverty among people with disabilities. Although it was recognized in the 1950s that they should receive disability pensions, these were set, as were other forms of direct economic help, at socially minimal levels. Thus, even though unemployed people with disabilities have been viewed by both governments as surplus labour since at least the 1970s (because of persistently high general rates of unemployment), and efforts to increase their employment opportunities have been minimal, they are kept at poverty level incomes[7] based on the 'incentive' principle. Poverty is the single most disabling social circumstance for people with disabilities, since it means that they can barely afford the things that are necessities for non-disabled people, much less the personal care, medicines, and technological aids they may need to live decent lives outside institutions, or the training or education or transportation or clothing that might enable them to work or to participate more fully in public life.

Failure or unwillingness to provide help often takes the form of irrational rules governing insurance benefits and social assistance,[8] long bureaucratic delays, and a pervasive attitude among those administering programs for people with disabilities that their 'clients' are trying to get more than they deserve. In her semiautobiographical novel, *The Body's Memory* (1989), Jean Stewart describes the cluster of assumptions a woman discovers behind the questions of her social worker when she first applies for some 'vocational rehabilitation,' that is, the money to buy a basic wheelchair:

> (1) The client-applicant is ineligible for services until proven eligible. (2) The client-applicant's Vocational Goals are outlandish, greedy, arrogant, must be trimmed down to appropriately humble scale. (3) The client-applicant's motive in seeking services is, until proven otherwise, to rip off the system. (4) The function of the Agency is to facilitate (favorite word) adaptation (second favorite) of client to job (client to world), not the reverse. (5) The client is a fraud. (6) The client is helpless. (Stewart 1989, 190)

I do not want to claim or imply that social factors alone cause all disability. I do want to claim that the social response to and treatment of biological difference constructs disability from biological reality, determining both the nature and the severity of disability. I recognize that many disabled people's relationships to their bodies involve elements of struggle that perhaps cannot be eliminated, perhaps not even mitigated, by social arrangements. But many of the struggles of people with disabilities and much of what is disabling, are the consequences of having those physical conditions under social arrangements (Finger 1983; Fine and Asch 1988) that could, but do not, either compensate for their physical conditions, or accommodate them so that they can participate fully, or support their struggles and integrate those struggles into the cultural concept of life as it is ordinarily lived.

Cultural Construction of Disability

Culture makes major contributions to disability. These contributions include not only the omission of experiences of disability from cultural representations of life in a society, but also the cultural stereotyping of people with disabilities, the selective stigmatization of physical and mental limitations and other differences (selective because not all limitations and differences are stigmatized, and different limitations and differences are stigmatized in different societies), the numerous cultural meanings attached to various kinds of disability and illness, and the exclusion of people with disabilities from the cultural meanings of activities they cannot perform or are expected not to perform.

The lack of realistic cultural representations of experiences of disability not only contributes to the 'Otherness' of people with disabilities by encouraging the assumption that their lives are inconceivable to non-disabled people but also increases non-disabled people's fear of disability by suppressing knowledge of how people live with disabilities. Stereotypes of disabled people as dependent, morally depraved, superhumanly heroic, asexual, and/or pitiful are still the most common cultural portrayals of people with disabilities (Kent 1988; Dahl 1993). Stereotypes repeatedly get in the way of full participation in work and social life. For example, Francine Arsenault, whose leg was damaged by childhood polio and later by gangrene, describes the following incident at her wedding:

> When I got married, one of my best friends came to the wedding with her parents. I had known her parents all the time I was growing up; we visited in each other's homes and I thought that they knew my situation quite well.
>
> But as the father went down the reception line and shook hands with my husband, he said, "You know, I used to think that Francine was intelligent, but to put herself on you as a burden like this shows that I was wrong all along." (Arsenault 1994, 6)

Here the stereotype of a woman with a disability as a helpless, dependent burden blots out, in the friend's father's consciousness, both the reality that Francine simply has one damaged leg and the probability that her new husband wants her for her other qualities. Moreover, the man seems to take for granted that the new husband sees Francine in the same stereotyped way (or else he risks incomprehension or rejection), perhaps because he counts on the cultural assumptions about people with disabilities. I think both the stigma of physical 'imperfection' (and possibly the additional stigma of having been damaged by disease) and the cultural meanings attached to the disability contribute to the power of the stereotype in situations like this. Physical 'imperfection' is more likely to be thought to 'spoil' a woman than a man by rendering her unattractive in a culture where her physical appearance is a large component of a woman's value; having a damaged leg probably evokes the metaphorical meanings of being 'crippled,' which include helplessness, dependency, and pitifulness.[9] Stigma, stereotypes, and cultural meanings are all related and interactive in the cultural construction of disability. I will discuss them, and some of their social consequences, more extensively in chapter 3.

The power of culture alone to construct a disability is revealed when we consider bodily differences—deviations from a society's conception of a 'normal' or acceptable body—that, although they cause little or no functional or physical difficulty for the person who has them, constitute major social disabilities. An important example is facial scarring, which is a disability of appearance only, a disability constructed totally by stigma and cultural meanings.[10] Stigma, stereotypes, and cultural meanings are also the primary components of other disabilities, such as mild epilepsy and not having a 'normal' or acceptable body size.

I believe that culture plays a central role in constructing (or not constructing) disability. However, I want to distinguish this view from approaches to cultural construction of 'the body' that seem to confuse the lived reality of bodies with cultural discourse about and representations of bodies, or that deny or ignore bodily experience in favour of fascination with bodily representations.[11] For example, this approach troubles me in Donna Haraway's "The Biopolitics of Postmodern Bodies: Constitutions of Self in Immune System Discourse" (Haraway 1991), where Haraway discusses the biomedical construction of "immune system discourse" as though discourse and its political context are all there is, without acknowledging either the reality of physical suffering (for example, by people with AIDS, ME, MS, Amyotrophic Lateral Sclerosis (ALS), rheumatoid arthritis), which surely has *some* relationship to the development of immune system discourse, or the effects of this discourse on the lives of people who are thought to be suffering from immune disorders.

I do not think my body *is* a cultural representation, although I recognize that my experience of it is both highly interpreted and very influenced by cultural (including medical) representations. Moreover, I think it would be cruel, as well as a distortion of people's lives, to erase or ignore the everyday, practical, experienced limitations of people's disabilities simply because we recognize that human bodies and their varied conditions are both changeable and highly interpreted. That I can imagine having an energetic, pain-free body or living in a society where my body is considered acceptable or normal and its limitations are compensated by social and physical arrangements does not make it any easier to get out of bed or to function as an academic in my present circumstances. In most postmodern cultural theorizing about the body, there is no recognition of—and, as far as I can see, no room for recognizing—the hard physical realities that are faced by people with disabilities. (Or would postmodernists deny that there are such 'realities,' suggestive as they are of something that is not constructed or constituted by discourse? I cannot tell, because nothing like it is discussed.) The experiences of people with disabilities are as invisible in the discourses of postmodernism, which has the virtue of being critical of idealized, normalized, and universalized representations of bodies, as they are in discourses which employ concepts of bodily 'normality' uncritically.[12]

I believe that in thinking about the social construction of disability we need to strike a balance between, on the one hand, thinking of a body's abilities and limitations as given by nature and/or accident, as immutable and uncontrollable, and, on the other hand, thinking of them as so constructed by society and culture as to be controllable by human thought, will, and action. We need to acknowledge that social justice and cultural change can eliminate a great deal of disability while recognizing that there may be much suffering and limitation that they cannot fix.

Social Deconstruction of Disability

In my view, then, disability is socially constructed by such factors as social conditions that cause or fail to prevent damage to people's bodies; expectations of performance; the physical and social organization of societies on the basis of a young, non-disabled, 'ideally shaped,' healthy adult male paradigm of citizens; the failure or unwillingness to create ability among citizens who do not fit the paradigm; and cultural representations, failures of representation, and expectations. Much, but perhaps not all, of what can be socially constructed can be socially (and not just intellectually) deconstructed, given the means and the will.

A great deal of disability can be prevented with good public health and safety standards and practices, but also by relatively minor changes in the built environment that provide accessibility to people with a wide range of physical characteristics and abilities. Many measures that are usually regarded as helping or accommodating people who are now disabled, such as making buildings and public places wheelchair accessible, creating and respecting parking spaces for people with disabilities, providing American Sign Language translation, captioning, and Telephone Devices for the Deaf,

45

and making tapes and Descriptive Video services available for people who are visually impaired, should be seen as preventive, since a great deal of disability is created by building and organizing environments, objects, and activities for a too-narrow range of people. Much more could be done along the same lines by putting people with a wide variety of physical abilities and characteristics in charge of deconstructing disability. People with disabilities should be in charge, because people without disabilities are unlikely to see many of the obstacles in their environment. Moreover, they are likely not to see them *as obstacles* even when they are pointed out, but rather as 'normal' features of the built environment that present difficulties for 'abnormal' people.

Disability cannot be deconstructed by consulting a few token disabled representatives. A person with a disability is not likely to see all the obstacles to people with disabilities different from her/his own, although s/he is likely to be more aware of potential inaccessibility. Moreover, people with disabilities are not always aware of the obstacles in our environment *as obstacles*, even when they affect us. The cultural habit of regarding the condition of the person, not the built environment or the social organization of activities, as the source of the problem, runs deep. For example, it took me several years of struggling with the heavy door to my building, sometimes having to wait until someone stronger came along, to realize that the door was an accessibility problem, not only for me, but for others as well. And I did not notice, until one of my students pointed it out, that the lack of signs that could be read from a distance at my university forced people with mobility impairments to expend a lot of energy unnecessarily, searching for rooms and offices.[13] Although I have encountered this difficulty myself on days when walking was exhausting to me, I interpreted it, automatically, as a problem arising from my illness (as I did with the door), rather than as a problem arising from the built environment having been created for too narrow a range of people and situations. One of the most crucial factors in the deconstruction of disability is the change of perspective that causes us to look in the environment for both the source of the problem and the solutions.

It is perhaps easiest to change perspective by thinking about how people who have some bodily difference that does not impair any of their physical functions, such as being unusually large, are disabled by the built environment—by seats that are too small and too close together, doors and aisles and bathroom stalls that are too narrow, desks and tables that are too low (or chairs that cannot be adjusted for height), the unavailability or expense of clothing that fits or of an automobile that they can operate comfortably. Of course, many people regard large people as unfortunate or (if they are fat) weak individuals whose abnormality creates their problems, which in itself illustrates the strength of the cultural demand that everyone meet body ideals. Nevertheless, although they are subjected to stigma, stereotypes, and cultural judgements, they are not surrounded by the same aura of hopelessness and pathology that many cultures project onto people with illnesses and injuries, nor does it seem as plausible that they should be kept out of public life. This makes it somewhat easier to see how the built and social environments create disability by failing to accommodate bodily difference.

How much difference can be practically accommodated? How large a group must find a public place, a product, or an activity inaccessible before we must accept a social obligation to change it? These are reasonable questions that are sometimes difficult to answer.[14] Although a great deal of disabling structure and organization can be prevented by creative, relatively inexpensive planning or correction,[15] sometimes it is quite costly to make an environment or activity accessible to a relatively small number of people, especially if it was planned originally to accommodate a narrow range of human beings (an example is equipping city buses with wheelchair lifts). Some increases in accessibility—such as making public places accessible to people with severe allergies to perfumes, solvents, cleaners, smoke, and a multitude of other chemicals—would require many changes and significant sacrifices by many individuals. I do not want to offer an ethical formula for making decisions about how much to change existing structures, objects, and ways of doing things in order to accommodate how many people. But I would like to suggest that in thinking about these questions, it is important to remember three things: First, it is likely that the number of people who will benefit from an improvement in accessibility is greater than expected, since many people are hidden in the private sphere because of assumptions that they belong there and because public spaces and facilities are inaccessible to them. Second, rates of disability increase dramatically with age, so that as populations age, improvements in accessibility will benefit larger proportions of the population, and those who work to increase accessibility now may very well benefit from it later. Third, the public presence of people with disabilities has many potential benefits for people without disabilities, including better knowledge of the forms of difference among people, better understanding of the realities of physical limitations and/or suffering, and a lessening of the fear of becoming disabled, which is exacerbated by the assumption that disability means exclusion from major aspects of social life.

Architectural changes and expansions of communication are the best known, and probably the most often recognized, efforts to deconstruct disability, along with 'changing the attitudes' of non-disabled people, which I will come to later. But it must be recognized that other changes and accommodations would make it possible for more people with disabilities to participate in all the major aspects of life in a society. Among these are accommodations of pace and expectations, which I discussed earlier in this chapter. Many more people with disabilities would be able to work, for example, if they could work part-time or flexibly, so that they could manage their work despite having more fatigue, pain, and/or interruptions for medical procedures than the average non-disabled worker.[16] People with disabilities are often forced to work less than they could, or at less creative and demanding jobs than they are capable of doing, because of inflexible workplaces. Those who acquire chronic illnesses often have to fight to continue working at a slower pace or with fewer hours. I was shocked to discover that the major insurer who administered disability insurance at my university had no policy to cover workers who remain 'partially disabled'[17] (i.e., able to work part-time, but not full-time) more than two years after returning to work. After two years, the insurance company expected workers to be "fully rehabilitated," that is, working full-time, or "fully disabled." Given the choice between the impossible (working full-time) and the undesirable (being on full disability leave), surely many people are forced to stop working altogether. This bad choice must cost insurers and employers a lot of money. Whether it is a price they choose to pay rather than making the organizational changes that would accommodate disabled workers, or simply the product of a cultural assumption that disabled people cannot work, I do not know. I do know that, when my university created a policy to cover ongoing 'partial disability' of professors, someone at the insurance company was said to have warned that, with this new policy, all the professors would want to be disabled.[18]

It is probably best to face this sort of objection squarely. Much disability policy and practice makes the assumption that disability must have enormous economic disadvantages, or else large numbers of people will want to be, or to pretend to be, disabled, presumably because they would not be expected or forced to work with a disability. Of course, if workplaces and the organization of work were fully accessible, or even considerably more accessible than they are now, and if employers stopped discriminating against people with disabilities, but hired them for their abilities, then many more people with disabilities could reasonably be expected to work. In the best circumstances, only people with the severest physical and mental impairments would be unable to work, and it is not plausible that many people would be motivated to acquire or pretend to such severe impairments in order to avoid work. So, even if the motivation argument were correct, improving access to work would seem to be an effective way of preventing the alleged desire for disability, which would make it unnecessary to impoverish people with disabilities in order to make disability undesirable. Of course, the motivation argument does not take adequate account of the disadvantages of pretending to have a disability, much less the disadvantages of having a disability, including the social burden of stigma.

Advocates for people with disabilities tend to argue for accessibility on the basis of rights, perhaps because rights, once recognized, can be written into laws. A rights-based approach to thinking about social assistance for people with disabilities is also appealing because it so clearly opposes the charity-based approach, and because it requires the recognition that people with disabilities are full citizens who belong in the realm of public rights and duties.

In "Disability and the Right to Work," the philosopher Gregory S. Kavka argued that people with disabilities in advantaged societies[19] have a right "not only to receive a basic income, but to *earn* incomes at—or above—the basic maintenance level" (Kavka 1992, 265). He described this right as follows:

> What specific sorts of treatment or "special opportunities" are entailed by handicapped people's right to work? First, a right of nondiscrimination in employment and promotion—that people not be denied jobs on the basis of disabilities that are not relevant to their capacities to carry out the tasks associated with those jobs. Second, a right to compensatory training and education, funded by society, that will allow disabled people the opportunity to overcome their handicaps and make themselves qualified for desirable employment. Third, a right to reasonable investments by society and employers to make jobs accessible to otherwise qualified people with disabilities. Fourth, and most controversially, a right to minimal (or tie-breaking) "affirmative action" or "preferential treatment": being admitted, hired, or promoted when in competition with other equally qualified candidates. Spelled out in this way, the right of handicapped persons to work is seen to be, in its various elements, a right against society, government, and private employers. (Kavka 1992, 265)

This sounds like a good beginning to me. However, I am wary of being satisfied with "desirable employment." People with disabilities should have opportunities equal to those of non-disabled people to develop their talents and work at the things they could do best, not just at any "desirable employment." How many potential Stephen Hawkings[20] might we have already condemned to lives of idleness, or boring, trivial labour in 'sheltered workshops?' In thinking about providing training and education, why not start with the assumption that people should receive a reasonable amount of help to make significant contributions to society according to their potential, both for their sakes and for the benefit of society? If schools, colleges, universities, and workplaces were designed or modified to be fully accessible, and if discriminatory practices were ended, the extra help that a person with a disability would need to meet her/his potential would not be very much greater than that needed by a non-disabled person.

Of course, help in achieving one's goals often has to be a compromise between what an individual wants to do and what a society is willing and able to offer. For instance, societies cannot reasonably be expected to restore all opportunities that are lost due to lack of ability. Some inabilities are widespread in the population, such as the inability to dance gracefully or to perform complex mathematical operations. Although these inabilities do result in lost opportunities, and although we might say that a dancer who lost her ability to dance or a mathematician who lost her ability to do mathematics had been disabled,[21] it would be wrong to consider them disabilities in any sense that would imply a social obligation to give those particular opportunities to the people who lack the abilities. Many other inabilities are not particularly important to full participation in the life of a society, and it would be inappropriate to consider them disabilities, even though they do deprive people of opportunities. Thus, I want to say that preventing disability requires providing the help necessary to create, wherever possible,[22] the ability to participate in all *major aspects* of life in a society, in which I would include (for Canada and the United States) at least work, social life, political life, religious life, cultural life, personal relationships, and recreation.

Yet I am not satisfied with this description either. I feel strongly that the ultimate goal of social assistance for people with disabilities should be to enable them to fulfill their potentials, enjoy their lives, and make as full a contribution to society as they can, not merely to enable them to participate. But here I encounter a conflict. Should the goals of social help for people with disabilities be higher than those currently operating for most people without disabilities? Yes, because they should be higher for everyone. But I do not want the just claims of people with disabilities to be drowned in a general discussion of social justice and political economy.

There are still so many obstacles to thinking clearly and accurately about the needs and claims of people with disabilities that it seems to me too early to attempt to weigh them in relation to the needs and claims of others.

Obstacles to the Deconstruction of Disability

As Ron Amundson points out (1992, 115–16), theorists and others tend to worry about potential "social hijacking" of resources by extremely needy people if accessibility is given the status of a civil right. Proposals to provide any assistance to people with disabilities inevitably raise concerns about cost and benefit, and possible drains on resources, partly because most people do not realize that different help could in many instances cut overall costs, partly because most people still think of disability as a personal or family responsibility, and partly because public aid to people with disabilities has long been characterized as pure charity, rather than as social investment in ability and productivity. It is questionable whether making Canada and the United States fully accessible to people with disabilities would be more or less costly than the widespread current approach of providing unearned subsistence incomes or expensive institutionalization for many people with disabilities who would not need them in an accessible society.

There is considerable disagreement among economists and rehabilitation researchers about the net monetary costs of rehabilitation and accessibility, and only a great deal of research (and probably some experimentation) will answer the questions.[23] There is also the question of who should pay for rehabilitation and modifications to create greater accessibility—employers, governments, or private insurers? I will make no attempt to offer answers to these questions here. I will, however, draw attention to the fact that the people of Sweden have created a much higher degree of accessibility in their country than we have in Canada or the United States[24] and suggest that they might be looked to for imaginative solutions to problems of rehabilitation and access. The Swedes are leaders in the technological development of aids for people with disabilities, which the Swedish government provides to those who need them (Milner 1989, 193). A 1987 study by Sven E. Olsson found that, in Sweden, "average household income for the severely handicapped was only slightly below that of households without handicapped members" (Milner 1989, 191). Recent statistics for the United States show that fifty-nine percent of adults with disabilities live in households with incomes of $25,000 or less, compared to thirty-seven percent of non-disabled adults.[25]

In the cost-benefit debates, it is essential to realize that the costs of the current welfare and warehousing approaches to disability are human, as well as economic. They deprive thousands of people of minimally decent lives and millions more of opportunities to participate in aspects of social life that non-disabled people consider essential to the meaningfulness of their own lives. Moreover, they hurt the non-disabled as well as the disabled, not only because many non-disabled people know and love people with disabilities whom these policies hurt, and because many people without disabilities must work much harder on behalf of their disabled friends and family members to make up for the inaccessibility and hardship created by these policies, but also because the non-disabled must live with the fear that illness, accident, or old age will render their own lives or those of their non-disabled loved ones worthless to themselves and society.

Attitudes that disability is a personal or family problem (of biological or accidental origin), rather than a matter of social responsibility, are cultural contributors to disability and powerful factors working against social measures to increase ability. The attitude that disability is a personal problem is manifested when people with disabilities are expected to overcome obstacles to their participation in activities by their own extraordinary efforts. The public adoration of a few disabled heroes who are believed to have 'overcome their handicaps' against great odds both demonstrates and contributes to this expectation. The attitude that disability is a family matter is manifested when the families of people with disabilities are expected to provide whatever they need, even at great personal sacrifice by other family members. Barbara Hillyer describes the strength of expectations that mothers and other caregivers will do whatever is necessary to 'normalize' the lives of family members, especially children, with disabilities—not only providing care, but often doing the work of two people to maintain the illusion that there is nothing 'wrong' in the family (Hillyer 1993).

These attitudes are related to the fact that many modern societies split human concerns into public and private worlds. Typically, those with disabilities and illnesses have been relegated to the private realm, along with women, children, and the old. This worldwide tendency creates particularly intractable problems for women with disabilities; since they fit two 'private' categories, they are often kept at home, isolated and overprotected (Driedger and Gray 1992). In addition, the confinement of people with disabilities in the private realm exploits women's traditional caregiving roles in order to meet the needs of people with disabilities (Hillyer 1993), and it hides the need for measures to make the public realm accessible to everyone.

There also seem to be definite material advantages for some people (people without disabilities who have no disabled friends or relatives for whom they feel responsible) to seeing disability as a biological misfortune, the bad luck of individuals, and a personal or family problem. Accessibility and creating ability cost time, energy, and/or money. Charities for people with disabilities are big businesses that employ a great many non-disabled professionals; these charities depend upon the belief that responding to the difficulties faced by people with disabilities is superogatory for people who are not members of the family—not a social responsibility to be fulfilled through governments, but an act of kindness. Moreover, both the charities and most government bureaucracies (which also employ large numbers of non-disabled professionals) hand out help which would not be needed in a society that was planned and organized to include people with a wide range of physical and mental abilities. The potential resistance created by these vested interests in disability should not be underestimated.

The 'personal misfortune' approach to disability is also part of what I call the 'lottery' approach to life, in which individual good fortune is hoped for as a substitute for social planning that deals realistically with everyone's capabilities, needs and limitations, and the probable distribution of hardship.[26] In Canada and the United States, most people reject the 'lottery' approach to such matters as acute health care for themselves and their families or basic education for their children. We expect it to be there when we need it, and we are (more or less) willing to pay for it to be there. I think the lottery approach persists with respect to disability partly because fear, based on ignorance and false beliefs about disability, makes it difficult for most non-disabled people to identify with people with disabilities.[27] If the non-disabled saw the disabled as potentially themselves or as their future selves, they would want their societies to be fully accessible and to invest the resources necessary to create ability wherever possible. They would feel that 'charity' is as inappropriate a way of thinking about resources for people with disabilities as it is about emergency medical care or basic education.

The philosopher Anita Silvers maintains that it is probably impossible for most non-disabled people to imagine what life is like with a disability, and that their own becoming disabled is unthinkable to them (Silvers 1994). Certainly many people without disabilities believe that life with a disability would not be worth living. This is reflected in the assumption that potential disability is a sufficient reason for aborting a fetus, as well as in the frequent statements by non-disabled people that they would not want to live if they had to use a wheelchair, lost their eyesight, were dependent on others for care, and so on.[28] The belief that life would not be worth living with a disability would be enough to prevent them from imagining their own disablement. This belief is fed by stereotypes and ignorance of the lives of people with disabilities. For example, the assumption that permanent, global incompetence results from any major disability is still prevalent; there is a strong presumption that competent people either have no major physical or mental limitations or are able to hide them in public and social life.

It seems that the cultural constructions of disability, including the ignorance, stereotyping, and stigmatization that feed fears of disability, have to be at least partly deconstructed before disability can be seen by more people as a set of social problems and social responsibilities. Until that change in perspective happens, people with disabilities and their families will continue to be given too much individual responsibility for 'overcoming' disabilities, expectations for the participation of people with disabilities in public life will be far too low, and social injustices that are recognized now (at least in the abstract), such as discrimination against people with disabilities, will be misunderstood.

To illustrate, let me look briefly at the problem of discrimination. Clearly, when considering whether some action or situation is an instance of discrimination on the basis of ability, the trick is to distinguish ability to do the relevant things from ability to do irrelevant things. But, given that so many places and activities are structured for people with a narrow range of abilities, telling the two apart is not always easy. No one has to walk to be a typist, but if a company is housed in a building that is inaccessible to wheelchairs, and therefore refuses to hire a competent typist who uses a wheelchair because it would be expensive to fix the building, has it discriminated against her on the basis of her disability? Laws may say yes, but people will resist the laws unless they can see that the typist's inability to work in that office is not solely a characteristic of her as an individual. Most people will be ready to recognize refusal to hire her to work in a wheelchair-accessible office, provided she is the most competent typist who applied, as discrimination against her because of her disability; they will regard her disability (like her race) as a personal characteristic irrelevant in the circumstances. But will they be ready to require a company to create wheelchair accessibility so that it can hire her? This is being tested now in the United States by the 1990 Americans with Disabilities Act. Although I expect the Act to have an invaluable educational function, I predict that it will be very difficult to enforce until more people see accessibility as a public responsibility. Only then will they be able to recognize inabilities that are created by faulty planning and organization as irrelevant.

Consider these sentiments expressed in the Burger King case, as described in *The Disability Rag and Resource* (March/April 1994, 43):

> When deaf actress Terrylene Sacchetti sued Burger King under the ADA for refusing to serve her when she handed the cashier a written order at the pickup window instead of using the intercom, Stan Kyker, executive vice-president of the California Restaurant Association, said that those "people (with disabilities) are going to have to accept that they are not 100 percent whole and they can't be made 100 percent whole in everything they do in life."

Had a woman been refused service because she used a cane to walk up to the counter, her treatment would, I think, have been recognized at once as discrimination. But since Ms. Sacchetti was refused service because she was unable to perform the activity (ordering food) in the way (orally) that the restaurant required it to be performed, the refusal to serve her was not immediately recognized as discrimination. Indeed, the representative of the restaurant association apparently felt comfortable defending it on the grounds that her individual characteristics were the obstacles to Ms. Sacchetti's being served.

When I imagine a society without disabilities, I do not imagine a society in which every physical and mental 'defect' or 'abnormality' can be cured. On the contrary, I believe the fantasy that someday everything will be 'curable' is a significant obstacle to the social deconstruction of disability. Instead I imagine a fully accessible society, the most fundamental characteristic of which is universal recognition that all structures have to be built and all activities have to be organized for the widest practical range of human abilities. In such a society, a person who cannot walk would not be disabled, because every major kind of activity that is accessible to someone who can walk would be accessible to someone who cannot, and likewise with seeing, hearing, speaking, moving one's arms, working for long stretches of time without rest, and many other physical and mental functions. I do not mean that everyone would be able to do everything, but rather that, with respect to the major aspects of life in the society, the differences in ability between someone who can walk, or see, or hear, and someone who cannot would be no more significant than the differences in ability among people who can walk, see, or hear. Not everyone who is not disabled now can play basketball or sing in a choir, but everyone who is not disabled now can participate in sports or games and make art, and that sort of general ability should be the goal in deconstructing disability.

I talk about accessibility and ability rather than independence or integration because I think that neither independence nor integration is always an appropriate goal for people with disabilities. Some people cannot live independently because they will always need a great deal of help from caregivers,[29] and some people with disabilities, for example the Deaf, do not want to be integrated into non-disabled society; they prefer their own, separate social life. Everyone should, however, have access to opportunities to develop their abilities, to work, and to participate in the full range of public and private activities available to the rest of society.

3 〽

Disability as Difference

Sociologist Erving Goffman's 1963 book *Stigma: Notes on the Management of Spoiled Identity* is still the most influential description of the processes of stigmatization. Goffman frequently uses disabilities as examples of stigmas, which has increased the influence of his book on those attempting to understand the social devaluing of people with disabilities. Although Goffman's work contains significant insights that apply to the experience of disability, I believe that his lumping together all sources of stigma, which causes him to overgeneralize, prevents him from seeing some crucial aspects of the stigmas of illness and disability. In addition, because he does not question the social 'norms' that stigmatize people with disabilities, he tends to adopt a patronizing tone in speaking of people who do not meet them, and to belittle and underestimate their efforts to live by different 'norms.'

Let us look first at how Goffman characterizes stigma:

> Three grossly different types of stigma may be mentioned. First there are the abominations of the body—the various physical deformities. Next there are the blemishes of individual character perceived as weak will, domineering or unnatural passions, treacherous and rigid beliefs, and dishonesty. . . . Finally there are the tribal stigma of race, nation, and religion, these being stigma that can be transmitted through lineages and equally contaminate all members of a family. In all of these various

> instances of stigma, however, . . . the same sociological features are found: an individual who might have been received easily in ordinary social intercourse possesses a trait that can obtrude itself upon attention and turn those of us whom he meets away from him, breaking the claim that his other attributes have on us. He possesses a stigma, an undesired differentness from what we had anticipated. (Goffman 1963, 4–5)

Here Goffman misses the importance of the specific symbolic meanings people with disabilities have for others in a society. It is interesting that his own language reflects those meanings. He refers unself-consciously to "physical deformities," even though the examples he uses throughout the book include all sorts of disabilities, including deafness and stuttering; then he calls them "abominations of the body," the strongest expression he uses for any of the types of stigma. Dishonesty, in contrast, is called a "blemish" of character. Elsewhere in the book, he uses such terms as "affliction," "victim," and "cripple," and introduces people as "cases." Of course he was writing in 1963, when such language was still widely used, so I am not drawing attention to it to criticize his personal attitudes toward disability. My point is that he exhibited subscription to the cultural stereotypes and meanings of disability far more than he examined it.

Later in his book, Goffman says of stigma that it "involves not so much a set of concrete individuals who can be separated into two piles, the stigmatized and the normal, as a pervasive two-role social process in which every individual participates in both roles, at least in some connections and in some phases of life" (Goffman 1963, 138). But then he says that "[t]he lifelong attributes of a particular individual may cause him to be type-cast; he may have to play the stigmatized role in almost all of his social situations" (138). He makes no attempt to explain why some attributes typecast a person and others do not; I do not see how he could explain it without considering the symbolic meanings of stigmatizing characteristics. I will return to the subject of symbolic meanings of disability later.

Goffman did contribute to the understanding of disability by bringing to public attention some of the social and psychological burdens of living as a person with a disability in the United States and places with similar cultures. He is particularly good on some of the dynamics of 'passing' as non-disabled (42), the obligation placed on 'different' individuals to 'manage' social situations with 'normals' in such a way as to protect the 'normals' from discomfort (especially 21–23 and 115–16), and the propensity of stigmatized people to place themselves along with others like them in hierarchies of value (107). Moreover, by comparing the stigmas of disability to those of race and ethnic origin, he at least implies, although he never explicitly supports, the possibility of seeing disability as a civil rights issue.

Nevertheless, Goffman repeatedly fails to appreciate the possibility that having at least some disabilities may be, like membership in some other groups that are stigmatized, as good as or better than 'normality.' He discusses valuing one's difference only as a coping strategy of the stigmatized, without calling into question the objectivity or permanence of the values that regard them as less than 'normal.' On the contrary, he rates valuing one's difference and identifying closely with those who share it rather low, even as a coping strategy:

> The first set of sympathetic others is of course those who share his stigma. Knowing from their own experience what it is like to have this particular stigma, some of them can provide the individual with instruction in the tricks of the trade and with a circle of lament to which he can withdraw for moral support and for the comfort of feeling at home, at ease, accepted as a person who really is like any other normal person. . . .
>
> Among his own, the stigmatized individual can use his disadvantage as a basis for organizing life, but he must resign himself to a half-world to do so. Here he may develop to its fullest his sad tale accounting for his possession of the stigma. . . .
>
> On the other hand, he may find that the tales of his fellow-sufferers bore him, and that the whole matter of focusing on atrocity tales, on group superiority, on trickster stories, in short, on the "problem," is one of the large penalties for having one. (1963, 20–21)

The possibility of genuinely felt group pride (such as Deaf pride) seems to escape Goffman's imagination. He can see solidarity among the different only as poor compensation for the acceptance as 'normals' that is denied them. He even seems to miss the genuineness of pride among stigmatized ethnic groups. Consequently, Goffman also misses an important difference between people with disabilities and other stigmatized people. Most stigmatized people are members of stigmatized groups that have subcultures within which the stigma may be made irrelevant or at least ameliorated by the group's own values. Most (but not all) people with disabilities grow up with non-disabled people and/or are constantly surrounded by them, absorbing their values and assumptions; they have little or no contact with a subculture that destigmatizes or positively values their difference from the non-disabled (Zola 1993, 167).[1] Perhaps Goffman's inability to imagine group pride is caused partly by his overgeneralizing from examples of people with disabilities.

Nevertheless, inability or unwillingness to imagine taking real (as opposed to defensive, self-deceptive) pride in a difference that is stigmatized by the majority indicates a failure to question the values of the majority; in effect, Goffman represents those values rather than examining them. Insofar as he holds out any collective hope for stigmatized people, he places it in the possibility that their differences may someday be ignored or at least considered unimportant relative to their other characteristics, not in the possibility that they might be revalued and appreciated. Difference remains a curse.

People with Disabilities as 'the Other'

In many ways, the concept of 'the Other' as developed in feminist theorizing is more fruitful than stigma for understanding the social position of people with disabilities. When Simone de Beauvoir used this term to elucidate men's views of women (and women's views of themselves), she emphasized that Man is considered essential, Woman inessential; Man is the Subject, Woman the Other. (Beauvoir 1952, xvi) In *Pornography and Silence* (1981), Susan Griffin expands upon this idea by showing how we project rejected aspects of ourselves onto groups of people who are designated 'the Other.' Thus, as I understand the concept of 'the Other,' it involves two essential processes: When we make people 'Other,' we group them together as the objects of our experience instead of regarding them as subjects of experience with whom we might identify, and we see them primarily as symbolic of something else—usually, but not always, something we reject and fear and project onto them. To the non-disabled, people with disabilities and people with dangerous or incurable illnesses symbolize, among other things, imperfection, failure to control the body, and everyone's vulnerability to weakness, pain, and death.

Griffin, in a characteristically insightful passage from "The Way of All Ideology" (1982), illustrates the dynamics of making another person symbolic to oneself:

As I was composing the notes toward this writing, I was forced to confront my own self-denial and projection. Waiting in line to be served in a restaurant, I began to notice an older woman who was sitting at a table alone. She was not eating, and she seemed to be miserable. I assumed she was waiting to be met. Her expression, the paleness of her skin, something in her posture all indicated to me that she might be ill, perhaps even seriously ill, perhaps dying. I imagined that she was nauseous. I was hungry. Yet as I looked at her I felt my appetite begin to ebb, a nausea seemed about to invade me by virtue of her presence. I was afraid that I might be seated at a table next to her, so that I might become more nauseous, or be contaminated. Slowly, despite another voice in me that urged reason and compassion, I felt an anger toward her. Why was she sick in this restaurant? Why force people who are eating to participate in her misery? I wanted to shout at her that she should go home, but of course, I did not. I was deeply ashamed of my feelings. And because of this shame I hid them away.

. . . And now as I looked at my imagined portrait of her son I saw myself. For according to my ideological explanation of male hostility toward women, men are afraid of women, and most particularly of their mothers, because they fear death. And was not that precisely what I had projected on her, my own fear of death, of the possibility that my body might fail me, and instead of giving me hunger, give me nausea? (1982, 648–49)

This sort of projection is something we can all do to each other, but the process is often not symmetrical, because one group of people has more power than another to call itself the paradigm of humanity and to make the world suit its own needs and validate its own experiences; the non-disabled are such a group in relation to people with disabilities. Non-disabled people may sometimes be 'the Other' to people with disabilities (as when disabled people refer to them as TABS, Temporarily Able-Bodieds), but the consequences of this 'Othering' for the able-bodied are minor. Most non-disabled people can afford not to notice that they might be 'the Other' to people with disabilities. The reverse is not true.

However, people with disabilities can and sometimes do make each other 'the Other,' for example by despising those who have less control over their bodily functions. There are often hierarchies of power and value in rehabilitative institutions, with those who act most like the non-disabled at the top, and those who have least control of their bodies at the bottom (Frank 1988). This suggests that failure to control the body is one of the most powerful symbolic meanings of disability.

The Symbolic Meanings of Illnesses and Disabilities

The symbolic meanings that disabilities and dangerous or incurable illnesses have are both products of and contributors to making people with them 'the Other.' Of course different disabilities and illnesses can have different meanings within a society (consider the different meanings of epilepsy and AIDS, or bipolar disorder and paraplegia), and the same disability or illness may have different meanings in different societies or in the same society at different times (tuberculosis is no longer considered romantic in Western societies, as it once was). Moreover other characteristics of a person, such as race, age, gender, class, or sexual identity, may alter the meaning of her/his disability. For example, Fine and Asch (1988, 3) point out that cultural associations of disability with dependency, childlikeness, and helplessness clash with cultural expectations of masculinity but overlap with cultural expectations of femininity, so that a disabled man is perceived as a "wounded male," while a disabled woman is redundantly fulfilling cultural expectations of her.

Susan Sontag has described in detail and with a critical eye the symbolic meanings of having tuberculosis, cancer, and AIDS in Western cultures: excess passion (in the past, for TB), repression of feeling, especially rage (for cancer), invasion by an alien force (cancer and AIDS), pollution (AIDS), cosmic punishment for immorality (AIDS) or for living unhealthy lives (cancer and AIDS), the possibility of moral or spiritual contagion with evil (cancer and AIDS), and so forth. (Sontag 1977, 1988) I find it interesting that myalgic encephalomyelitis, or chronic fatigue immune dysfunction syndrome, was for a while described in the media primarily in terms of the symbolic meanings that were created for it in the mid 1980s; it was the "yuppie flu," a punishment of nature visited upon the ambitious, especially ambitious women. Even now, few people realize that it occurs in many children, old people, and people in all socioeconomic classes, or that it can be a chronic, debilitating illness; the mythic descriptions are more exciting and more reassuring to the healthy than the reality. Moreover, a disease that causes profound fatigue was perfect for symbolizing the fatigue that many people experienced or feared when attempting to meet the demands of the 1980s for higher performance at a faster pace in all aspects of life. It is interesting that the words "Immune Dysfunction" are usually omitted from its name (which was given to it by the Centers for Disease Control) in popular reference. I find that friends and acquaintances often forget that the primary symptom of my disease now is chronic pain; the extreme fatigue that dominated the first few years of my illness captured people's imaginations, and they still tell me that their own experiences of exhaustion make them realize what it must be like for me.

Although different illnesses carry different symbolic meanings, there are, I think, meanings associated with being chronically ill with anything. In my society, acceptance of the chronicity of one's illness is generally perceived as 'giving up hope,' which clearly implies that the chronically ill person is not good enough as s/he is but needs hope of getting better. Chronic illness also seems to mean chronic misery or unhappiness. I have the impression that people expect me to be miserable as long as I am ill. If I say I am doing well, they tend to assume that my health has improved. I have experimented with saying, in answer to "How are you?," "I'm sick but happy,"[2] but so far it has produced a lot of silence and puzzled looks. Most people who know me are aware that I live a complex life of work and relationships, just as they do, but it seems to be hard to reconcile that fact with the fact that I have a disabling illness. I understand the difficulty all too well; for most of the first few years of my illness, I could not imagine having a good life with it. I wonder frequently if some people think I am not as ill as I say I am, and others think I am putting on a brave face. I feel the weight of a social obligation to be either healthy or miserable. Nevertheless, I have concluded that I am always sick and often happy, and that this seems very peculiar in my culture.

As with illnesses, although different disabilities have different meanings within a society, there seem to be meanings associated with having any physical disability. (See Mason 1987 and Morris 1991 on England; Vargas 1989 and Dahl 1993 on Canada; Zola 1993 on the United States.) There also seem to be some similarities in the meanings of having a physical disability across societies and over time.[3] Disability tends to be associated with tragic loss, weakness, passivity, dependency, helplessness, shame, and global incompetence.[4] In the societies where Western science and medicine are powerful culturally, and where their promise to control nature is still widely believed, people with disabilities are constant reminders of the failures of that promise, and of the inability of science and medicine to protect everyone from illness, disability, and death. They are 'the Others' that science would like to forget. In the societies where there are strong ideals of bodily perfection to which everyone is supposed to aspire, people with disabilities are the imperfect 'Others' who can never come close enough to the ideals; identifying with them would remind the non-disabled that their ideals imply a degree of control that must eventually elude them too.[5]

Some people with disabilities, the 'disabled heroes,' symbolize heroic control against all odds, and their public images comfort non-disabled people by reaffirming the possibility of overcoming the body. Disabled heroes are people with readily apparent disabilities who receive public attention because they accomplish things that are unusual even for the able-bodied. It is revealing that, with few exceptions (Helen Keller and, recently, Stephen Hawking are among them), disabled heroes are recognized for performing feats of physical strength and endurance. While disabled heroes can be inspiring and heartening to the disabled, they may give the non-disabled the false impression that anyone can 'overcome' a disability. Disabled heroes usually have extraordinary social, economic, and physical resources that are not available to most people with those disabilities. In addition, many disabled people are not capable of performing physical heroics, because many (perhaps most) disabilities reduce or consume the energy and stamina of people who have them and do not just limit them in some particular kind of physical activity. The image of the disabled hero may reduce the 'Otherness' of a few people with disabilities, but because it creates an ideal that most people with disabilities cannot meet, it *increases* the 'Otherness' of the majority of people with disabilities.

Some Consequences of Being 'the Other'

For people with disabilities, the consequences of being 'the Other' to non-disabled people include all those aspects of the social construction of disability that result from the failure of non-disabled people to identify with people with disabilities, or to identify themselves as potentially disabled, including planning and structuring society for a narrow range of abilities, refusing to take responsibility for creating ability, rigid and unimaginative expectations of performance, and false or inadequate cultural representation. This is a self-perpetuating social system, since the exclusion of people with disabilities from many aspects of life in a society prevents non-disabled people from getting to know them, and also prevents people with disabilities from making their own mark on culture, both of which contribute to their remaining the symbolic 'Other' to non-disabled people.

Like other people who are made 'Other,' people with disabilities are subjected to high rates of verbal, physical, and sexual abuse (Matthews 1983; Ridington 1989; Sobsey 1989).[6] For people whose disabilities are readily apparent, every appearance in the public world means risking insult, ridicule, and embarrassment, but also physical assault. Diane DeVries, who was born with short arms, no hands, and no legs, describes an incident in her childhood:

> I just knew I was different. Certain things could happen during the day to make me sad or mad, 'cause I could go . . . weeks without it bothering me at all, because nothing happened. But something *could* happen, like once when I was a little kid. I was in the wagon and we were in this trailer park, and some kid came up to me with a knife. He said, "Aw, you ain't got no arms, you ain't got no legs, and now you're not gonna have no head." He held me right there, by the neck, and had a little knife. It was one of those bratty kids that did weird things. (Frank 1988, 48)

As Anne Finger points out (Fellows and Razack 1994, 1055), people with disabilities are also subjected to forms of abuse, such as public stripping in hospitals, which are extremely damaging to their self-esteem and sexual identity, but which might not even be recognized as abuse by people who regard them as 'Other.' One has to be aware of the subjectivity of a person to imagine her/his experience of events and how s/he might be affected by one's actions.

'Otherness' is maintained by culture but also limits culture profoundly. Canadian and United States culture rarely include people with disabilities in their depictions of ordinary daily life, and they exclude the struggles, thoughts, and feelings of people with disabilities from any shared cultural understanding of human experience. This tends to make people with disabilities feel invisible (except when they are made hypervisible in their symbolic roles as heroes or tragic victims), and it deprives the non-disabled of the knowledge and perspectives that people with disabilities could contribute to culture, including knowledge of how to live well with physical and mental limitations and suffering. Because disabled people's experience is not integrated into the culture, most newly disabled people know little or nothing about how to live with long-term or life-threatening illness, how to communicate with doctors and nurses and medical bureaucrats about their problems, how to live with limitation, uncertainty, pain, and other symptoms when doctors cannot make them go away. Nor do they have any idea that they might gain something from their experiences of disability. There is a cultural gulf between the disabled and the non-disabled; to become disabled is to enter a different world. Yet experiences of living with a disability are not by their nature private, separable from the rest of life and the rest of society. They can and should be shared throughout the culture as much as we share experiences of love, work, and family life.

I have found that people who realize concretely and vividly their own physical and mental limitations, or who understand from their own lives that they cannot control everything, not even the things that are most important to them, are more open to identifying with people with disabilities, less inclined to regard and treat them as 'the Other.'[7] On the other hand, I am uncomfortable with efforts to undermine the 'Otherness' of people with disabilities by overextending the category of disability, for example by claiming that everyone is 'disabled' in some way because everyone has some limitations and 'imperfections'; this can lead to underestimating the struggles of people whose limitations or sufferings are much greater because of their physical and/or mental conditions and because of the many socially constructed obstacles in their lives besides their 'Otherness.'[8]

Disability as Difference

Disability may be looked at as a form of difference from what is considered normal or usual or paradigmatic in a society. Difference is a more general concept than either 'Otherness' or stigmatization, both of which are forms of difference. Difference is also more value-neutral than either stigmatization or 'Otherness,' and it is therefore possible and necessary to ask whether a particular kind of difference is as good as or better than 'normality.' Because it leaves open the question of value, I prefer to speak of disability as a form of difference, while recognizing that both stigma and being 'the Other' are aspects of the social oppression of people with disabilities.

It is not uncommon for a difference to be valued for being exotic and interesting, even as the people who embody it or are associated with it are kept on the outskirts of society (Fiedler 1984). People with disabilities are subject to this double-edged form of appreciation, which plays a role in their token cultural representation. Since their difference is what is seen to make them interesting, it is highlighted, and their similarity to people without disabilities is minimized or else commented upon as amazing or amusing in order to maintain focus upon the difference. Of course, to those with a disability, their difference is not exotic, and it may be valued for itself, or for the different knowledge, perspective, and experience of life it gives them. Among people without disabilities, it is somewhat more unusual to view disabilities as *valuable* forms of difference without treating the people who have them as curiosities, but this attitude is repeatedly demonstrated in the writings of the neurologist Oliver Sacks.

Sacks's appreciation of difference is shown in his descriptions of the lives of people with diagnoses of major neurological 'disorders.' First, he explores respectfully the meanings that their 'symptoms' have for the people who experience them. Second, although Sacks does not minimize the suffering of his patients, he is very willing to see the intrinsic value (and sometimes extrinsic advantages) of some of the forms of consciousness that are consequences of pathology. Third, he makes us aware of the contextuality of disability by describing situations in which his patients' differences from the 'normal' are not disadvantages.

For example, Sacks discusses the complex situation of "Witty Ticcy Ray," a man with Tourette's syndrome who was "almost incapacitated by multiple tics of extreme violence coming in volleys every few seconds" (Sacks 1987, 97). Ray had been fired from a dozen jobs because of his tics, was frequently embroiled in crises because of "his impatience, his pugnacity, and his coarse, brilliant 'chutzpah,'" and had marital difficulties caused by his loud, involuntary outbursts of obscenities, all of which were manifestations of Tourette's. On the other hand, Tourette's was also the source of his famous, wild improvisations as a weekend jazz drummer and his extraordinary ability at Ping-Pong.

When Sacks treated Ray with Haldol, Ray eventually became free of tics and able to work steadily. His marriage improved, and he had children and many friends. But he also lost something:

> During his working hours, and working week, Ray remains 'sober, solid, square' on Haldol—this is how he describes his 'Haldol self.' He is slow and deliberate in his movements and judgments, with none of the impatience, the impetuosity, he showed before Haldol, but equally, none of the wild improvisations and inspirations. . . . He is less sharp, less quick in repartee, no longer bubbling with witty tics or ticcy wit. He no longer enjoys or excels at ping-pong or other games . . . he is less competitive . . . and also less playful; and he has lost the impulse, or the knack, of sudden 'frivolous' moves which take everyone by surprise. He has lost his obscenities, his coarse chutzpah, his spunk. . . .
>
> Most important, and disabling, because this was vital for him—as a means of support and self-expression—he found that on Haldol he was musically 'dull,' average, competent, but lacking energy, enthusiasm,

extravagance and joy. He no longer had tics or compulsive hitting of the drums—but he no longer had wild and creative surges. (Sacks 1987, 100–101)

Eventually Sacks and Ray worked out a solution. Ray took Haldol during the working week, and stopped taking it at weekends, so that he could still experience the "wildness" of Tourette's syndrome while having the rest of the life he wanted.

Another of Sack's patients, Natasha K., came to him at the age of ninety, explaining that shortly after her eighty-eighth birthday she began to notice a change in her state of mind. "I felt more energetic, more alive—I felt young once again." (Sacks 1987, 102) This change was, as she suspected, caused by the advent of neurosyphilis after a latent period of seventy years following a primary, uncured infection with syphilis. She knew that it could progress to a severe dementia, which she did not want, but she did not want it 'cured' either, since she felt better with the neurosyphilis than she had in twenty years. Sacks treated her with penicillin, which halted the progress of infection but fortunately did nothing to reverse the changes that had already occurred in her brain. She was well satisfied with the treatment. Sacks says of Natasha K., Ray, and related examples:

> We are in strange waters here, where all the usual considerations may be reversed—where illness may be wellness, and normality illness, where excitement may be either bondage or release, and where reality may lie in ebriety, not sobriety. It is the very realm of Cupid and Dionysus. (Sacks 1987, 107)

In Western scientific-medical culture, it is far more common to assume that states of mind that are caused by or associated with pathological states of the body are themselves pathological, and to dismiss both their perspective and their content as illusory. This attitude, which seems to be based on a model of temporary illness, total recovery, and complete return to one's former self, makes it unlikely that we will be open to regarding illness and disability as either sources of knowledge or valuable ways of being.[9]

Yet as Sacks's work demonstrates, if one looks at disabilities as forms of difference and takes seriously the possibility that they may be valuable, one begins to notice the lived reality of people one may have assumed were simply less able and less fortunate versions of oneself. Then it becomes obvious that people with disabilities have experiences, by virtue of their disabilities, which non-disabled people do not have, and which are sources of knowledge that is not directly accessible to non-disabled people. Some of this knowledge, for example, how to live with a suffering body, would be of enormous practical help to most people, as I have already pointed out. Much of it would enrich and expand our culture, and some of it has the potential to change our thinking and our ways of life profoundly.

For example, because people with disabilities cannot do or be many things that non-disabled people feel they themselves must do or be in order to be 'normal,' sane, and happy, people with disabilities are in better positions to notice and criticize cultural myths about the body and mind,[10] as well as such matters as self-worth, intimacy, sexuality, dependency, and independence. When people cannot ground their self-worth in their conformity to cultural body-ideals or social expectations of performance, the exact nature of those ideals and expectations and their pervasive, unquestioning acceptance become much clearer. So does the fact that most people must fail eventually to conform to them, a fact that those who can currently conform do not usually want to face. When people's genitals are numb or paralyzed, they may discover things about the nature of intimacy and sexuality that remain unknown to people who can participate in cultural obsessions with goal-oriented, genital sex. (See Bullard and Knight 1981; Morris 1989.) And an adult who needs someone else's daily help to eat, wash, dress, and use the toilet may see very clearly how a culture despises this kind of dependency, but also how the same culture promotes the self-deception that 'independent' adults do not need each other's help, that we are not all profoundly dependent on one another.[11]

A Standpoint Epistemology for People with Disabilities?

These observations about the knowledge of people with disabilities raise questions that have been disputed extensively in feminist theory, questions about the epistemic advantages of oppressed groups and the plausibility of standpoint epistemologies. In *The Science Question in Feminism* (1986), Sandra Harding describes the feminist standpoint epistemologies, that is, feminist descriptions of the nature of knowledge and the processes of creating knowledge, thus:

> The logic of the standpoint epistemologies depends on the understanding that the "master's position" in any set of dominating social

relations tends to produce distorted visions of the real regularities and underlying causal tendencies in social relations—including human interactions with nature. The feminist standpoint epistemologies argue that because men are in the master's position vis-à-vis women, women's social experience—conceptualized through the lenses of feminist theory—can provide the grounds for a less distorted understanding of the world around us. (Harding 1986, 191)

Harding (1986, chapter 7) and others have pointed out the questionable assumptions of the standpoint epistemologies: that women, or even feminists, are a social group in the sense required by these epistemologies; that identities/social positions that cut across gender, such as race, class, and culture, are not as important to knowledge as gender; that other identities/social positions, and also historical contexts, do not profoundly affect how gender is experienced. Harding and others have labelled the critiques of these assumptions "postmodernist." They include the critiques of "universalization" and "essentialism" that have been very influential in feminist theory since the early 1980s.[12] These point out, among other things, that efforts to describe 'women' as a social group and to honour 'women's experiences' ignored and made invisible differences among women, including differences of race, class, sexual identity, age, ethnicity, and (dis)ability, often falsely universalizing the social positions and experiences of small groups of relatively privileged women (Spelman 1988; Fine and Asch 1988; Higginbotham 1992).

I want to avoid making the same mistakes with the category "people with disabilities" that were, and still are, frequently made with the category "women." We now know, from the extensive writings of women with disabilities, that living with similar disabilities is different for females and males. An emerging literature also reveals that living with similar disabilities is different for women of different races, classes, sexual identities, and ethnicities. (See, for example, Rooney and Israel 1985; *Canadian Woman Studies* 1993.) Moreover, we know that living with disabilities is different for people with different disabilities, such as paraplegia and blindness, and different for people whose disabilities are readily apparent compared to those whose disabilities can be hidden (Todoroff and Lewis 1992). It is therefore important not to assume that people with disabilities identify with all others who have disabilities or share a single perspective on disability (or anything else), or that having a disability is the most important aspect of a person's identity or social position.

It is worth noting that some of the most influential tendencies toward false universalizing about disability arise from the medical model of disability. Doctors, researchers, and rehabilitation specialists tend to universalize the experience of a given disease or disability because they are trying to fit people's experiences into 'scientific' descriptions of the disease or disability. It is true that people with the same physical condition, such as osteoarthritis of roughly the same severity affecting the same joints, will usually have quite a lot of bodily experiences and struggles in common. Nevertheless, their social experiences, their opportunities, their economic welfare, and their status in their communities may be very different, and these will have profound effects on how disabling their arthritis is (i.e., how it limits their participation in major aspects of life in their societies) and on how they experience their disability. The medical model, with its tendency to over-generalize in this particular way, still has a very strong presence in most people's thinking about disability.

Nevertheless, much of the risk of obscuring differences among people with disabilities also comes from choosing categories upon which to build analyses or politics. As Jane Roland Martin points out (1994, 637), all categories mask some differences, although some categories mask fewer differences than others. "People with disabilities" masks all differences but disability. "Disabled women" does not mask gender differences, but does mask differences of race, class, sexual identity, age, and different disabilities, among others. "Working-class African-Canadian heterosexual middle-aged women with rheumatoid arthritis" masks fewer differences, but even this category masks differences; for example, it does not say whether the women are mothers, whether they are employed, whether they are labelled as "former mental patients," and many other things that might be relevant to understanding their situations and their perspectives. Yet it is impossible to engage in social analysis without choosing some categories with which to work, or to engage in political activity without choosing categories around which to organize, and all categories mask differences. Martin suggests: "The question of which categories we should choose cannot be answered in advance of inquiry or decided upon once and for all because the contexts of our investigations change over time and so do our interests and purposes" (Martin 1994, 637–38).

Categories must be chosen, but they need not be chosen forever, and they need not be used in all contexts. The categories that mask the fewest differences contain the fewest people, which is an important consideration for both social analysis and political activity. Differences can be unmasked by choosing a category for a particular context or purpose, working with it, and listening carefully to those who do not identify with it or who disagree with generalizations made about members of the category and their experience. The question whether everyone in the category has anything significant (for analytical or political purposes) in common is an open question, which can only be answered by learning about all the people in a category. Practically speaking, it is answered by attempting to work with the category and remaining aware of its possible inadequacies, and by unmasking the differences it is found to mask.

A second important concern remains. Insofar as identities/social positions are interactive, rather than additive, we cannot arrive at an understanding of a person's epistemic perspective or social position by creating understandings of the effects of (dis)ability, the effects of race, the effects of gender, the effects of sexual identity, and so forth, and adding together the relevant ones for each person (Spelman 1988). The interaction of identities/social positions means that we will not have an accurate understanding of what it is to be disabled until we hear from everyone who is disabled. It also means that their stories may or may not have anything in common; that remains an open question, to be kept constantly under investigation.

Although the feminist standpoint epistemologies Harding originally discussed made some false and damaging assumptions, the idea that some groups of people have access to experiences that are not directly available to others, and that those experiences could give them, not only a different, but a truer and more complete perspective on some aspects of the world still seems plausible to many people, and standpoint epistemologies have not been abandoned. Patricia Hill Collins has developed a standpoint epistemology of Black feminist thought (Collins 1989; 1991), which she defines as follows:

> Black feminist thought consists of theories or specialized thought produced by African-American women intellectuals designed to express a Black women's standpoint. The dimensions of this standpoint include the presence of characteristic core themes, the diversity of Black women's experiences in encountering these core themes, the varying expressions of Black women's Afrocentric feminist consciousness regarding the core themes and their experiences with them, and the interdependence of Black women's experiences, consciousness, and actions. (Collins 1991, 32)

Collins builds the expectation of diversity into her standpoint epistemology of Black women and into her definitions of Black feminist thought. She does not assume that all Black women, or even all Black feminists, think alike. She looks and listens to discover how much similarity there is. She identifies the core themes of Black women's standpoint by investigating the writings and sayings of Black women and discovering the themes, such as the legacy of struggle, that are central in their thought. She starts with the assumption that experience affects consciousness, including how and what people know, but she does not assume that similar experiences always produce similar points of view.

> Black women's work and family experiences and grounding in tradi-
> tional African-American culture suggest that African-American women as
> a group experience a world different from that of those who are not Black
> and female. Moreover, these concrete experiences can stimulate a distinc-
> tive Black feminist consciousness concerning that material reality. Being
> Black and female may expose African-American women to certain com-
> mon experiences, which in turn may predispose us to a distinctive group
> consciousness, but it in no way guarantees that such a consciousness will
> develop among all women or that it will be articulated as such by the
> group. (Collins 1991, 25)

Does having a disability in itself give a person a particular point of view or a less distorted and more complete perspective on certain issues? No. Following in the footsteps of Patricia Hill Collins, I want to say that having a disability usually gives a person experiences of a world different from that of people without disabilities, and that being a woman with a disability usually gives a person different experiences from those of people who are not female and disabled, and that these different experiences create the possibility of different perspectives which have epistemic advantages with respect to certain issues.[13] I do not want to claim that all people with disabilities, or all women with disabilities, have the same epistemic advantages, or that they all have the same interpretations of their experiences, or even that they all have similar experiences. We are just beginning to investigate how much we have in common. But (and here I am following Collins's empirical approach to epistemological issues), having read and listened a great deal to the thoughts of people with disabilities, I do want to claim that, collectively, we have accumulated a significant body of knowledge, with a different standpoint (or standpoints) from those without disabilities, and that that knowledge, which has been ignored and repressed in non-disabled culture, should be further developed and articulated.

The Politics of Similarities and Differences

While questions of similarities and differences among people with disabilities are still open, many people with disabilities are, of course, already engaged in political work on behalf of people with disabilities.[14] The problems of being 'the Other' to a dominant group are always politically complex. Many of them tend to centre around the question of whether to emphasize similarities to the dominant group or differences from them.

Emphasizing similarities between people with and people without disabilities seems to hold the promise of reducing the 'Otherness' of those who are disabled by enabling the non-disabled to identify with them, recognize their humanity and their rights, paving the way to increasing their assimilation into all aspects of social life. Many people with disabilities are tired of being symbols to the non-disabled, visible only or primarily for their disabilities, and they want nothing more than to be seen as individuals rather than as members of the group, 'the disabled.'

Emphasizing similarities to the non-disabled, attempting to make people's disabilities unnoticeable in comparison to their other human qualities, may be a good strategy for bringing about assimilation one-by-one.[15] It does not directly challenge the non-disabled paradigm of humanity, just as women emphasizing their similarities to men and moving into traditionally male arenas of power does not directly challenge the male paradigm of humanity, although both may produce a gradual change in the paradigms. Moreover, assimilation of most people with disabilities may be very difficult to achieve. Although the non-disabled like disabled tokens who do not seem very different from themselves and who seem to confirm the possibility of 'overcoming' great adversity, they may need someone to carry the burden of the negative body as long as they continue to idealize and try to control the body; the subject needs 'the Other' to carry the subject's fears and rejected qualities. People without disabilities may therefore resist the assimilation of most disabled people.

Emphasizing differences from the dominant group, on the other hand, often creates a strong sense of solidarity among those who share them and makes it easier to resist the devaluation of those differences by the dominant group. In addition, some people with disabilities do not particularly want to be assimilated into non-disabled social life or non-disabled political groups, either because they fear that unless social values are changed quite radically, they will always be at a disadvantage in integrated settings, or because they value qualities of their separate lives and organizations.[16]

In separate groups of people with disabilities, powerful 'givens' of the larger culture that put them at a disadvantage, such as the non-disabled paradigm of humanity, the idealization of the body, and the demand for control of the body, can be challenged openly and even made irrelevant. Values that are highly esteemed in non-disabled culture, such as the value of independence from the help of others, can be more safely questioned and debated in a context where the stereotype of all people with disabilities as dependent and incompetent is known to be false.[17] Where these values have been questioned and debated in relation to the lives of people with disabilities, they are not as likely to be used unthinkingly to the detriment of those who cannot conform to them. Why should people who need a great deal of physical or mental help from others, for example, seek the company of those who take naive pride in their own imagined 'independence,' when they can have the company of those whose values and understanding are more sophisticated?

The desire to preserve culture is another powerful motive for avoiding assimilation into non-disabled society. Many of the Deaf do not want to be assimilated into 'hearing' society because they want to preserve the separate culture Deaf people have created. Oliver Sacks quotes the message of a Deaf student at the California School for the Deaf, who signed on television: "We are a unique people, with our own culture, our own language (American Sign Language, which has just recently been recognized as a language in itself), and that sets us apart from hearing people" (Sacks 1988, 28).

It would be hard to claim that disabled people as a whole have their own culture. Nevertheless, there is an extensive and growing literature on disability by people with disabilities, as well as drama, poetry, and art that express experiences of disability and the ideas that arise from them. Moreover, people with disabilities have both knowledge and ways of knowing that are not available to the non-disabled. Although I hope that their knowledge will ultimately be integrated into all culture, I suspect that any culture that stigmatizes and fears disability would rather ignore and suppress that knowledge than make the changes necessary to absorb it. It may have to be cultivated separately until non-disabled society is transformed enough to receive and integrate it.

Despite the advantages, emphasizing differences from the non-disabled in disability politics and organizing separately from the non-disabled carry perils that should not be underestimated. First, when we do so, we identify ourselves by the categories of those who stigmatize us and to whom we are 'the Other.' Second, proclaiming and valuing one's difference may contribute to the dominant group's assumptions that they are the paradigm human beings and that they have a valid basis for discriminatory actions. Feminist politics and theory have struggled a long time with the problems created by valuing difference from a group that has greater power to describe the differences and to control their consequences (Snitow 1990; Kimball 1995). It would be good to avoid these problems, but can they be avoided? How can people fight collectively an oppression based on a category without using that category, without organizing around it? But then, if they do use it, do they not build a collective interest in maintaining the category? How can people preserve their valuable differences from dominant groups without proclaiming them and asserting their importance? But then, if they do proclaim their valuable differences, do they not increase the likelihood of remaining 'the Other' indefinitely? Is it possible to use a collective identity, preserve the differences we value, and undermine our 'Otherness' too? Questions like these, to which I do not know the answers, lead me to value a diversity of political groups and strategies in disability politics (and in feminist politics), including both groups and strategies that emphasize similarities to the non-disabled and those that emphasize differences.

Perhaps the type of disability I have also influences my appreciation of diversity in disability politics. Because my disability is no longer readily apparent, and because it is an illness whose symptoms vary greatly from day to day, I live between the world of the disabled and the world of the non-disabled. I am often very aware of my differences from healthy, non-disabled people, and I often feel a great need to have my differences acknowledged when they are ignored. Moreover, I identify strongly with people with disabilities, and thinking about disability issues has become the centre of my intellectual life. On the other hand, I am very aware of how my social, economic, and personal resources, and the fact that I can 'pass' as non-disabled among strangers, allow me to live a highly assimilated life among the non-disabled; I have more choices in this respect than many other people with disabilities. Because of these circumstances, I repeatedly experience in my daily life advantages and disadvantages of both emphasizing similarities to the non-disabled and emphasizing differences from them.

The Politics of Language

Not surprisingly, disputes over whether to emphasize similarities or differ-ences in relation to people without disabilities are reflected in disagreements over what we should call ourselves—"handicapped," "dis-abled," "differently abled," "challenged?" I have my own preferences, some of which I have explained, and some of which I will explain soon, but first I want to discuss why the issue of labels tends to have so much importance to people with disabilities. I believe it is because our own languages so often betray us—by offering so many ways of derogating us, by containing the assumption that we are 'Other,' and by failing to describe our experi-ences[18]—and because both deliberate verbal abuse and unintentional insult of people with disabilities is so common. Part of asserting our similarities to people without disabilities is demanding that we not be set apart by dis-paraging and/or unnecessary labels, and that the words used to describe or refer to us be as respectful as the words used to describe or refer to non-disabled people. Part of asserting the value of our differences is taking control of language to describe ourselves, adopting realistic and positive self-descriptions.

There is a large number of terms (not all of which were originally derogatory) in English that are used for insulting people with disabilities, such as "cripple," "gimp," "spastic," "retard," "invalid," and "psycho." Some of these terms, as well as relatively neutral terms for describing dis-abilities, are used to insult people without disabilities, by way of implying insultingly that they have disabilities, as in, "What, are you blind (spastic, deaf, etc.)?" They are also used to refer to defects in physical objects. (Once, when I was shopping with my cane, a store clerk advised me not to buy a piece of clothing with a sewing mistake she noticed because, she said, "It's gimpy.") Thus, even people with disabilities who are lucky enough not to encounter much direct insult are exposed frequently to uses of language that remind them that they are stigmatized and/or 'the Other.'

There are extended discussions of language and the politics of disability in the work of Irving Kenneth Zola (1993) and Barbara Hillyer (1993, chapter 3).[19] In these discussions, both emphasize the importance of con-text concerning the acceptability and consequences of using particular expressions. Both draw attention to the fact that even "cripple" has acceptable uses among people with disabilities (Zola, 169; Hillyer, 23). Zola points out that for some stages of coping with a disability, and for a political coming out as disabled, the personal "ownership" expressed by "I am disabled" may be essential, whereas, on the other hand, "where coalition politics is needed, the concept of 'having' vs. 'being' may be a more effective way of acknowledging multiple identities and kinship. . . ." (Zola, 171). Zola did, however, generally favour the use of prepositions, and I agree with his reasons for this:

> 'a disabled car' is one which has totally broken down. Could 'a disabled person' be perceived as anything less? Prepositions, on the other hand, imply both 'a relationship to' and 'a separation from'. At this historical juncture the awkwardness in phrasing that often results may be all to the good, for it makes both user and hearer stop and think about what is meant, as in the phrases 'people of color' and 'persons with disabilities'. (Zola 1993, 170)

Zola concluded his discussion of language by expressing his concern that demanding 'politically correct' usage among ourselves and criticizing anyone who deviates from it will damage the unity disability activists need and distract us from the main problem: "Our struggle is necessary because we live in a society which devalues, discriminates against and disparages people with disabilities. It is not our task to prove that we are worthy of the full resources and integration of our society. The fault is not in us, not in our diseases and disabilities but in mythical demands, social arrangements, political priorities and prejudices" (171). While more than twenty-five years of feminist politics have made me wary of calls for unity when there is disagreement, I share Zola's concern that acrimonious divisions over language could weaken our ability to work together and distract us from more central problems.

Hillyer tackles the same issue. I like her honest acknowledgement of political fashions in language and of the difficulties of always speaking/writing acceptably to every group one supports, given that there are conflicting and constantly changing opinions about what language is acceptable.

> The politics of both movements (feminist and disability) are such that the implications of each term are constantly reexamined and criticized. The word "disabled" itself was once considered less acceptable than "handicapped," then more acceptable, then acceptable in its noun but not in adjective form (as in "a person with a disability," not "a disabled per-

son"). Language is controversial and political acceptability changes. (Hillyer 1993, 21)

Hillyer provides many examples of changing and conflicting usage. Nevertheless, she is not just complaining about the difficulties this presents. She appreciates the value of political self-consciousness about language usage and of the controversies it generates. She concludes:

> What I deduce from all this is the value of a rich, complex language. Instead of creating dichotomies between good and bad words, we can use accurate, individual descriptors. Instead of taking for granted the meanings assigned by one or another political group, we can struggle with distinguishing our own definitions from theirs. The process is awkward; it slows down talk; it is uncomfortable. It slows down thought and increases its complexity. (Hillyer 1993, 46)

Although I do not want to list and defend all my linguistic preferences in relation to disability, and, in agreement with Zola and Hillyer, I think that context is vitally important, I do want to discuss two recent trends in usage that have generated some controversy. I hope they will illustrate some of the perils of attempts to reform language. The first is the introduction of new and (to my mind) euphemistic expressions for disabilities and people with disabilities. One such expression is "differently-abled," which has found favour among feminists since the early 1980s. I assume the point of using this term is to suggest that there is nothing wrong with being the way people with disabilities are, just different. It also seems as though it might have some educational value: It could remind the non-disabled that to be disabled in some respects is not to be disabled in all respects, and it suggests that a person with a disability may have abilities that the non-disabled lack in virtue of not being disabled.

Yet to call someone "differently-abled" is much like calling her "differently-coloured" or "differently-gendered." It says: "This person is not the norm or paradigm of humanity." If anything, it increases the 'Otherness' of people with disabilities, because it reinforces the paradigm of humanity as young, strong, and healthy, with all body parts working 'perfectly,' from which this person is different. Using the term "differently-abled" also suggests a (polite? patronizing? protective? self-protective?) disregard of the special difficulties, struggles, and suffering people with disabilities face. We are dis-abled. We live with particular social and physical struggles that are partly consequences of the conditions of our bodies and/or minds and partly consequences of the structures and expectations of our societies, but they are struggles that only people with bodies and/or minds like ours experience. Expressions that attempt to put a cheerful face on this reality invite denial, placing social pressure on people with and without disabilities to pretend that everything is fine.

Another trend in usage also, to my mind, invites denial. Perhaps so far it is not so much a trend as a demand for change in linguistic practices, which I have now heard in several circumstances, and which Hillyer discusses briefly (Hillyer 1993, 29–30). The demand is that we should avoid metaphoric use of words which refer to abilities which some people lack; I have always heard it in relation to metaphors of sight, such as, "Do you see what I mean?" or, "She can't see the forest for the trees," although the same objection would surely apply to metaphors of other abilities that some people lack.

It seems likely that the abundance of sight metaphors in English usage might hurt or at least get on the nerves of anyone who cannot see.[20] Moreover, people who can see often experience sudden awareness of sight metaphors in the presence of blind people, as well as concern about whether they are hurtful. But, while I feel strongly that we should avoid using "blind" as an insult, trying to eliminate sight metaphors from English usage would be setting out on a road that, ultimately, no one will want to travel. For why stop at sight? If metaphors are offensive because they refer to abilities some people do not have, or activities in which some people cannot participate, then metaphors of hearing, walking, running, crawling, swimming, and dancing are offensive for the same reason. There are people who cannot smell, taste, touch, perceive colours, feel pain, talk, read, write, remember anything, or feel love. Metaphors of these abilities must sometimes hurt people who lack them, but we would impoverish language if we stopped using metaphors of all abilities that some people lack. Moreover, do we know that metaphors of abilities are more hurtful to people who lack the abilities than other references to those abilities and their consequences, which we cannot always avoid? Is using the word "insight" really more hurtful than, "Oh, your garden looks beautiful," said to someone else in the presence of a blind person?

Hillyer presents another objection to this demand to reform language: "To avoid all visual imagery in deference to the blind may discriminate against the deaf for whom visual experience is central, as well as against any sighted person for whom visual ability is very important to her self-concept" (1993, 30). The strength of this objection is obvious when one considers how far it extends. For most people with disabilities, our remaining abilities are extremely important, and for every ability remaining in one person, there is another person who lacks it.

Speaking personally, I would not want people to avoid metaphoric uses of or references to energy, which I lack in abundance, or to running, dancing, hiking, climbing, and opening doors, all of which are difficult or impossible for me. I do sometimes feel bad when people go on at length about someone's great energy, especially when their attitude seems to be that it is a moral virtue. And I do sometimes feel sad, or envious, hearing about other people's hiking expeditions or trips to places that are too exhausting for me. But I would not want to be protected from these feelings, and I would not want other people to pretend that they do not have abilities I lack, or that they are not important, even central, in their lives. Both of the attempts to reform language that I have discussed seem to me to invite denial, if not of difference, then of painful consequences of difference. I regard denial as far more dangerous than feeling angry, sad, or envious.

The Future of Difference

The final group of issues I want to consider in this chapter concerns the preservation of difference. If we value the differences of people with disabilities, what implications does that have for efforts to prevent or cure disabilities? Is saying, "Everyone wants a healthy baby," morally and politically similar to saying, "Everyone wants a white baby?" If not, how is it different? Is there as much reason to preserve the functional impairments and structural imperfections of human bodies as there is to preserve their genetic diversity? Feminist ecologists often urge us to value and protect the vulnerability and imperfections of nature. Should the vulnerability and imperfections of our bodies also be valued and protected, or should we attempt to transcend them?

Some of these questions arise practically now in relation to medical technologies that offer genetic 'diagnosis' of potential disabilities in a person's offspring and prenatal detection of potential disabilities in fetuses. Although I will discuss them again in chapter 6 in relation to a feminist ethics of abortion, I want to point out here that widespread ignorance of the lives of people with disabilities, fear of disablement, and the assumption that disability is primarily a biologically determined, rather than a socially constructed, phenomenon, contribute to the desire to prevent disability by preventing difference from the physical and mental 'norms' of a society. To people who value disabilities as differences, attempts to prevent disability by preventing the birth of people with disabilities can seem analogous to attempts to guarantee the birth of male babies because they are more highly valued, or to wipe out colour differences by genetic technologies.

It might be argued that it is hard to appreciate disabilities as differences where disabilities have devastating social consequences. The fact is that a child born with spina bifida or Down's syndrome will face many socially created obstacles to living well. Of course the same thing is true for children-of-colour in white-dominated societies, but few people-of-colour would argue that it is a sufficient reason not to bring a child-of-colour into the world. Rather, it would be argued, it is a reason to fight for just treatment of people-of-colour. I think we have to admit that it is the fact of physical and/or mental difference, usually perceived as 'abnormality' or 'pathology,' that makes it seem so much more obvious to many people that potential disability is a sufficient reason not to bring a child into the world. Moreover, unlike children-of-colour in white-dominated societies, who are most often born into families or communities of people-of-colour, children with disabilities are not usually born into a family or community of people with disabilities who are already committed to valuing their differences and fighting for their rights.[21] At best, adults thinking of parenting a child with disabilities know they will have to find or create a community of support for themselves and their child; at worst, they believe they will have to cope on their own. If they are afraid of the burden of raising a child with a disability in a society where accessibility and help are far from adequate, they have reason to be afraid.

Another consideration enters into questions about the practical implications of valuing disabilities as differences. How much physical and/or mental suffering is inherent in the difference itself, that is, how much suffering that could not be eliminated by any social arrangements, no matter how supportive they might be to the lives of people with disabilities? Part of what is at work in the sentiment, "Everyone wants a healthy baby," is a desire that children be spared suffering. Although ignorance of disability probably exaggerates the physical suffering (and underestimates the social suffering) of most people with disabilities in the minds of people without disabilities, the importance of ineliminable suffering must not be overlooked. Even people with disabilities who identify strongly with being disabled and have very happy, fulfilling lives might want to be cured, not for social reasons, but because they want to have less pain or physical or mental difficulty.

Who can and who should answer the question: Is the suffering too high a price to pay for the difference? Certainly people with disabilities who have intimate knowledge of the suffering involved in a disability, and who also have sufficient experience to know and value the differences it makes possible, are better qualified to answer this question than others. Yet even for them, this may be a hard question to answer, especially since the social components of the suffering of many people with disabilities, such as loneliness, alienation, poverty, constant blows to self-esteem, and frustration due to lack of accessibility and services are hard to separate clearly from the socially ineliminable physical and/or mental components. Difficult circumstances make both physical and mental suffering worse and harder to bear. These factors are likely to cause error on the "yes" side of the question, but not, I think, as much error in that direction as the ignorance and fear of most people who have little or no experience of disability.

Like the development of technologies to prevent people with disabilities from being born, the drive to find 'cures' for disabilities can be seen, by those who appreciate disabilities as differences, to be as much an attempt to wipe out difference as an effort to relieve suffering. There is so much emphasis on possible 'cures' in biomedical talk and charity talk (and indeed most talk) about disability, and so little recognition of the potential and value of disabled people's actual lives, that this interpretation of motives is justified. The widespread message that they are not good enough until they are 'cured' places the self-respect of people with disabilities in conflict with any desire to be 'cured.'

I find that my own resistance to the attitude that I need to be 'cured' in order to be a whole or fully acceptable person infuses my desire for a 'cure' with ambivalence. I want to have more energy and less pain, and to have a more predictable body; about that there is no ambivalence. Moreover, I feel heartsore when I hear about someone being diagnosed with ME; how could I not want a cure for everyone else who suffers with it? Yet I cannot wish that I had never contracted ME, because it has made me a different person, a person I am glad to be, would not want to have missed being, and could not imagine relinquishing, even if I were 'cured.' For example, I cannot imagine that I would ever stop identifying myself as a person with a disability, and when I think about the probability that others would stop identifying me as one if I were 'cured,' it is hard to imagine how I would deal with the dissonance. Perhaps the best summary of my attitude toward 'cure' is this: I would joyfully accept a cure, but I do not need one. If this attitude toward 'cures' were taken for granted in my society, then the search for them would not be accompanied by insulting implications, as it often is now.

People who take it for granted that it would be a good thing to wipe out all biological causes of disability (as opposed to social causes) are far more confident that they know how to perfect nature and humanity than I am. Even supposing that everyone involved in such an effort were motivated entirely by a desire to prevent and alleviate suffering, what else besides suffering might we lose in the process? And would they know where to stop?[22] Certainly, those who do not value the differences of people with disabilities cannot be trusted to decide where to stop trying to 'perfect' human beings. Moreover, promises to eliminate the biological causes of disability assume that some culturally neutral, biomedical definition of disability can be agreed upon, and they obscure the fact that disability is socially constructed from physical and mental difference.

What would it mean, then, in practice, to value disabilities as differences? It would certainly mean not assuming that every disability is a tragic loss or that everyone with a disability wants to be 'cured.' It would mean seeking out and respecting the knowledge and perspectives of people with disabilities. It would mean being willing to learn about and respect ways of being and forms of consciousness that are unfamiliar. And it would mean giving up the myths of control and the quest for perfection of the human body.

4

The Flight from the
Rejected Body

In the commercial-media-soaked societies of North America,[1] the body is idealized and objectified to a high degree; these cultural practices foster demands to control our bodies and to attempt to perfect them, which in turn create rejection, shame, and fear in relation to both failures to control the body and deviations from body ideals. Implied in any idealization of the body is the rejection of some kinds of bodies or some aspects of bodily life. I use the terms "rejected body" and "negative body" to refer to those aspects of bodily life (such as illness, disability, weakness, and dying), bodily appearance (usually deviations from the cultural ideals of the body), and bodily experience (including most forms of bodily suffering) that are feared, ignored, despised, and/or rejected in a society and its culture. In this chapter I discuss some forms of idealization and objectification of the body, how they affect people with and without disabilities, and how they contribute to cultural demands that we control our bodies. I then describe and criticize some influential contemporary versions of the myth that the body can be controlled.

Our real human bodies are exceedingly diverse—in size, shape, colour, texture, structure, function, range and habits of movement, and development—and they are constantly changing. Yet many cultures, especially modern commercial cultures, do not seem to absorb or reflect these simple facts. Instead, they idealize the human body; the ideals change from time to time, but there always seem to be ideals. Body ideals include not only ideals of appearance, which are particularly influential for women (Bartky 1990), but also ideals of strength, energy, movement, function, and proper control; the latter are unnoticed assumptions for most people who can meet them, but they leap to the foreground for those who are sick or disabled. In Canada and the United States, we are bombarded everywhere with images of these ideals, demands for them, and offers of products and services to help us achieve them.

Clearly, idealization of the body is related in complex ways to the economic processes of a consumer society. Idealization now generates tremendous profits, and the quest for profit demands that people be reminded constantly of existing body ideals and presented regularly with new ideals. Moreover, never before in history have images of real people who meet the latest cultural ideals of beauty, health, and physical performance been so often presented to so many people. Now it is possible for the images of a few people to drive out the reality of most people we actually encounter. (For example, I find that few people realize that the average North American woman is much fatter than the average woman we see on television.) This tends to conflate body ideals with our concept of what is physically 'normal,' increasing the number of people whose bodies are regarded by themselves and others as abnormal and socially unacceptable.

Idealization also contributes to objectification of the body, along with other factors, such as the cultural splitting of mind from body and derogation of the body, strong cultural emphasis on physical appearance, medical ways of seeing and treating the body, sexual exploitation, pressures to perform, and some forms of competition. To objectify another person's body is to ignore (at least temporarily) the consciousness that is embodied there and to fail to concern oneself with her/his subjective bodily experience. Objectifying one's own body is more complex; one must, in a sense, split one's consciousness from it and ignore one's inner subjective experience of it in order to regard or treat it as another person might. Widely accepted current forms of objectifying one's own body include treating it primarily as an instrument for accomplishing one's goals, regarding it as a physical object to be viewed, used, and manipulated, and treating it as a material possession to be maintained, exploited, and traded (Sheets-Johnstone 1992b). They all assume and require considerable control of the body in order to maintain its suitability as an object of that type. Observing and participating in constant cultural objectification of other people's bodies encourages us to objectify our own. Some objectification of one's own body is probably inevitable, and not always harmful, but if it becomes the primary mode of experiencing one's body, it is a source of profound alienation from feeling, from nature, from the unconscious, from every aspect of oneself and others that resists control.

The Disciplines of Normality

Feminist analyses of the cultural treatment of women's bodies have shaped a great deal of my thinking, and Sandra Lee Bartky has done more than anyone to illuminate for me the social construction of femininity through idealization, objectification, and demands for control of the female body. Expanding upon Michel Foucault's account of the disciplinary practices that produce the "docile bodies" required by modern social institutions (Foucault 1979), she has provided a detailed examination of "those disciplinary practices that produce a body which in gesture and appearance is recognizably feminine," including "those that aim to produce a body of a certain size and general configuration; those that bring forth from this body a specific repertoire of gestures, postures, and movements; and those directed toward the display of this body as an ornamented surface" (Bartky 1990, 65). Moreover, she has argued that because these disciplinary practices, which include (among other things) dieting, exercise, control of facial expression and careful constraint of movements, removal of body hair, application of skin-care preparations, hairdressing, and the 'correct' application of cosmetics, are not forced upon women by anyone in particular (indeed, they are often self-imposed, although there are also severe external sanctions), they appear to be natural or voluntary while they wield tremendous power in women's lives:

> the disciplinary power that is increasingly charged with the production of
> a properly embodied femininity is dispersed and anonymous; there are
> no individuals formally empowered to wield it; it is . . . invested in
> everyone and in no one in particular. This disciplinary power is peculiarly
> modern: It does not rely upon violent or public sanctions, nor does it
> seek to restrain the freedom of the female body to move from place to
> place. For all that, its invasion of the body is well-nigh total: The female
> body enters "a machinery of power that explores it, breaks it down and

> rearranges it." The disciplinary techniques through which the "docile bodies" of women are constructed aim at a regulation which is perpetual and exhaustive—a regulation of the body's size and contours, its appetite, posture, gestures, and general comportment in space and the appearance of each of its visible parts. (Bartky 1990, 80)

I believe that there are also disciplinary practices of physical normality that are in many ways analogous to the disciplinary practices of femininity Bartky describes. Unlike the disciplines of the body described by Foucault, which are specifically linked to participation in certain modern social institutions, such as armies, schools, hospitals, and prisons, but like Bartky's disciplines of femininity, the disciplines of normality are "institutionally unbound" (Bartky 1990, 75), internalized by most of us, and socially pervasive. Like the disciplines of femininity, they require us to meet physical standards, to objectify our bodies, and to control them.

The disciplines of normality are preconditions of participation in every aspect of social life, yet they are unnoticed by most adults who can conform to them without conscious effort. Children are very aware of the requirements of normality; among children, conformity to standards of normality in body size, carriage, movement, gesture, speech, emotional expression, appearance, scent, ways of eating, and especially control of bodily functions such as salivation, passing gas, urination, and defecation, are enforced by teasing, taunting, and the threat of social ostracism, beginning at an early age. (When I was a child in New York City public schools, peeing in your pants in school or on the playground was one of the most shameful things that could happen to you; nothing you might do deliberately, no matter how morally rotten, could compare in shamefulness.) Those of us who can learn to be or seem 'normal' do so, and those of us who cannot meet the standards of normality usually achieve the closest approximation we can manage.

The disciplines of normality, like those of femininity, are not only enforced by others but internalized. For many of us, our proximity to the standards of normality is an important aspect of our identity and our sense of social acceptability, an aspect of our self-respect. We are unlikely to notice this until our ability to meet the standards is threatened in some way. An injury or a prolonged illness often draws the attention of non-disabled people to this previously unnoticed facet of their self-images. For people who already have disabilities, the prospect of more disability can have the same effect. Shame and self-hatred when we cannot measure up to the standards of normality are indications that they are enforced by a powerful internalized disciplinarian.

People who do not appear or act physically 'normal' draw attention to the disciplines of normality, just as women who do not practice the disciplines of femininity make them more apparent. In both cases, there are rules at work, but most of us are trying to ignore the existence of the rules, trying to pretend that things are 'naturally' and effortlessly the way they seem, not socially enforced. (Consider how rarely anyone admits in public that s/he is depressed, having intestinal cramps, or even just desperate for a toilet, compared to how often you feel that way. Stating such a thing would be at least as embarrassing as a woman's remarking in public that she did not have time to shave her legs.) Moreover, since almost everyone tries to appear as 'normal' as possible, those who appear clearly 'abnormal' according to their society's standards are constant reminders to those who are currently measuring up that they might slip outside the standards. In this aspect, people with disabilities arouse fear. But they are also reassuring, in that encountering them can make 'normals' feel more 'normal' by comparison (which in turn may arouse guilt).[2] These reactions are completely understandable, given the disciplines of normality, and they all contribute to the 'Otherness' of people with disabilities.

It is not easy to distinguish standards of physical normality from ideals of health, appearance, and performance, just as it is not easy to distinguish between feminine body ideals and minimal standards of femininity. One would expect the range of social normality (not medical 'normality,' which is different) to be considerably broader than the physical ideals of a culture, because otherwise very few people would be considered normal. Nevertheless, in practice, the two are linked. When the ideals of physical health, appearance, and performance become more difficult to meet, the social standards of normality follow suit, threatening more of us with the possibility of falling below the minimum required for self-esteem and social acceptability. Moreover, for many people, falling within the 'normal' range is not enough, especially when they are constantly pressured and encouraged to try to meet the ideal. By pursuing the cultural ideal, people can raise the standards of normality.

Kathryn Pauly Morgan discusses this phenomenon in relation to plastic surgery for women:

> In the technical and popular literature on cosmetic surgery, what have previously been described as normal variations of female body shapes or

described in the relatively innocuous language of "problem areas," are increasingly described as "deformities," "ugly protrusions," "inadequate breasts," and "unsightly concentrations of fat cells"—a litany of descriptions designed to intensify feelings of disgust, shame, and relief at the possibility of recourse for these "deformities." Cosmetic surgery promises virtually all women the creation of beautiful, youthful-appearing bodies. As a consequence, more and more women will be labelled "ugly" and "old" in relation to this more select population of surgically created beautiful faces and bodies. . . . I suspect that the naturally "given," so to speak, will increasingly come to be seen as the technologically "primitive"; the "ordinary" will come to be perceived and evaluated as the "ugly." (Morgan 1991, 41)[3]

Other ideals can sneak up on us, becoming standards of normality because they enter into a society's competitive structure. For example, when the pace of life increases, stamina becomes more important to participation in every aspect of society, and what was once regarded as an ideal level of energy gradually comes to be regarded as normal. Everyone who cannot keep up is urged to take steps (or medications) to increase their energy, and bodies that were once considered normal are pathologized. In my society, I have noticed that it has become increasingly unacceptable to "slow down" as one ages, when not long ago it was expected.

Bartky argues that the disciplinary practices of femininity "must be understood as aspects of a far larger discipline, an oppressive and inegalitarian system of sexual subordination. This system aims at turning women into the docile and compliant companions of men just as surely as the army aims to turn its raw recruits into soldiers" (Bartky 1990, 75). Here I think there are disanalogies between the disciplines of femininity and those of normality. Although the standards of normality are certainly aspects of the subordination of people with disabilities, and although the disciplines of normality do generate profits in a consumer society (much advertising offers products to help us hide or correct our physical 'abnormalities,' such as 'excess' fat, lack of teeth, lack of hair, flabby muscles, and weak bladders), and therefore serve some people's direct interests, they also weigh heavily upon all people without disabilities. Under the disciplines of femininity, women must fear becoming less feminine, but men need not fear becoming women of any kind. Under the disciplines of normality, everyone must fear becoming a member of the subordinated group; everyone who does not die suddenly will become a member of the subordinated group. Who does not suffer from these standards?

Some people can have the temporary self-acceptance that comes from believing that their bodies are 'close enough' to current body ideals, but this gives them an investment in the ideals and draws them into the endless task of reconciling reality with them. Most people learn to identify with their own strengths (by cultural standards) and to hate, fear, and neglect their own weaknesses. Everyone is subjected to cultural pressure to deny bodily weaknesses, to dread old age, to feel ashamed of and responsible for their distance from the ideals, and to objectify their own bodies at the expense of subjective bodily awareness. These pressures foster a desire to gain/maintain control of our bodies; conversely, the myth that we can control our bodies encourages us to strive to meet body ideals.

Most people with disabilities cannot even attempt to make their bodies fit the physical ideals of their culture. They may wish for bodies they cannot have, with frustration, shame, and sometimes self-hatred; they may reject the physical ideals as narrow, unimaginative, and/or oppressive; or, like myself, they may fluctuate irrationally between these points of view. In any case, they must struggle harder than non-disabled people for a self-image that is both realistic and positive, and this is made more difficult by other people's reactions to them.[4] In a society that idealizes the body, people who cannot come close enough to the ideals, and those whose bodies are out of control, become devalued people because of their devalued bodies (Hannaford 1985). Moreover, they are constant reminders to the temporarily 'normal' of the rejected body—of what the 'normal' are trying to avoid, forget, and ignore (Lessing 1981).

Of course, it is not just from fear of being or becoming abnormal that the rejected body is shunned. It is also shunned from fear of pain, illness, limitation, suffering, and dying. Yet the cultural banishment of the rejected body contributes to fear of those experiences by fostering ignorance of them. Even though everyone has or will have experiences of the negative body, if the cultural concept of the 'normal' body is a young, healthy, energetic, pain-free body with all parts present and a maximum range of graceful movement, then experiences of the negative body need not be confronted and understood. They belong to those with disabilities and illnesses, who are marginalized, not 'ordinary' people, not 'us.'

People with disabilities and illnesses learn that most people do not want to know about the suffering they experience because of their bodies. Curiosity about medical diagnoses, physical appearance, and the sexual and other intimate aspects of disability is common; interest in the subjective experience is rare (Matthews, 1983). This is also understandable. If we tell people about our pain, for example, we remind them of the existence of pain, the imperfection and fragility of the body, the possibility of their own pain, the inevitability of it. The less willing they are to accept all these, the less they will want to know. If they cannot avoid confronting pain in our presence, they can avoid us. They may even blame us for being in pain. They may tell themselves that we could have avoided it, in order to believe that they can avoid it. They may want to believe they are not like us, not vulnerable to this; if so, they will cling to our differences, and we will become 'the Others.' Our shared culture offers this solution and makes the distance between our experiences difficult to bridge. It is not surprising that many people who can, hide their disabilities from everyone but their closest friends.

Are there sources of resistance to the disciplines of normality, analogous to the oppositional discourses and practices (many of them feminist) that Bartky identifies as emerging forms of resistance to the disciplines of femininity? Certainly I see disabled people's re-valuing of their own bodies and ways of living, and the forms of culture that are emerging from disability pride, as oppositional discourses and practices. They do weaken the internal hold of the disciplines of normality over those of us who have disabilities. But do they undermine commitment to those disciplines and fear of abnormality in those who meet the social standards of normality, or do they only, at best, change some attitudes toward 'the Others'? I do not think we can answer that question yet. There has been only a small, recent increase in the general presentation of disability culture, and there is still a flood of cultural idealizations of the body.[5]

Feminist Idealizations of the Body

Feminists have always criticized the idealization and objectification of women's bodies, recognizing them as sources of exploitation and alienation.[6] They have particularly focussed on ideals of appearance, grooming, and bodily comportment for women, and on sexual and medical objectifications of women's bodies. Yet feminist movements have expressed their own body ideals, often insisting on women's strength and overlooking the fact that many women's bodies are not strong. We have celebrated those aspects of women's bodily experience that are sources of pleasure, satisfaction, and feelings of connection, but we have underestimated the bodily frustration and suffering that social justice cannot prevent or relieve. Feminists have also criticized and worked to undo men's control of women's bodies, without undermining the myth that women can control our own bodies. In one of the most influential feminist books that discussed bodily life, *Of Woman Born*, Adrienne Rich wrote: "In order to live a fully human life we require not only control of our bodies (though control is a prerequisite); we must touch the unity and resonance of our physicality, our bond with the natural order, the corporeal ground of our intelligence" (Rich 1976, 21).[7]

Until feminists criticize our own body ideals and confront the weak, suffering, and uncontrollable body in our theorizing and practice, women with disabilities and illnesses are likely to feel that we are embarrassments to feminism. In a 1992 article in *Ms.*, Canadian feminist filmmaker Bonnie Klein described her experience at a feminist film festival—the first she had attended since being disabled by a stroke.

> The women who had organized the festival—also Canadian filmmakers—had promised to "accommodate" me, but they make no provision for my needs. I am expected to fit in and keep up. They schedule my films late at night when I am too tired; they do not include me in panel discussions or press conferences; they arrange social events in inaccessible places. I miss the informal personal exchanges catalyzed by the shared film experience.
>
> I can no longer move in what had been my world. I feel I have been used for my films, but neglected and made invisible as a person. I feel as if my colleagues are ashamed of me because I am no longer the image of strength, competence, and independence that feminists, including myself, are so eager to project. There is clearly a conflict between feminism's rhetoric of inclusion and failure to include disability. My journals reveal that this is the only moment in which I think of suicide. (Klein 1992, 72)

The Myth of Control

A major obstacle to coming to terms with the full reality of bodily life is the widespread myth that the body can be controlled. Conversely, people embrace the myth of control in part because it promises escape from the rejected body. The essence of the myth of control is the belief that it is possible, by means of human actions, to have the bodies we want and to prevent illness, disability, and death. Like many myths, the myth of control contains a significant element of truth; we do have some control over the conditions of our bodies, for example through the physical risks we take or avoid and our care for our health. What makes it a myth is that people continue to cling to it even where there is overwhelming evidence against it, and that most versions of it are formulated in such a way that they are invulnerable to evidence against them.

When people are blamed or made to feel responsible for having nonideal bodies despite their reasonable care, when unproveable theories are generated to explain how someone could have avoided becoming ill, when people with disabilities are seen as having their psychological, moral, or spiritual failures written upon their bodies, and when every death is regarded as a defeat of human efforts, the myth of control is at work. This myth is shared by scientific, nonscientific, and antiscientific worldviews. It persists in many forms, but I will focus my discussion on those forms that most affect people with disabilities and illnesses in my society.

Scientific Western Medicine and the Myth of Control

The myth that the body can be controlled is part of the general assumption of the modern Western scientific project that nature can be controlled. Neither the larger assumption about nature nor the more specific myth about the body is seriously questioned in the light of failures; they are heuristics, guiding long-term goals and scientific projects, not propositions meant to be tested by experience. Yet there is a strong tendency in scientific medicine to pretend that the myth of control is the truth. Collectively, doctors and medical researchers exhibit very little modesty about their knowledge, rarely admitting to patients or the public the vast remaining gaps in scientific medicine's understanding of the human body or their inability to repair or heal most physical conditions that cause suffering, limitation, and death. Scientific medicine participates in and fosters the myth of control by focussing overwhelmingly on cures and lifesaving medical interventions, and by tending to neglect chronic illnesses, rehabilitation, pain management, and the quality of patients' experiences, including their experiences of dying. Research, funding, medical care, and the numbers and status of various types of medical professionals all reflect this emphasis.

Sherwin Nuland (1993, 71), points out that there are only 4,084 geriatricians (they specialize in total care of elderly patients), but 17,000 heart specialists in the United States. Those specializations that involve surgery and saving lives carry by far the most prestige; they also bolster the illusion of control much better than does the long, patient process of rehabilitation or the management of long-term illness. These latter, less visible functions of medicine tend to be performed by nurses, physiotherapists, and other low-prestige members of the profession, and by some primary-care physicians, whose prestige and incomes are much lower than those of physicians who specialize in cures.

All doctors in the Western scientific tradition are trained to do something to control the body, to 'make it better' (Kleinman 1988). Moreover, people who crave control may be attracted to medicine. Nuland, a surgeon of many years and a teacher of surgery and the history of medicine, says that he has observed in many doctors "a need to control that exceeds in magnitude what most people would find reasonable" (Nuland 1993, 258); he believes this need often leads them to deal badly with loss of control over a patient's condition.

> There is a specific form of abandonment that is particularly common among patients near death from cancer, and it requires comment. I refer here to abandonment by doctors. Doctors rarely *want* to give up. As long as there is any possibility of solving The Riddle, they will keep at it, and sometimes it takes the intervention of a family or the patient himself to put an end to medical exercises in futility. When it becomes obvious, though, that there is no longer a Riddle on which to focus, many doctors lose the drive that sustained their enthusiasm. As the long siege drags on and one after another treatment has begun to fail, those enthusiasms tend to fall by the wayside. Emotionally, doctors then tend to disappear; physically, too, they sometimes all but disappear. (Nuland 1993, 257–58)

It would be too easy to blame this and other manifestations of medicine's participation in the myth of control on the personalities and socialized attitudes of doctors. Doctors seek heroic control in part because they are cast as the heroes of medicine. They may enjoy being in the role of hero, but the rest of us also like them in that role and try to keep them there, because *we* want to believe that someone can always 'make it better.'[8] We (nondoctors) are allowed to maintain this illusion partly because the most obvious loss of control over the body, death, has been medicalized, hidden from us and 'managed' by medical institutions. Eighty percent of

Americans now die in hospitals, compared to 50 percent in 1949 (Nuland 1993, 255).[9] Nuland has this to say about the neglect of dying in a society that does not want to know about death:

> We live today in the era not of the art of dying, but of the art of saving life, and the dilemmas of that art are multitudinous. As recently as half a century ago, that other great art, the art of medicine, still prided itself on its ability to manage the process of death, making it as tranquil as professional kindness could. Except in the too-few programs such as hospice, that part of the art is now mostly lost, replaced by the brilliance of rescue and, unfortunately, the all-too-common abandonment when rescue proves impossible. (Nuland 1993, 265)

Scientific medicine's participation in the myth of control is perhaps most obvious in the fact that no one is acknowledged to have died of old age anymore. In fact, Nuland tells us that, by fiat of the World Health Organization and by the rules of local authorities everywhere in the world, it is now illegal to record old age as the cause of death (Nuland 1993, 43). Refusal to believe that old age inevitably leads to death is also manifested in the ways that diseases that commonly kill the very old are discussed. It often seems to me lately, when I hear reports on medical research, or pleas for donations to medical research charities, or warnings of the dangers of eating fat, smoking, or not exercising, in which it is said in tones of deep concern that so many millions of Americans or thousands of Canadians die of stroke or heart disease every year, that medical scientists and public health experts actually hope, even expect, to eliminate death altogether. Of course I support efforts to prevent people dying before old age, but I find it odd that no distinction is made between dying young of these diseases and dying of them after a long life. Do I not have to die of something? Is not dying of a heart attack or stroke sometimes better than dying of Alzheimer's disease or cancer? Why do I never hear anyone saying this in public?

Ironically, the more successful medicine is at warding off death, the more people with disabilities it keeps alive, thus increasing the need for the long-term support that it is least interested in delivering. Moreover, those of us who have chronic illnesses and disabilities, and those who are dying of incurable illnesses, symbolize the failure of medicine and the Western scientific project to control nature. We carry this stigma in medicine and in our cultures.

Alternative Therapies and the Myth of Control

Many patients who cannot be helped significantly by scientific Western medicine, and those who feel abandoned by it because their conditions are considered incurable, seek attention and relief from alternative practitioners. I value some of these alternatives very highly, in part because I believe that incurable suffering is more bearable if someone is willing to pay attention to it, and in part because I think that they employ techniques that can offer relief to patients who cannot be cured.[10] Some non-Western and nontraditional medical practices define healing not as cure but as improvement in the quality of the patient's experience, an approach that seems particularly well suited to helping those with chronic or life-threatening illnesses. I have been helped a great deal, but not cured, by massage therapy, naturopathy, therapeutic touch, and traditional Chinese medicine.

On the other hand, I know people who have been made to feel guilty or recalcitrant when they were not cured by practitioners of non-Western or nontraditional healing methods. Practitioners of these methods can be as reluctant to accept failure to cure their patients as practitioners of scientific Western medicine. Patients may be made to feel that they are not getting well because they do not want to, do not live sufficiently 'pure' lives, are not visualizing their health properly, or are not confronting psychological or spiritual issues that are harming their bodies.[11] Although these reactions may run counter to the philosophies of the treatment practices, it is not surprising to encounter them in practitioners who are working in a cultural context where patients (and sometimes the practitioners themselves) have been taught to expect control and cure.

The very availability of a virtually unlimited number of treatments protects the myth of control from evidence against it, because there is always another method of control to be tried. People with disabilities or incurable illnesses often find that long after they have accepted the conditions of their bodies, their friends and acquaintances want them to continue looking for cures. Out of kindness and a wish to help, but also frequently because of a frantic desire not to be forced to believe that the body cannot be controlled, people offer endless advice about possible treatments. "I know you've tried naturopathy, but you haven't been to my naturopath." To turn down a suggestion is to risk the judgement that you do not want to get well. To pursue every suggestion is a full-time job (with a price tag instead of a paycheque). For people with life-threatening illnesses, pressures from their loved ones to seek a cure can consume their remaining time in medical and quasi-medical quests.

I am convinced that there is no solution to the inadequacies of biomedicine as a healing art without changing its social context. The answers are not to be found in simply switching to alternative therapeutic approaches, nor in combining Western medical knowledge with, say, traditional Chinese medicine or Eastern-derived psychological techniques or spiritual practices. As long as the goal is to control the body, there is great potential in all healing practices for blaming the victims, and for discarding or ignoring all those whose bodies are out of control, including people who are terminally ill, disabled, chronically ill, fat, or addicted. The context of any attempt at healing in my society is a culture that considers controlling one's body a criterion of full humanity and of social acceptability. This must be changed if medicine is to address the needs of most people throughout their lives.

Mind over Body and the Myth of Control

The influence of psychoanalysis on both medicine and popular culture has contributed the concepts of psychosomatic illness and imagined illness to the myth of control, and it has strengthened the older and vaguer notion that the mind can control the body. Although there may be genuine psychosomatic conditions and forms of mental illness in which people imagine physical symptoms, both these explanations are employed too readily by medical practitioners and lay people when they can find no other explanation for a patient's complaints or when a patient does not benefit from medical treatment.

In 1972, Irving Zola warned of the re-introduction, through psychosomatic diagnoses, of the idea that individuals are responsible for their illnesses:

> it is not clear that the issues of morality and individual responsibility have been fully banished from the etiological scene itself. At the same time as the label 'illness' is being used to attribute 'diminished responsibility' to a whole host of phenomena, the issue of 'personal responsibility' seems to be re-emerging within medicine itself. Regardless of the truth and insights of the concepts of stress and the perspective of psychosomatics,

whatever else they do, they bring man, not bacteria to the center of the stage and lead thereby to a re-examination of the individual's role in his own demise, disability and even recovery. (Zola 1972, 491)[12]

The literature describing experiences of disabilities and chronic illnesses abounds with accounts of early diagnoses of "psychosomatic illness," even when the patients had diseases and conditions well known to medical science. For example, in a study of 21 women and 14 men with multiple sclerosis in Canada, Susan Russell found that 7 of the women and 1 of the men (note the gender difference), that is 22.8 percent of the 35 patients, had been told by physicians that their symptoms were psychological in origin (Russell 1985, 56).[13] No doubt the physicians would reply in their own defense that MS is notoriously difficult to diagnose, presenting as it often does at first with fatigue, dizziness, or brief episodes of numbness. But if they know that MS (and certainly this is true of many other physical ailments as well) is difficult to diagnose, why are they telling their patients that their symptoms have psychological causes, instead of telling them that they do not yet know what is wrong and they must wait and see?

If patients with well known physical diseases and conditions are likely to receive diagnoses of psychosomatic illness, patients with little-known or unknown physical problems are in great danger of being told that their symptoms are psychological in origin. Toni Jeffreys, who was so ill with ME in the late 1970s (before ME was more widely recognized) that she could not walk, was repeatedly told that her illness was psychosomatic. When she was completely bedridden, her partner Jim, who had made an emergency call to a specialist they had consulted because he was frightened by the severity of Toni's symptoms, was advised by the doctor to abandon her: "He said you'd soon pull yourself together" (Jeffreys 1982, 85). Since I am a somewhat public person with ME, I have been contacted by dozens of people with ME who have discussed their experiences with me. If they became ill before about 1988 (when ME, or chronic fatigue immune dysfunction syndrome, began to be recognized as a 'legitimate' physical illness in medical circles, most notably at the Centers for Disease Control), they were usually sent to psychiatrists. If they became ill after 1988, they were not. The difference was not in the symptoms, but in their doctors' recognition of physical disease. Psychosomatic illness was not being diagnosed on the basis of positive evidence of psychological problems; it was a *default* diagnosis for physical symptoms.[14] Why do physicians burden their patients with self-doubt, not to mention expensive and unnecessary psychological treatment, when they could admit that they do not know what is wrong?

Toni Jeffreys suggests an answer:

> An undiagnosed patient, or a patient whose account 'conflicts' with laboratory findings represents an untidiness, an affront. This is where psychiatry has made it possible for medicine to be, not a science in its infancy groping its way toward understanding, but a 'perfect science.' For what could be more convenient? A patient is sent to a psychiatrist for evaluation when the doctor fails to determine what is wrong. The psychiatrist, convinced the doctor has found nothing organically wrong, will naturally find a reason for the undiagnosed illness, a mental reason.[15] It is a perfect symbiosis: the doctor is relieved of a problem, the psychiatrist gains a patient. It reminds one of the sex-lives of snails. (Jeffreys 1982, 175)

The diagnosis of psychosomatic illness props up the myth of control in two ways. First, it contributes to the illusion that scientific medicine knows everything it needs to know to cure us (provided we cooperate fully), because there is no physical problem for which it cannot provide a diagnosis. Second, it transfers responsibility for controlling their bodies to the minds of those patients who cannot be cured; the problem is not that medicine cannot control their bodies, it is that their minds are working against them.

Moreover, the idea that the mind is controlling the body is employed even when physical causes of a patient's symptoms are identified clearly. Doctors, families, friends, and patients themselves speculate about psychological reasons for patients' illnesses and even accidents, and for the course of their recovery or failure to recover. As an explanation for the failure of treatments, the idea that the patient's mind is resisting recovery is useful in maintaining the illusion of medical omnipotence. The thought that "she could be cured if only she wanted to get well" is comforting to both healers and those who want to believe in their power. As an explanation for an accident or the onset of an illness, it is comforting to those who need to assign a cause and cannot find another, and to those who want to believe that they will avoid a similar disaster because they have healthier, or at least different, psyches.

Psychological speculation about illnesses and accidents may be fueled by the metaphorical meaning of some illnesses in the culture. For example,

Susan Sontag describes the widespread belief in the so-called 'cancer personality,' allegedly marked by depression, difficulties in maintaining relationships, inability to recover from loss, and self-pity. She contrasts this contemporary explanation for affliction with cancer with the nineteenth-century belief that cancer was caused by hyperactivity and hyperintensity of emotion (Sontag 1977, 50–55). Dr. Barry J. Marshall (Monmaney 1993) describes how difficult it was to persuade physicians even to consider his evidence that peptic ulcers were an infectious disease caused by bacteria, because the partially metaphorical belief that they were psychosomatic diseases (patients 'eating away at themselves' with stress or unfilled needs) was deeply entrenched.[16] The meanings that a society or an individual patient[17] gives to particular illnesses or disabilities are readily confused with their causes, or even with motivations, conscious or unconscious, for illness, accident, or persistent physical limitations.

Arthur Kleinman is a psychiatrist who has an intense interest in experiences of chronic illness and how people make these meaningful. His attention to the particularities of patients' lives, their social and cultural contexts, and their interpretations of the experience of illness is unusually intelligent, compassionate, and understanding. Yet even Kleinman slips into some of the popular versions of the myth of control when he discusses people with diseases or syndromes that are not fully recognized or understood by modern scientific medicine. He occasionally writes as though social, psychological, and cultural factors are *motivating* the patients to remain ill, as though the context and meaning patients have constructed for their illness are *causing* the illness. For example, in chapter 6 of *The Illness Narratives* (Kleinman 1988), Kleinman discusses two patients who suffer from chronic fatigue and pain, one in China and one in the United States. He mentions historical and contemporary controversies over whether their symptom-patterns are caused by an unknown infectious agent, but in summing up his view of the two cases, he says:

> Neither person has insight into the way her chronic illness expresses and helps resolve tensions in her life. And this may be a salient similarity worldwide. The chronically ill are caught up with the sheer exigency of their problems; what insight they possess into its structural sources and consequences they are not expected to voice. This is a social fiction of the illness role. The patient, in order to legitimately occupy that role, is not expected to be consciously aware of what she desires from it, what practical uses it has. (Kleinman 1988, 119)

Such a view of illness places people with chronic illnesses in a "Catch-22" position. If they manage to create meaningful lives within the limitations of illness, they must be motivated to be and remain ill. If they do not create meaningful lives within the limitations of illness, they have not made a successful adjustment, which in itself will be taken to be a sign of psychological inadequacy or illness. Either way, there is something wrong psychologically; so the very existence of chronic illness implies psychological dysfunction. Scientific medicine's inability to cure patients with chronic illnesses is explained away, preserving the medical myth of control while fostering the myth that a healthy mind will guarantee a healthy body.

I do not deny that there may sometimes be controllable psychological forces at work in creating or prolonging ill health or disability. But somehow we must find responsible ways to employ this hypothesis and test it in individual cases, and to avoid using it as an all-purpose face-saving device when scientific medicine cannot offer a diagnosis or a cure. Freewheeling speculation about psychological causes can delay appropriate treatment and/or impede scientific investigation of physical processes that are poorly understood. Speculation also causes a great deal of suffering by generating guilt, blame, and self-disgust in people who are already struggling with illness, disability, and/or impending death.

Another widespread mind-over-body version of the myth of control is that recovery from illness or disability can be accomplished with the right attitude; this, of course, has the implication that everyone who did not recover had the wrong attitude. Our cultural desperation to believe that it is always possible to ward off the disasters of illness and accident is reflected in many such cruel fictions. In 1993 I saw an interview with an artist who had been infected with HIV for fifteen years. (Doctors know this because his blood samples were being stored for an unrelated study begun in the late 1970s.) He had never had an HIV-related illness, and researchers were studying his immune system to find out why. When the interviewer asked the man what he thought about why he had not become ill, he explained at length, and with total confidence, that he had the right attitude. He always tried to see the good in any situation and to appreciate life. This, he claimed, had kept him alive, and it would continue to protect him from AIDS. The interviewer was impressed. It did not seem to occur to either of them that this man's claim implied that everyone who has died of AIDS so far, including the infants, had the wrong attitude toward life.

People often justify psychologizing illness and disability by observing that the mind has profound effects on the body. I agree. The mind does affect the body, and not just in the obvious sorts of ways, for example, that I can decide to raise my arm (the classic philosophical example). For instance, my own experiences of living with chronic pain have taught me that fear of pain and resistance to it amplify pain, and that pleasure, excitement, and intense concentration decrease it (provided it is not already extremely intense).[18] What is wrong with much of the psychologizing of illness and disability is not the claim that the mind affects the body, but a naive, simplistic picture of both what is going on in the mind and how it affects the body. The idea that I can make my body do anything I really want it to do, such as making the pain go away completely, is a form of the myth of control, a childish belief in the omnipotence of what I want. It is a failure to admit that the human mind is much bigger than our egos, and, even more obviously, that the rest of nature is bigger than our egos (facts for which we should be thankful, in my opinion).

Because our minds are much bigger than our egos, and because we are not consciously aware of most of what takes place in our minds, the mind-body relationship is far more mysterious and complex than the mind-over-body versions of the myth of control imply. Moreover, these versions of the myth seem to have a peculiar metaphysical underpinning: They tend to discount the body as a *cause* of events. People who would not deny that an earthquake could devastate someone's life without any cooperation from her/him are anxious to deny that a disease or disability could do so. People who readily recognize that drinking alcohol could impair their judgement are unwilling to admit that a physical abnormality could make them incurably depressed or cause them pain for the rest of their lives. This suggests very strongly that something irrational, such as a myth that is untouchable by evidence, is at work.[19]

More Versions of the Myth

There are other popular versions of the myth of control. One is the belief that if you take proper care of your body, you will stay well and fit until you die (presumably death will be both instantaneous and inexplicable). This has the ugly implication that if you are ill or disabled, you must have failed to take care of yourself. Another is that people 'make themselves' ill or disabled by mismanaging their lives, their psyches, or their spirits in some way.

I spent a lot of the time I was confined to bed probing the question of whether I fell ill because I had mismanaged my life in some way. I find this is the most common hypothesis among women who, like myself, were struck down suddenly by ME in the midst of busy lives. This may be due partly to the popular media characterization of ME as a disease of 'over-achievers.' It may also reflect feelings of guilt or uncertainty about having worked toward goals which were widely considered 'inappropriate' for us. It may be part of a rationalizing rejection of one's former, healthy self, in order to adjust to a new body and a new way of life. I discarded the mis-management hypothesis eventually, partly on the reasoned basis that I know dozens of healthy people who have always taken far worse care of themselves than I ever did, and partly on the emotional basis that I liked (and still do like) the woman I used to be, even though I have become a different woman. If I mismanaged my life, it was not in any way I could have known at the time, nor in any way I can see now.

When people remake their lives in order to live with an illness or dis-ability, and especially when they come to like their new lives better or find them more fulfilling than their previous lives, they and others often infer that they became ill or disabled in *order* to change their lives or because their lives needed changing. And, as I have mentioned, when people make their illnesses or disabilities meaningful in their lives, the meanings they give them are often interpreted as the *reasons* for their having become ill or dis-abled. Both these responses strike me as manifestations of the myth of control, as well as attempts to believe that nothing really devastating happens without a good purpose.

The mismanagement hypothesis is not the only one of the control hypotheses I explored personally. Several friends suggested that conflicts we were having at the time might have been responsible for my falling ill. Some suggested that unconscious hostility toward me, which they had since become aware of, might have hurt me physically. These attempts to take responsibility were both touching and rather frightening. They made me think about possible forms of vulnerability I had not seriously consid-ered. I did not and do not dismiss them, because I do not imagine that my own worldview is complete or even very accurate, and because I know that wise and compassionate people believe that such things happen and live according to those beliefs.[20] But because neither the friends who suggested them nor I come from cultures in which these hypotheses are supported, their suggestions, and my reactions, made me realize how hard we were all trying to believe that we had some control over my being ill.

Doctors[21] and mothers are popular targets of the desire to blame somebody in order to maintain the myth of control. In her discussion of "mother-blaming," Barbara Hillyer (1993, chapter 6) points out that the mothers of children with disabilities are often blamed for the existence or severity of their children's disabilities, for their lack of 'independence,' or for their inability to progress, thrive, or respond to treatment. As Hillyer says, this blaming of individual women focusses attention away from social structures and responsibilities, but I would point out that it is also a way of denying that no one had or has control over some painful, frustrating, and frightening situations.

Some Consequences

The various versions of the myth of control have powerful effects on people who are incurably ill or attempting to adjust to a permanent disability. We become acutely aware that, as Robert Murphy pointed out, the first commandment of sickness is: Get well (Murphy 1990, 20). My version is harsher: Get well or die.[22] Your not getting well depresses everyone—the doctors and nurses who have tried to fix you, your friends and relatives, even people who hardly know you. Your hanging around without recovering reminds them that not everything, not even everything terribly important, can be fixed.

Cheri Register writes about the shame felt by people with chronic illnesses:

> Even illnesses that do not carry the stigma of manic-depression and epilepsy can generate shame. In a culture that is literally overrun by joggers in quest of complete physical self-control, a body that defies control is a source of humiliation. Feeling defective and dysfunctional is far worse than being just out-of-shape. In addition, some of the newly popular forms of healing and self-help approaches to "wellness" reinforce the notion that complete health is accessible to anyone, as long as you find the right diet or exercise program or have the right mental attitude. By drawing too simplistic a cause-and-effect link between will and bodily function, they deepen the sense of failure that many of us already feel. The emphasis on healing yourself becomes just another form of blaming the victim. (Register 1987, 44–45)

The price of the illusion that most of us are in control is the guilt and stigma we inflict on those whose bodies are out of control. I believe it is a major contributor to the stigma of disability. It is reflected in the fact that the media like people with disabilities best when they are engaged in some form of 'overcoming,' when an interviewer can draw the conclusion, "people can do anything they really want to." Imagine the self-doubt and psychological pain this inflicts on people who want to get up and walk away from a wheelchair, or just not to die. More subtly, it also inflicts a constant fear of losing control on those who feel they are in control now.

Ironically, by creating a culture of individual responsibility for illness and accident, the myths of individual control and medical control through cure discourage any search for possible social and environmental causes of diseases and disabilities, thus inhibiting efforts to prevent them.[23] However, some patients' groups have begun to focus on finding environmental causes of illnesses, notably the large number of women's cancer research groups studying the epidemiology of cancer and its relationship to industrial pollutants.[24] Efforts to uncover the preventable environmental causes of some diseases and disabilities are extremely valuable and important, and, unlike other quests for control, they may lift the burden of blame and guilt from some people who are ill or disabled by demonstrating that conditions beyond their control, not their own 'lifestyles' or bad attitudes, caused their illness or disability.

On the other hand, there is some danger of their adding to the burden of blame and guilt. If you suspected that the chemical plant you lived near or worked in might be dangerous to your health, why did you not move or quit? If you suspected that your food might be contaminated with pesticides, why did you not buy organic? In societies where corporate or governmental neglect or exploitation is habitually reinterpreted in terms of individual choice and responsibility, prevention efforts carry the risk of creating greater burdens of blame and guilt for individuals whose choices are in fact very limited. I hope that prevention efforts based on environmental improvement do not produce new versions of the myth of control that will further stigmatize people who become ill or disabled. As with efforts to find a cure versus willingness to accept the reality of illness or disability, there has to be a balance struck between efforts toward prevention, which require a faith that some causes can be found and removed, and willingness to accept the fact that life is full of risks.

Bad Things Happen

Feminist theorists have probed the causes of European patriarchal cultures' demands for control of the body, postulating fear of death, fear of the strong impulses and feelings the body gives us, fear of nature, and fear and resentment of the mother's power over the infant (Beauvoir 1952; Dinnerstein 1976; Griffin 1981). I will not rehearse these theories here, since they are widely available in better form than I could give them. I think the evidence is strong that all four factors, in addition to the idealizations and objectifications of the body by a culture, contribute to the demand for control of the body. But I think there is another, more general contributor.

Most people are deeply reluctant to believe that bad things happen to people who do not deserve them, or seek them, or risk them, or fail to take care of themselves. To believe this as a general proposition is to acknowledge the fragility of one's own life; to realize it in relation to someone one knows is to become acutely aware of one's own vulnerability.

The philosopher Susan Brison, who survived rape and attempted murder by a stranger, eloquently describes the reluctance to believe in unavoidable disaster that she encountered:

> My sense of unreality was fed by the massive denial of those around me—a reaction I learned is an almost universal response to rape. Where the facts would appear to be incontrovertible, denial takes the form of attempts to explain the assault in ways that leave the observer's world view unscathed. Even those who are able to acknowledge the existence of violence try to protect themselves from the realization that the world in which it occurs is their world and so they find it hard to identify with the victim. They cannot allow themselves to imagine the victim's shattered life, or else their illusions about their own safety and control over their lives might begin to crumble. The most well-meaning individuals, caught up in the myth of their own immunity, can inadvertently add to the victim's suffering by suggesting that the attack was avoidable or somehow her fault. One victims' assistance coordinator, whom I had phoned for legal advice, stressed that she herself had never been a victim and said that I would benefit from the experience by learning not to be so trusting of people and to take basic safety precautions like not going out late at night. She didn't pause long enough during her lecture for me to point out that I was attacked suddenly, from behind, in broad daylight. (Brison 1993, 11)

Reactions to illness or accident are often similar to the reactions Brison describes. Most people cannot resist suggesting ways in which it was avoidable, or at least seeking causal factors over which a person might exert control to avoid it. The ill and injured themselves, like the victims of any personal disaster, usually prefer blaming themselves to believing that they could not have prevented it. Brison says: "I felt angry, scared and helpless, and I wished I could blame myself for what had happened so that I would feel less vulnerable, more in control of my life" (Brison 1993, 13).

Of the vulnerability that people with disabilities both symbolize for others and feel themselves, Mary Jane Owen says:

> Those of us with disabilities are precisely the people who prove to society how frail and vulnerable the human creature is. We prove in every way that "it" can happen to anyone, anywhere, anytime. That reality often frightens non-disabled people into avoiding us.
>
> It also frightens many of us. We know, from the gut out, what it feels like to have some system of the body fall apart. The sword has fallen and broken our thin thread of potential perfection. We are already flawed. And if it happened once, it can happen again and again.
>
> Maybe we have learned to compensate at our present level of functioning. But what about the next assault? How much can we be expected to overcome? We are vulnerable, in the worst way, to the future. (Owen 1994, 8)

Affirming that bad things happen to people who do not deserve them, or seek them, or risk them, or fail to take care of themselves not only frightens most of us, it also raises challenging religious or spiritual issues for people who believe that God is omnipotent, omniscient, and benevolent, for those who believe that one or more powerful transcendent beings are caring for them, and for those who believe (or just feel) that the universe itself is, if not benevolent, at least benign. On rereading Job, I was amused to discover that Job's friends and colleagues offered (unsolicited) many theories of how he had brought an unremitting plague of misfortunes upon himself by his own actions and omissions. Reactions to other people's disasters do not seem to have changed much. The book also portrays Job's own agonized attempts to understand why God is punishing him so harshly. In fact, as the reader knows, God is not punishing him but allowing Satan to test Job's faith. That God would allow God's faithful servant to be tortured for so long to prove a point to a fallen angel does not offer an attractive or comforting picture of God. Job is a vivid story of terrible things happening to someone who did not deserve them, seek them, risk them, or fail to take care of himself, with which the writer forces the reader to think beyond a religious faith based on the fantasy of the perfect parent. Job presents the spiritual challenge: Can you love and seek to know

God even if God might be like this? Or, put more generally (in Platonic terms): Can you love and seek to know Reality even if Reality might be like this? Desire to avoid such spiritual challenges is liable to lead religious people to attribute too much responsibility to victims of disaster and to look for moral and spiritual flaws in those whose lives have been devastated by violence, accident, or disease.

Knowledge Lost

The idealization of the body, the myth of control, and the marginalization of people with illnesses and disabilities mean that much knowledge about how to live with limited and suffering bodies is not transmitted in cultures where these influences are powerful. Consequently, many of us are ill-equipped to cope with the problems of illness and disability, having had no opportunity to learn. Cultural silence about pain, limitation, suffering, and dying also increases our fear of them, and thus contributes to our need to believe that we can control our bodies.

Consider again the example of pain. It is difficult for most people who have not lived with prolonged or recurring pain to understand the benefits of accepting it. Yet some people who live with chronic pain speak of "making friends" with it as the road to feeling better and enjoying life. How do they picture their pain and think about it; what kind of attention do they give it and when; how do they live around and through it, and what do they learn from it? We could all learn this as part of our education. Some of the fear of experiencing pain is a consequence of ignorance and lack of guidance. The effort to avoid pain contributes to such widespread problems as drug and alcohol addiction, eating disorders, and sedentary lives. People with painful disabilities can teach us about pain, because they cannot avoid it and have had to learn how to face it and live with it. The pernicious myth that it is possible to avoid almost all pain by controlling the body gives the fear of pain greater power than it should have and blames the victims of unavoidable pain. The fear of pain is also expressed or displaced as a fear of people in pain, which often isolates those with painful disabilities. All this is unnecessary. People in pain and knowledge of pain could be fully integrated into culture to everyone's benefit.

If we knew more about pain, about physical limitation, about loss of abilities, about what it is like to be 'too far' from our cultural ideals of the body, perhaps we would have less fear of the negative body, less fear of our own weaknesses and 'imperfections,' of our inevitable deterioration and death. Perhaps we could give up some of our idealizations and relax our desire for control of the body; until we do, we maintain them at the expense of people whose bodies do not fit the ideals, and at the expense of much of everyone's ability to live comfortably with our own real bodies.

The myth that we can control the body also contributes to perpetuating non-disabled people's failure to identify with people with disabilities, and to the lottery approach to social (lack of) planning. Most people who are not disabled now will be disabled in the future. If they faced up to that, instead of hoping that medicine, diet, exercise, attitude, and moral goodness will save them from it, they would take social measures to provide for the needs of people with disabilities, increase accessibility to the public sphere, and guarantee good opportunities for everyone to participate in all aspects of social and creative life.

Some Conclusions

I am far from wanting to advocate that we give up all forms of trying to control the body. Scientific Western medicine's quest for control of bodily injury and disease has prevented a great deal of suffering and premature death. I am especially impressed by its accomplishments in dealing with traumatic injury. When my partner fell headfirst down the stairs, breaking three vertebrae in his neck, I was acutely aware in the first few weeks after the accident that it was the modern techniques of scientific Western medicine that saved his life. Moreover, it provided the treatments that prevented damage to his spinal cord while promoting good (well-aligned) healing of the vertebrae. He was lucky both in the nature of the accident (the cord missed being damaged by one millimeter) and in his access to the best response that medicine has to offer to traumas of that kind. Someone discovered the drugs that prevented swelling around the injury which might have damaged his spinal cord in the first few days, someone invented traction, someone invented the bone-imaging techniques and machines which were used to evaluate his condition, someone invented the halo-thoracic brace that enabled him to avoid the months in traction that are dangerous to health, and probably there was more research and invention behind his treatment of which I know nothing. He also owed a lot of his recovery to the emergency-response team who arrived at the house, the emergency-room doctor who identified the injury, the highly trained specialists who prescribed and administered treatment, the nurses who helped him cope with the treatments, and the physiotherapists who helped restore function to the muscles in his back. There can be no doubt that the impulse to save life and to cure injuries resulted in the medical care that enabled him to recover from a very dangerous accident. It allows thousands of others to survive (with and without disability) accidents and infections that, here in the recent past and in many parts of the world even now, would have killed them.

I do not even want to abandon all aspects of the myth of control. There are truths contained in most versions of that myth. Medicine can sometimes prevent death and suffering and cure disease and disability. There are psychological causes of illness and contributions to it. Some people do neglect or abuse their bodies, sometimes from self-hatred or despair, and sometimes to try to fulfill the physical ideals of their culture (as with dieting). Attitudes do seem sometimes to affect the progress of an illness or a recovery, and there are spiritual and other lessons a person can learn from being ill or disabled. It is the overgeneralization and misapplication of these truths, combined with a strong cultural demand for control of the body, that cause the damage I have described.

We need to recognize that scientific Western medicine's quest for prevention and cure has prevented and relieved, but also caused, a great deal of suffering. We need to recognize that most people experience disability in the course of their lives. We need to demand that medical practice devote more attention and resources to improving the quality of patients' experiences, to helping people to live with incurable physical limitations and suffering, and to enabling those who are fatally ill to die as well as possible. We need to integrate the experience and knowledge of people with disabilities and those who are dying into the mainstream of our cultures, into our concept of life as it is ordinarily lived. We need to learn to accept that people are not always able to control their bodies and to stop holding them responsible for doing the impossible. In short, we need to become more willing to face the realities of bodily life.

Many aging or old people in the United States and Canada now fear something at the end of life more than they fear death: becoming mere physical objects in the hands of medical doctors/technicians who, rather than letting them die, will pursue cures or prolong their lives while remaining unaware of and unconcerned about their patients' subjective experiences of the 'procedures' they inflict on them. This increasingly widespread fear is a hopeful sign, a possible source of resistance to the medical versions of the myth of control and to some of the other collective self-deceptions about avoiding death. Honest discussion of death and the process of dying could introduce more realism into our cultural picture of the human body.

Sherwin Nuland is somewhat pessimistic about this issue:

> Mine is not the first voice to suggest that as patients, as families, and even as doctors, we need to find hope in other ways, more realistic ways, than in the pursuit of elusive and danger-filled cures. In the care of advanced disease, whether cancer or some other determined killer, hope should be redefined. Some of my sickest patients have taught me of the varieties of hope that can come when death is certain. I wish I could report that there were many such people, but there have, in fact, been few. Almost everyone seems to want to take a chance with the slim statistics that oncologists give patients with advanced disease. Usually, they suffer for it, they lay waste their last months for it, and they die anyway, having magnified the burdens they and those who love them must carry to the final moments. Though everyone may yearn for a tranquil death, the basic instinct to stay alive is a far more powerful force. (Nuland 1993, 233–34)

Doctors, as well as patients, need to be released from the frantic, unrealistic pursuit of cures. This will require a cultural change, not simply the injection of "medical ethics" into the practice of medicine. As long as patients want rescue from death more than anything else from their doctors, doctors will feel the ethical pull of fulfilling their patients' expectations of them, and rightly so.[25]

Yet despite his pessimism, Nuland repeatedly emphasizes that there are sources of hope even when rescue is impossible. Of his own anticipation of death, he says:

> When my time comes, I will seek hope in the knowledge that insofar as possible I will not be allowed to suffer or be subjected to needless attempts to maintain life; I will seek it in the certainty that I will not be abandoned to die alone; I am seeking it now, in the way I try to live my life, so that those who value what I am will have profited by my time on earth and be left with comforting recollections of what we have meant to one another. (Nuland 1993, 257)

I am convinced that if we knew our society would help us to prepare for death and support us in the process of dying, at least some of our fear of death, and thus some of our need for control, would be diminished. Certainly a society that hides and denies death feeds people's fears of it. People with AIDS and cancer who are describing their dying to the rest of us are beginning to show us that dying can be a rich part of human experience, and not the monolithic suffering and despair that we might imagine from our cultural avoidance of those who are dying. If helping people to die as comfortably and peacefully as possible were treated as an indispensible part of medicine and psychology, and if preparing to die and dying were considered to be important, creative stages of life in which friends and families normally participated, perhaps our cultural obsession with keeping people alive could be allowed to diminish.

I do not imagine that it would be easy to reduce the cultural attachment to the myth of control. Having an unpredictable chronic illness keeps me acutely aware of the strength of my own desire for control of my body. Although for more than ten years I have repeatedly had to give in to the sickness of my body, to surrender to deep fatigue, weakness, and pain, I still resist it every time, because the need to give in is a violation of my autonomy, my ability to plan, to make commitments, to choose. It makes me feel helpless and ashamed. Cheri Register says of chronic illness: "Dealing with loss of control is the most difficult aspect of acceptance. The single most frightening feature of chronic illness is the uncertainty" (Register 1987, 208). I do not doubt that losing much of my personal sense of control of my body, as well as other people's reactions to my illness and my greatly increased awareness of the struggles of people with disabilities, have made me unusually sensitive to the myth of control at work in my culture. I feel out-of-step culturally, uncomfortable with many assumptions about bodily life I encounter in daily interactions.

I regard the current level of cultural idealization, objectification, quest for perfection, and demand for control of the body as a collective sickness of the soul, an alienation from experience and reality. I believe that people with and without disabilities would benefit from lessening the desire to control one's body and increasing the desire to live in respectful harmony with it, whatever its weaknesses and failures. Barbara Hillyer says it well: "Positive body awareness . . . comes not from striving for an ideal but from accepting the reality—that we change, age, become ill or disabled, and will die" (Hillyer 1993).

I close this chapter with a poem by Barbara Ruth, in which I see a desperate, wearisome, and humourous wrestling, like my own, with the contemporary myths of control.

Pelvic Mass Etiology

for all the people who say or think,
"Barbara, why are you doing this? Again?"

I think it all started with moving to Oakland
The fact that I took birth control pills for fourteen years
My neurotic desire for a child
It's proof of bad karma in the second chakra
It's related to Halley's comet
Due to the fact I started menstruating early
It's caused by the patriarchy
By racism
Anti-semitism
Being on welfare
Or maybe it's sunspot activity
It's something I made because I want to be mutilated
It's punishment for enjoying sex too much
The wrong kind of sex
The wrong kind of partner
It's because I eat the wrong foods
It's choosing the wrong acupuncturist
The wrong Chinese herbs
The wrong visualization technique
It's too much vitamin C
It's my father trying to make me his son
It's this hard rock of anger
It's blaming myself
It's forgiveness refused
It's being an anarchist under advanced capitalism
It's my tax dollars
Invading Nicaragua
Investing in apartheid
It's not being a tax resister
It's going to jail in South Carolina to protest nukes

More Cesium in their water
Than anywhere else in the world
And that's what I lived on
It's being kicked in the belly by cops in Philadelphia
And then refusing to let the male ER doctor
Examine my bleeding ass
It's too much resistance
Or not enough
It's my great aunt kicked in the head
By Cossacks' horses
It's my father's family bombed on reservation Redeye
Then sedated by condominium whiskey
It's the persecution of the peyote church
It's too many psychedelics when I was a hippie
It's something I do
In order to get post-surgical morphine
It's something I do for attention
I do it in order to help
The surgeons work out their karma
I do it in order to meet the x-ray technicians
I do it in order to write this poem
It's punishment for being bad
For doing something so bad I forget what it is
But it probably happened before I was five
Or maybe before I was born
It's afflicted planets in my natal chart
It's genetic propensity
An unlucky roll of the chromosomes
It's having no homeland
Having my homeland taken away
It's forced relocation
It's Big Mountain
It's the Golan Heights
It's Thanksgiving and Christmas
Coming too close together
It's the long nights of winter
It's being battered by people I loved
As a child
As a wife
As a dyke

The Rejected Body

It's the toxins I breathe
It's the polar caps melting
It's the Coriolis effect.

I think it's the problem of entropy
The body's, the world's
Rushing toward ever increasing chaos
And I'm afraid there's not enough love medicine
In the whole universe
To make it stop hurting
To make me ever be well.

5

The Cognitive and Social Authority of Medicine

In my society and many others where it holds sway, scientific Western medicine has both the cognitive and the social authority to describe our bodies to ourselves and to others. "Cognitive authority" is a term I borrow from feminist philosopher Kathryn Pyne Addelson (1983). It means the authority to have one's descriptions of the world taken seriously, believed, or accepted generally as the truth. H. Tristram Englehardt says of this: "Medicine molds the ways in which the world of experience takes shape; it conditions reality for us" (Englehardt 1986, 157). Susan Sherwin, elaborating upon Englehardt's view, says: "The reality that medicine creates is socially accepted; given the power and authority that are awarded to medical expertise, its reality is generally socially dominating" (Sherwin 1992, 191).

The *social* authority of doctors, researchers, and other medical professionals derives partly from their cognitive authority within and outside their professions and partly from their positions in powerful institutions, their social status, and their professional and social connections. Their authority operates far beyond medical institutions—inside and in relation to government bureaucracies, insurance companies, courts, schools, charities, rehabilitative organizations, and institutions for long-term care. Medical professionals also exercise considerable authority with all types of employers, certifying people medically capable or incapable of working.

In 1972, Irving Kenneth Zola warned us that "medicine is becoming a major institution of social control, nudging aside, if not incorporating, the more traditional institutions of religion and law. It is becoming the new repository of truth, the place where absolute and often final judgments are made by supposedly morally neutral and objective experts" (Zola 1972, 487). Zola pointed out that, although considerable attention had been focussed on the increasing social power of psychiatry, it was not yet widely recognized that similar powers and dangers extended beyond psychiatry to the entire medical profession. It is still the case that psychiatry tends to be the focus of people's criticism of and resistance to medicine's social authority. Perhaps this is because its cognitive authority to describe our minds and behaviour still has strong competition from less reductionistic, for example, religious, worldviews, unlike the cognitive authority of scientific medicine to describe our bodies, which is nearly uncontested in many societies, including my own. Perhaps also there is more criticism of psychiatry's authority because, as John R. Woodward claims, most people already know enough to fear it.

> Whether or not you believe that the human mind should be studied scientifically, you have to acknowledge that the psychiatric profession is very powerful. Psychiatrists influence our lives in court, in the workplace and in school. In most states, they are the only officials that the law allows to confine you against your will for an indeterminate period of time, without the benefit of a trial. They preside over the expansion of the fastest-growing segment of the pharmacopoeia. While the entertainment media exploit them as figures of fun, jokes about them are funny precisely because psychiatrists have such power. After all, a cop can beat you up or throw you in jail, but a psychiatrist can persuade you that your mind, that thing that is most intimately and inescapably *you*, is defective. (Woodward 1995, 17)

Criticism of psychiatry often contrasts the lack of agreement among its practitioners and the lack of careful scientific testing of its hypotheses with the high degree of agreement upon an accepted body of knowledge and the careful application of scientific procedures in other medical specialities.[1] In other words, psychiatry's cognitive and social authority is often criticized on the basis that, unlike the rest of medicine, psychiatry is not scientific. This approach does not foster criticism of the authority of the other medical specialities. Because the authority of medicine to describe our bodies tends to be neglected (or taken for granted), I will focus my discussion in this chapter on that, rather than on medicine's authority to describe our minds or behaviour. Nevertheless, many of the concerns I raise may be applicable to psychiatry, and I hope that they will cast doubt on the view that the main problem with psychiatry's having cognitive and social authority is that it is not as scientific as the rest of medicine.

The cognitive and social authority of medicine to describe our bodies affects how we experience our bodies and our selves, how our society describes our experiences and validates/invalidates them, how our society supports or fails to support our bodily sufferings and struggles, and what our culture knows about the human body. It also affects profoundly the relationship of medical providers to patients and the quality of medical care. The authority of medicine tends to delegitimize our experiences of our bodies as sources of knowledge about them, because the authoritative, that is, the medical and scientific, descriptions of our bodies are third-person descriptions of physical conditions. For example, our own, phenomenological descriptions are at best treated as weak evidence for the truth of medical and scientific descriptions. They are almost never treated as even weak evidence *against* a medical or scientific description of our bodies.

In the rest of this chapter I will discuss some of the consequences of the authority of medicine. Throughout the discussion, it should be remembered that although the authority of medicine affects everyone, healthy or ill, disabled or non-disabled, its consequences are compounded for people who have little cognitive or social authority of their own, and for people who are routinely treated as though they are without such authority, such as most women, and many men who are poor, old, disabled, and/or subjected to racism.

Alienation

The authority of scientific medicine to describe our bodies contributes to our alienation from our bodies and our bodily experiences, an alienation that is already fostered by other aspects of the commercial cultures of North America, including the objectification and commodification of women's (and, to a lesser but increasing extent, men's) bodies, and the quest for physical 'perfection' that results from widespread acceptance of body ideals. Maxine Sheets-Johnstone (1992b) points out that the "popular body noise" representing the body as purely physical object and as material possession fits well with the objectifying perspective of scientific medicine. In the popular attitude toward the body, medicine takes on the role of a high-technology service industry that helps us maintain and improve a potentially valuable possession. She describes what is lost as a consequence:

> When the body is treated as a purely material possession, our human-ness is diminished. Popular body noise drowns out the felt sense of our bodies and a felt sense of our individual aliveness. In place of these felt senses is a preeminently visual object groomed in the ways of quite specific, all-pervasive, culturally-engrained attitudes and values. What is diagnosed as needing thinner thighs, increased fiber, stress-reduction, or an at-home aerobic device, is precisely a culturally-selected visual object. We no longer listen to our bodies directly, but only to what modern science tells us about our bodies, and not just at the level of food, sex, and stress, but at the level of neuroanatomical/physiological facts: how our brains work, how our eyes see, how our hearts react to trauma, and so on. The living sense of ourselves vanishes in the din of popular body noise. (Sheets-Johnstone 1992b, 3)

Philosophical phenomenologists Richard M. Zaner (1983) and Drew Leder (1990) both point out that the body as *corpse*, not the body as lived experience, is at the heart of Western medicine. Leder draws attention to the effects of this on medical practice. When the patient is conceived of as a physiological machine, "(d)iagnosis and treatment seek to address the observed lesion, the quantified measurement, more than a person living in pain. The patient's own experience and subjective voice become inessential to the medical encounter" (Leder 1990, 146–48). I believe, moreover, that the cognitive authority of medicine in the doctor-patient encounter gives far more weight to the doctor's metaphysical stance, undermining the epistemic confidence of patients in the importance of their bodily experiences. When that happens, patients cease to expect acknowledgement of their subjective suffering or help in living with it. This can leave them not only isolated with their experience but feeling obliged to discount or ignore it, alienating them further from their own bodies.[2]

Zaner emphasizes the cultural effects of medicine on our sense of ourselves as living bodies:

> precisely to the extent that medicine's powerful presence in our culture positively induces persons in the wider culture to view themselves in ways medicine itself views them and human life, and the latter includes the concept of the alive body as based on the dead body (the cadaver), so we are encouraged to view ourselves: as mechanisms and thus as funda-

mental enigmas. We are led eventually to the conviction that our every-day, life-worldly understanding and experience of our own alive bodies are fundamentally wrong, specious, and thus to think that our own most fundamental experiences are yet fundamental deceptions. Not trusting ourselves, thus, we perforce are led to place our trust in others—in experts in the body—to tell us about ourselves: whether, for example, our complaints are real diseases in need of professional treatment and cures. In short: coming to view ourselves in the ways medicine views us, and our bodies, we come to be alienated from ourselves and our most intimate experiences. (Zaner 1983, 154)

The authority of medicine to describe what is or should be going on in people's bodies also provides justification for medical management of bodily processes—management that may alienate people from their bodies by organizing and controlling the experience of some bodily events. For example, in their discussions of the management of childbirth in hospitals, Robbie Pfeufer Kahn and Meg Fox maintain that medical management reduces the highly variable, utterly absorbing experience of giving birth to a prescribed and clocked sequence of mechanical processes; women who do not keep to the expected timetable are usually medicated or operated upon. In contrast, a woman whose labour is not so carefully time-managed "leaves behind that quantifiable time which rushes past her attendants. The relentless rhythym of her contractions takes over the function of time-keeping, submerges objective, clock time in the eternity of bodily time, the endless succession of the heartbeat" (Fox 1989, 127).

The quest for control of the body that I discussed in chapter 4 undoubtedly plays a role in our acceptance of medicine's authority to describe our bodies. However alienating it may be, the scientific third-person perspective on the body fosters the illusion of control. As Susan Griffin points out, in our visually dominated culture, we often operate with the illusion that to see something is to control it (Macauley 1991, 124). The illusion of control is probably most desired when experience of the body seems most out-of-control, as in pregnancy and birth, illness, injury, or dying. Medicine is there to explain what is happening at these times with its objective, distancing perspective. Moreover, Drew Leder suggests that the alienation from our bodies fostered by scientific medicine offers us a means of dealing with the fear of death:

The terror of the body inaugurated by the approach of first-person death is countered by the figure of the third-person corpse. For this body yields up all its secrets to the scientist/physician. Moreover, the shift from the first- to the third-person perspective makes death a less threatening thing. Bodily death becomes not my death exactly, but modeled first and foremost on that of the Other. The true self cannot be threatened by the demise of that which from the start was mere mechanism. The dangerous body has been desubjectified, devitalized, demystified by Cartesian science. The corporeal threat is, as far as possible, subdued. (Leder 1990, 148)

Epistemic Invalidation

The cognitive and social authority of medicine includes the power to confirm or deny the reality of everyone's bodily experience. Thus medicine can undermine our belief in ourselves as knowers, since it can cast authoritative doubt on some of our most powerful, immediate experiences, unless they are confirmed by authorized medical descriptions, usually based on scientific laboratory results. Moreover, this power of medicine also subjects us to possible private and public invalidation by others—invalidation as knowers and as truth-tellers.

It might be observed that there is no necessary conflict between my experience of my body and medical descriptions of what is happening in my body. Medicine, society, and I could acknowledge that I am feeling what I am feeling regardless of whether medicine can explain it in objectively observable terms. But because one (albeit not the primary one) of medical science's goals is to explain our bodily experiences in terms of observable causes—to explain our aches, pains, and twitches, so to speak—it is a sign of the inadequacy or incompleteness of that science when it cannot explain my experience of my body. Since modern medical science does not exercise much modesty about the extent of its knowledge (more about this later), it has a tendency to ignore, minimize the importance of, or deny outright any of my bodily experiences that it cannot explain. It can get away with this response, moreover, because the third-person, scientific view of my body has become the socially authoritative one, in comparison to which my descriptions of my bodily experience are highly personal and too subjective to have much social weight. Thus scientific medicine's goal of explaining my experience is in some conflict with its desire to work entirely within its own third-person perspective on my body and its cognitive and social authority to do so. The upshot for me is that my subjective descriptions of my bodily experience need the confirmation of medical descriptions to be accepted as accurate and truthful.[3]

Englehardt (1986) attributes this to a historical change in medicine. What are now considered symptoms of underlying diseases were once considered diseases in their own right. For example, "pains" were, in the eighteenth century, a disease-classification. Now they are "complaints," which may or may not be symptoms of real disease.[4] This change was the result of the development of anatomy, physiology, pathology, and microbiology in the nineteenth century, and the successful correlation of laboratory findings with clinical findings. But gradually clinical findings lost their importance, and the explanatory models based on laboratory findings took precedence.

> Patient problems came to be understood as bona fide problems only if they had a pathoanatomical or pathophysiological truth value. Absent a lesion or a physiological disturbance to account readily for the complaint, the complaint was likely to be regarded as male fide. This requirement was credible because the laboratory sciences had become the basic medical sciences in an important ontological sense. They were seen as disclosing the reality underlying clinical findings. On the other hand, clinical observations . . . now became secondary. . . . This was in a very restricted sense correct with regard to the development of explanatory models. Accounts of disease were now formulated in terms of underlying pathophysiological and pathoanatomical mechanisms. The error lay in failing also to accent the goals and purposes of medicine. As an applied science, medicine remains focused on caring for human suffering. Clinical medicine begins from and returns to the problems of patients. However, the changes in explanatory assumptions, and the development of the basic sciences, led to certain unfortunate changes in the ideology of symptoms. (Englehardt 1986, 183–84)

One consequence is that, if a patient goes to doctors with symptoms (which medicine calls "complaints," to bracket the question of whether they have any 'real' causes) that the doctors cannot observe directly or verify independently of what the patient tells them, such as dizziness or numbness or visual problems or weakness or pain or difficulty concentrating, and if they cannot find an objectively observable cause of those symptoms (preferably laboratory test results), the patient is liable to be told, "There is nothing wrong with you," regardless of how acute or debilitating her/his condition feels to the patient.[5] I do not believe that most doctors realize how frightening and confusing such a pronouncement is, how it can shake a patient's self-confidence and undermine her/his relationship to reality.

When a doctor says to a patient who feels terribly ill or has acute pain, "There's nothing wrong with you," that doctor obliges the patient to choose between discounting her/his own experience and distrusting the knowledge of someone s/he may have trusted and respected for years. If the patient receives the same judgement from many doctors, or from one or more highly regarded specialists, s/he is forced to choose between asserting her/his own subjectively based ability to know her/his own body and discarding her/his belief in the expertise of medical science. Although most people may concede vaguely that science does not know everything, there is little social support for concluding that science is inadequate in one's own individual case.

One of the women Cheri Register interviewed in her study of chronic illness (Register 1987), Gloria Murphy (a pseudonym), experienced acute dizziness, numbness in her legs, inability to walk at times, double vision, bladder, kidney, and bowel problems. During most of the five years between the onset of her symptoms and her receiving a diagnosis of multiple sclerosis, she was told, by the Mayo Clinic and others, that she had "housewife's syndrome" and needed only to get busy and to get away from her children to feel better. In other words, the medical authorities pronounced that there was nothing physically wrong. What interests me here is not the failure of a few doctors to diagnose a known disease, but their patient's response to their authoritative dismissal of her symptoms. She responded by doubting her strong feeling that something was very wrong and, in order to "get busy and get away from her children," she took a job and became extensively involved in volunteer work, increasing her activities to a frantic pace. Instead of feeling better (as predicted by the doctors), she repeatedly collapsed and was hospitalized for more tests, including exploratory surgeries. Eventually, a neurologist specializing in MS gave her a diagnosis. She describes her reaction to the diagnosis as follows:

> And with that came this wonderful sense of relief. I giggled and laughed. I was joyous. My husband was the same way. We were just like two kids running through a park. We had a name to something. We could deal with it. I was not a neurotic lady. It was O.K. to slow down, to quit work. It was O.K. to say no to things. (Register 1987, 5)

This response was not the result of any failure to understand the seriousness of the diagnosis. It was the result of being rid of a terrible cognitive and social conflict—between how Gloria felt and what it was demanded that she believe about herself. Moreover, Register points out that Gloria's reaction is not unusual. Many people whose disabling physical conditions were not diagnosed for months or years describe increasing worries about their own sanity and judgement, and part of the relief of receiving a diagnosis, any diagnosis, is the confirmation by medical authority that they are not 'crazy' after all. This is not surprising. What can I know if I cannot know what I am feeling in my own body? How can I remain connected to a world that denies I am in pain, or dizzy, or nauseated, when I myself cannot deny that I am (or *can* deny it, but only at the cost of distrusting what is present to my consciousness most of the time)?

In Gloria's case, there turned out to be an explanation that medical science recognized and offered, and so anyone who reads the account of her efforts to discover what was wrong believes her, sympathizes with her, and understands her dilemma. Those who are diagnosed can tell their stories without fear of epistemic invalidation. But what of those who do not receive a diagnosis, either because they have not been to the right doctors, or because what is wrong with them is still unknown to medical science (a possibility that one rarely hears admitted in public)? Can their cognitive and social authority as individuals stand up to the cognitive and social authority of medicine? Imagine the self-confidence and inner strength it would take to continue to believe in one's own sanity, perceptions, and judgement, when they are called into question by medical experts. I think we have no idea how many people this happens to. I suspect that many people keep quiet about their pain or other physical sufferings once the doctor says, "There's nothing wrong with you," because they are unwilling to expose themselves repeatedly to such profound invalidation.

Moreover, when medicine recognizes that there is something physically wrong, that recognition by no means guarantees that a person will not be subjected to epistemic invalidation. Some people who have a diagnosis find that their experiences of their disease/disability are denied by medicine, because medicine claims to know more about the nature of their physical problems than they do. For example, a small percentage of people with advanced multiple sclerosis experience severe pain in their bones, muscles, and/or skin. Until recent studies confirmed that the disease processes of MS could indeed cause this pain, patients were told that the pain they reported was *impossible* (James 1993, 241).

Other patients find that their experiences are dismissed by medical practitioners as insignificant compared to other, more severe 'cases.' Arthur Frank, a medical sociologist who has written about his experience with a heart attack and testicular cancer, describes how medical professionals commonly respond to their patients' expressions of suffering by telling them that others are "much worse off." He says of these doctors and nurses: "Continuing suffering threatens them, so they deny it exists. What they cannot treat, the patient is not allowed to experience" (Frank 1991, 100–101).

Even when a person's experience of her/his body is recognized by medicine, it may be redescribed in ways that are inaccurate from the patient's standpoint. Oliver Sacks mentions that patients long reported "clear consciousness of the intended movements in their amputated limbs," while physicians described their experiences as "purely psychic hallucinations conjured up by bereavement, mourning, or yearning" (Sacks 1992b, 45). Then in 1872, Silas Weir Mitchell, a physician, described "phantom limb" phenomena and hypothesized that they had a neurological basis in the excitation of the brain, the spinal cord, and the remaining nerves to the limb, lending credence to the patients' own descriptions. Today, these patients' descriptions are recognized as accurate reports of neurophysiological processes. Using such reports, biomechanical engineers are now attempting to develop sophisticated artificial limbs which could actually carry out the "phantom" motions.

In a society where scientific medicine is powerful, one's status as a knower is quite precarious in relation to one's own body. No matter how trustworthy you may be considered now, you need only contract a rare[6] or previously unknown illness to become a suspect witness and to have your sanity questioned. Few medical practitioners will admit to patients that their personal medical knowledge or the collective knowledge of scientific medicine is incomplete. As discussed in chapter 4, people who have physical symptoms which their doctors cannot explain, especially women, are liable to be given 'diagnoses' that can be summed up as, "You're imagining it," or, "You're doing it to yourself." They may receive vague or specific psychiatric diagnoses and/or be committed to psychiatric hospitals (Jeffreys 1982; Hannaford 1985; Ramsay 1986; Register 1987; Rudner 1992; Thorne 1993).[7] Since most people take the cognitive authority of medicine for granted, these 'diagnoses' have considerable social force. Even if they do not convince the patients themselves that their problems are psychological, the doctors' verdicts often convince families, friends, employers, insurance companies, social service agencies, and courts that the patients are in some sense 'faking' illness or else mentally ill and resisting treatment. Thus a single unexplained illness can destroy the cognitive and social authority of any individual.

I once thought that if anyone were likely to be exempt from this sort of epistemic invalidation by medicine, surely it would be medical professionals themselves, when they became ill. Moreover, it seemed to me that if there were an 'epistemically safe' way to get an unknown illness, it would be as part of an epidemic. So I was surprised to discover A. Melvin Ramsay's account (Ramsay 1986) of how a 1955 epidemic of encephalomyelitis among doctors, nurses, and other staff at the Royal Free Hospital in London was later interpreted as "mass hysteria." Two hundred ninety-two staff members became ill between 13 July and 24 November with a range of symptoms including fever, headache, sore throat, swollen glands, dizziness, severe pain in the neck, back, and limbs, widespread muscle weakness, bladder dysfunction, and (sometimes severe) neurological problems. In 1970 Doctors C. P. McEvedy and A. W. Beard, having examined the records of the nurses[8] who fell ill in the epidemic, but not having seen any patients, published a paper in the British Medical Journal arguing that the epidemic was an instance of "mass hysteria." In a later paper in the same journal, they argued that some features of fourteen other epidemics of very similar illness justified a similar diagnosis, but that they were less "pure" examples of "mass hysteria" (Ramsay 1986, 33). These papers were very influential, and their verdict was accepted and widely publicized in the popular press, including Time magazine and the London Sunday Times.

The reasons for being suspicious of the "mass hysteria" hypothesis seem so obvious that I find it hard to believe that it was so readily accepted. If some epidemics of fever, sore throat, swollen glands, muscle pain, and other symptoms are instances of "mass hysteria," then why not conclude that all influenza epidemics are "mass hysteria?" How could we distinguish between genuine influenza outbreaks and "mass hysteria?" How is "mass hysteria" supposed to occur, and how does it produce fevers, sore throats, and swollen glands? Could it also produce sneezing, coughing, organ damage, paralysis, death? Could "mass hysteria" mimic any infectious disease or only some? Why believe in epidemic infectious diseases at all, if the "mass hysteria" hypothesis offers an adequate account of this sort of outbreak of illness? What I conclude from this particularly bizarre example of medical desperation to explain away an outbreak of a new, puzzling disease is that the power of some medical professionals to make people believe them, rather than accept the reports of patients, should never be underestimated. The cognitive and social authority of medicine is strong enough to foist wildly improbable theories upon the public and to question the sanity and cognitive integrity of large numbers of people, who, although they

127

once had their own medical authority, lost all credibility as soon as they became patients.[9]

Toni Jeffreys, who points out that, in the modern, scientific world, an illness "DOES NOT EXIST" until the medical profession says it does, remarks on the changed circumstances of patients:

> When people took to their beds in other centuries, their families, the community, assumed they had a good reason for doing so. They did what was necessary for them. The lives of Theresa of Spain, Florence Nightingale, and Charles Darwin are examples of people chronically ill for many years, but never 'diagnosed'. They were just ill, and that was enough for the rest of the world. But in the twentieth century, if one takes to one's bed and does not seek the medical 'seal of approval' for illness—medical diagnosis and treatment—one is suspect. (Jeffreys 1982, 183)

Jeffreys's observation suggests a solution to at least some of the epistemic invalidation that modern medicine inflicts on patients: Acknowledge the possible ignorance of individual practitioners and the incompleteness of medical science, and assume the reality of patients' symptoms unless there is overwhelming *positive* evidence that they are imagined or pretended. Unfortunately, many people with medical authority seem to lack the courage, self-confidence, or modesty to say simply: "We know you are in pain (or dizzy, nauseated, etc.), but we do not know why."[10] But this should not be attributed entirely to personal failures of character on the part of physicians. Medicine seems to me to be the only science that rarely admits publicly that it has unsolved puzzles, that is, important questions about which it knows little or nothing. One sees astronomers, physicists, and all sorts of nonmedical biologists on television describing unknown or relatively unexplored areas of their fields with excitement and anticipation. Medical scientists use a different discourse altogether when presenting their work to the public—a discourse of disease enemies versus heroic scientists. Failures of medicine are projected on to the temporarily more powerful diseases and rarely, if ever, described in terms of scientific ignorance.

Perhaps its unwillingness to acknowledge ignorance publicly (and often even privately to patients) is due to scientific medicine's continued connection to the mystique of the healer. The idea that the more power the patient believes the healer has, the more the patient will benefit from the treatment, seems to justify surrounding those whose business is healing with an unblemished aura of knowledge and power. Unfortunately it also rationalizes a great deal of deception and unwillingness to admit to mistakes and ignorance, for which both patients and physicians pay a price.

If any healing science or art is believed to have full knowledge and control of the body, then only the individual players—patient and doctor/healer—can be blamed when things go out of control, when the patient dies or remains ill or disabled. It is not surprising that patients and their families so often blame their doctors, even when no doctor could have done more. Why should patients accept that medicine cannot do everything if medicine will not admit it? Thus, to some extent, the cognitive and social authority of medicine is maintained at the expense of individual practitioners.

Nor is it surprising that doctors find ways to blame their patients for illnesses or disabilities they cannot explain. Patients pay the price of medicine's inflated image in loss of confidence in themselves and loss of other people's trust in them. Sometimes, they also lose their jobs, their families, their friends, their homes, their incomes, their freedom, and even their lives.

Social Abandonment

It is a consequence of the cognitive and social authority of medicine, combined with the limitations of medical knowledge and the unwillingness of medical practitioners to admit those limitations, that many people who are very ill and disabled are abandoned out of reach of any social safety net. People who are ill or disabled without a medical diagnosis are not eligible for the social programmes they may need in order to survive. Surprisingly many of them are also abandoned by friends and families. In Ingrid Deringer's (1992) interview-study of eight women who were eventually diagnosed with ME, four of the women reported having great difficulty getting insurance benefits or qualifying for social programmes when they were far too ill to work but still seeking definite diagnoses. One of the women had no money for rent or groceries for two months and was kept alive by neighbors who brought her food. All the women reported that they received little or no support—emotional, physical, or financial—from friends or family members before they had been diagnosed 'officially' by medical professionals (Deringer 1992, 84). Typically, one woman said, "My friends and family saw me so sick and they knew I was sick but because the doctors couldn't come up with a name, they'd say 'maybe it is all in your head' or 'if the doctors can't find anything, it can't be too serious'" (Deringer 1992, 87).

No wonder it is not uncommon for people to weep with happiness and relief upon receiving, after a long period of uncertainty, a definite diagnosis of a severely debilitating or even life-threatening illness. The diagnosis, however grim, restores them to society. Six of Deringer's eight interviewees reported feeling "euphoric" when they were diagnosed with ME, an incurable, disabling long-term illness (Deringer 1992, 59). In her book on living with chronic illnesses, Cheri Register comments that many of the people she interviewed had the same reaction to diagnosis. For example, one said the following about receiving a diagnosis of Crohn's disease, a terribly painful and unpredictable long-term illness:

> There was a great relief and feeling of euphoria when they told me I had Crohn's disease. "Gee, I was right. Something was wrong and this is what it is." I remember feeling kind of special and important. I could have just hugged that doctor for taking me seriously and deciding to get to the bottom of this. He didn't say, "It's all in your mind. Go away and don't bother us." (Register 1987, 15)

In 1972 the primary concern Zola expressed about medicine was that more aspects of daily life were being "medicalized" and coming under the formal jurisdiction and informal influences of medical "experts." Since then, concern about the cognitive and social authority of medicine has tended to centre upon the dangers of over-medicalization—of behaviour (Zola 1972) or ways of life (Englehardt 1986) that are socially unacceptable, of all forms of limitation (Rawlinson 1983), and of ordinary physical conditions and processes (especially those of women), such as pregnancy, menstruation, and menopause (Sherwin 1992). Less attention has been paid to the dangers of having physical experiences of illness or disability ignored or invalidated by medicine in societies where medicine has great cognitive and social authority, although both Engelhardt (1986) and Sherwin (1992) express concern about this problem.

Englehardt recognizes that medical diagnosis is "a complex form of social labeling" (Englehardt 1986, 185) that determines, among other things, a person's entitlement to treatment and social support. He also rejects explicitly the idea that medical classifications are objective scientific construals of reality. He says, "Concerns with evaluation and explanation . . . intertwine in health care in decisions about whether problems are medical problems, and about how medical problems ought to be understood and classified" (193). Moreover, he recognizes that different, sometimes conflicting interests may be involved in such decisions. The solution he suggests is greater democratization of the processes of medical classification:

> Communities must begin with a recognition of the constructed character of medical reality. This recognition underscores our choices and indicates our responsibilities as individuals who not only know reality but also know it in order to manipulate it. One must also recognize that these manipulations tend to be communal. Systematic programs for treatment and for the assessment of treatment, or communal insurance policies, are in principle not the undertakings of isolated individuals. As a result, communities of physicians, insurers, and the general public will need to negotiate regarding the characterization of medical reality where the interests of these three groups do not coincide. Such negotiations may take on either a formal or an informal character. In either case, they represent a democratization of reality. (Englehardt 1986, 194)

Sherwin, while acknowledging the value for feminists of Englehardt's social-constructionist account of health and illness and his call for democratization, warns that unequal positions of power in the 'democratic community,' combined with preexisting, widespread negative attitudes toward the physical processes of being female, create a danger for women. Democratic processes of medical classification, under these conditions, are liable to lead to continuing overmedicalization of ordinary female bodily events (Sherwin 1992, 195–96).

Sherwin's reminder that no democratic process takes place in a vacuum, that everyone enters into it with a position in a society and a cultural background, is very important to assessing the usefulness, to those of us who are already ill or disabled, of Englehardt's call for democratization of some aspects of the cognitive and social authority of medicine. There is reason to be skeptical that individuals who are ill and disabled, unable to work, isolated or bedridden, impoverished and begging for financial and social support, could really enter into negotiations on an equal basis with doctors, insurance company executives, social workers, and healthy non-disabled citizens over whether they have medically classifiable problems. Even if they could, there would be reason to worry, in such a democratic process, about whether people who have never experienced prolonged disability, and who have been exposed to a deep cultural fear of it, could contribute fair-mind-ed opinions to negotiations about which physical conditions constitute disabling medical problems.

In considering Englehardt's call for democratization of medical reality, Sherwin expresses uneasiness about a decision process that does not "grant special status to the input of an already oppressed group on a question that primarily affects its own members" (Sherwin 1992, 195). For example, some sort of special status could be granted to women's opinions about women's physical conditions and processes in Englehardt's scheme, and perhaps he would support such a move. But no such solution seems possible for people who are trying to obtain recognition of their own disability, because the outcome of the decision process itself would have to determine whether they were members of that particular oppressed group or not, and there are major, conflicting interests at stake.

I believe that Englehardt underestimates the potential role of conflicting interests in a democratized approach to medical classification. It is clearly in the direct financial interest of insurers of all types to recognize as few medical problems as they can while still making a convincing case to consumers that they offer valuable coverage. It is in the financial interest of government bureacracies that provide various forms of relief and support to people with disabilities to recognize as few disabling conditions as they can while avoiding major political opposition. It is in the interest of everyone who experiences bodily suffering and/or limitation to have it recognized by her/his society and to receive help and support in living with it. In a climate of acute public awareness that healthy people without disabilities pay (in part) for the treatment and support of those who are ill and/or disabled, widespread resentment of that fact, and the lottery approach to life, in which many people prefer betting on the unlikely probability that they themselves will never need help rather than supporting social programmes, there are bound to be bitter disagreements over medical recognition and classification. People with illnesses and disabilities, and their friends and supporters, would be outnumbered in these conflicts.

Sherwin addresses the problem at a deeper level, by pointing out that "social need should not have to be screened through the filter of medical values and authority" (Sherwin 1992, 194). This is a fundamental insight that many disability activists would cheer. If we were willing to assess realistically what each person needs to participate as fully as possible in the major activities of our societies, medical classifications would have far less social importance than they have now. Moreover, as a category, "disability" would either become more inclusive or else lose much of its social importance. It would also become obvious that disability is rarely total unless a society chooses to make it total.

But this introduces long-range political ideals into the discussion, and Sherwin cautions against undermining "the support now available under the rubric of health language" (194) before social structures of assistance to those who need it have been transformed. She says, "In a society that restricts provision of most forms of social assistance to those who have been designated as ill, it is strategically important that we maintain a broad understanding of the conditions that constitute illness" (194). I would add that it is also important to ensure that doctors are trained to use their cognitive and social authority responsibly, with full awareness of the social consequences of their pronouncements about patients' health and abilities. Moreover, the public should be better informed about the limitations of medical knowledge so that most people are aware of the genuine possibility that someone they know, or they themselves, might become very ill or disabled without a definite diagnosis.

Failures of Communication and Gaps in Knowledge

I believe that the cognitive authority of medicine causes us to censor the descriptions we offer to doctors, to pre-form them in what we hope will be scientifically acceptable descriptions of definite, recognizable symptoms.[11] This prevents doctors and medical researchers from receiving valuable information that might change their understandings of human bodies, illnesses, patients' needs, and appropriate treatments.

Biomedical ethicists have worried about the effects of doctors' authority on the flow of information from doctor to patient (Sherwin 1992). But the flow of information from patient to doctor is equally important and at least equally liable to distortions and failures due to the imbalance of power between them and the cognitive authority of the doctor. Kleinman (1988) argues that physicians are not currently trained to elicit, listen to, or respect patients' experiences of illness, and that the explanatory models of biomedicine too often drown out the information that patients want to communicate to doctors, and that doctors would benefit from hearing. Distortions and failures in this flow of information hinder medical care, protect medical science from its own mistakes, and sometimes have hurtful, even lethal consequences for patients.

Toni Jeffreys (1982, 174) remarks that although she consulted dozens of doctors while attempting to be diagnosed, only two of them asked, "How do you feel?" The others asked her to respond "Yes" or "No" to a list of symptoms. It need hardly be pointed out that this common procedure, although efficient for processing patients, is not likely to elicit information about unfamiliar medical problems or to increase doctors' understanding of patients' experiences of disease.

Not describing one's symptoms in the right language can also be quite dangerous. Jeffreys relates a story of a woman who tried to tell her doctor "that there was a crab inside her, tearing at her with its claws, eating her" (Jeffreys 1982, 172–73). No physical evidence was found at the time, because the technology available was not capable of detecting the problem, and she was placed in a mental hospital. Years later, when another doctor (the doctor who told Jeffreys the story) was called upon to perform emergency surgery on the same woman, he discovered that she had a stomach ulcer greater in diameter than a grapefruit. (This is very large for a stomach ulcer.) The original failure to find physical evidence, *plus her phenomenologically excellent but metaphorical description of her symptoms* had doomed her to disbelief, deprived her of freedom, and endangered her life.

The more I have learned about medicine, the more nervous and careful I have become about describing my own symptoms. I once told a specialist that relapses of my disease could happen so suddenly that it felt like being injected with strong poison. This still seems to me to be a good metaphor that most people would grasp at once, and other ME patients have agreed with the description, but I have never used it again in the presence of medical professionals. The look on the specialist's face told me that I was in danger of being sent to a psychiatrist forthwith. Yet who knows, at this early stage of investigation, that my metaphor might not provide a valuable clue to the nature of the disease?

The vocabulary of illness has become a vocabulary of third-person scientific and quasi-scientific description, which is inadequate for both medical practitioners and patients. In *Cancer in Two Voices*, Barbara Rosenblum, who was suffering at the time from advanced cancer, complained that it was hard to articulate how she felt because there is so little vocabulary to describe the sensations of bodily illness (Butler and Rosenblum 1991, 138). Toni Jeffreys asks, "If there are no words, how can those who care for the sick understand?" (Jeffreys 1982, 173). For example, patients often describe how they feel as accurately and in as much detail as they can for several minutes, only to have a doctor write a single word in his/her notes, "malaise," which is the only medical term for feeling ill over most of one's body. "Malaise" includes everything from feeling a bit off to feeling that death is imminent. This lack of vocabulary for the phenomenology of illness is one reason why patient-support groups are important and highly valued by patients. They offer a context in which people who are ill can work together to articulate their experiences of their bodies, to find or invent a phenomenological vocabulary that is adequate.[12]

For example, the best short description of the fatigue experienced by ME patients was, I think, invented by a doctor who has the disease herself. She calls it "cellular exhaustion."[13] This expression interests me, because it is not a standard biomedical description, yet it employs a scientific concept, "cellular." The fact that it strikes me as a perfect phenomenological description of my experience implies that my experience of my own body is partly mediated or structured by scientific understandings. Certainly I do not experience my body as cellular, but I experience the exhaustion as so deep and pervasive that it feels as though something is wrong throughout my body on the cellular level. (Clearly, my concept of "the cellular level" was created by my scientific education.) In addition, unlike the usual medical description, "fatigue," which is misleading because it suggests a normal condition experienced by healthy people—a condition that can be corrected by rest, food, or other strategies of renewal—"cellular exhaustion" suggests an abnormal condition, of a quality, severity, or persistence not experienced by healthy people, that is not responsive to normal strategies. The latter is much closer to the experience of ME patients.

This description differs from the understandings of both doctors of Western medicine and doctors of traditional Chinese medicine. A doctor of Western medicine would say something like this: that I have a long-term or chronic illness of unknown etiology, characterized by sudden, acute onset with flu-like symptoms, increasing fatigue, malaise, myalgia, and arthralgia, and so forth, with significant immunological abnormalities during the first year, and a good subsequent adjustment to ongoing disability. By the Centers for Disease Control diagnostic criteria, I have chronic fatigue syndrome. The English and Canadian designation for the same disease is myalgic encephalomyelitis. I do not dispute this description; it is accurate, as far as it goes.

A doctor of traditional Chinese medicine has told me something like this: that I have a complex imbalance of energy, that is, chi, caused by the fact that I worked too hard and exhausted my "heart" (by which she means something more like the Western literary understanding of "heart" than the

Western medical understanding, in that she told me I think with my heart), that I still work too hard and think too much, and that I need plenty of good sleep. This description too is accurate, as far as it goes.

Thus, I do not mean to suggest that there is some 'pure,' uninterpreted experience of the body, untouched by culture, which we need to liberate from medical and other social constraints and for which we need to develop a vocabulary. On the contrary, I believe that bodily experience is often, perhaps usually, highly interpreted and influenced by cultural, including scientific, understandings of the body. What I mean is that the vocabulary and understandings of the body produced by biomedicine often interfere with, rather than support, our abilities to communicate the phenomenology of bodily suffering. The conceptual categories that are most useful to medical science often exclude or distort those aspects of patients' experience that are most important to them. When the language of scientific medicine dominates encounters between doctors and patients, it contributes to alienation between them, to the objectification of patients, and to alienation of patients from their own experience.

In her study of an early eighteenth-century physician's record of the symptoms, diagnoses, and treatments of more than eighteen hundred of his female patients in Eisenach, Germany, Barbara Duden remarks, "The language of pain and the articulation of suffering, as cultural achievements in enduring pain, are historical phenomena" (Duden 1991, 88). The historical specificity of the language of pain is evident in the list Duden compiled of Dr. Johannes Storch's patients' complaints. Here is a brief exert from that list:

> A rising of the blood toward the breast, shortness of breath, a tight shortness of breath, choking in the breast, stinging pains around the breast, anxiety, fearfulness, a wooden stake in the heart, squeezing in the pit of the heart, heart anxiety, a pain in the breast that felt as though something was eating inside, anxiousness, throbbing of the heart, burning under the breastbone.
>
> Painful womb colic, womb fear, womb anxiety, womb trouble, cramps, a cold womb that was open too wide, a knot in the womb, a closed-in wind turning toward the womb, a womb cramp manifesting itself mostly in the mouth and in the tongue and rendering the latter useless for speaking. (Duden 1991, 90)

What interests me in this and many other examples from Duden's book is that, although some of the descriptions of symptoms are identical to descriptions anyone might offer to a doctor of Western medicine now, others seem very strange, evidently highly dependent on conceptions of the human (and specifically female) body that are very different from the conceptions of modern Western scientific medicine. The patients' complaints are, of course, reported by their doctor, and we have no way of knowing how he might have altered or reinterpreted them, but their strangeness to modern Western minds strongly suggests that patients once articulated their sufferings within very different conceptual schemes that they shared, to a significant extent, with their doctors, and that they may also have *experienced* their bodies very differently from those of us who live with the cultural authority of modern Western medicine.

I would like to see more exploration of the ways that the vocabulary and understandings of the body produced by biomedicine shape and limit the possibilities of our bodily experiences, as well as our abilities to articulate bodily suffering. I think that some of the attraction of Westerners to non-Western and 'alternative' medical practices reflects an intuition that different conceptualizations might lead to different experiences of the body, as well as a hope that practitioners with different conceptual schemes will listen more attentively to patients' experiences of their bodies and understand them better. As someone with chronic pain who has tried many alternative approaches to treating and living with it, I suspect that modern Western medicine may be among the worst medical systems ever to exist for dealing with chronic pain.[14] Not only does modern medicine take little interest in treating suffering that it cannot eliminate, but its conceptual schemes deprive suffering of meaning and context in a patient's life, when meaning and context are often essential to living with chronic pain.

It should not be surprising that scientific Western medicine is bad at dealing with chronic pain. The myth of control and the desire to control the body contribute significantly to determining medicine's priorities; medical practice is strongly oriented toward life-saving interventions and relatively unequipped to help patients live with conditions that cannot be cured. Knowledge of how to live with the suffering and limitation it cannot cure remains on the margins of medicine, and medicine's cognitive and social authority helps to perpetuate cultural ignorance about disability and incurable illness (as discussed in chapter 4).

Because of its 'scientific' identity and its participation in the myth of control, Western medicine is often in conflict with the needs of its patients. Medical practitioners tend to measure their success by the 'objective' state of the patient's body and to regard death as their greatest failure. Patients, on the other hand, are more likely to measure a healer's success by the quality of their subjective experiences, and to consider medicine's greatest failures to be cases of unrecognized, unsupported, meaningless, or hopeless suffering. Kleinman (1988, 255) says that medical education would have to be restructured completely to reduce this conflict. Nuland describes "the subtle progression by which a young medical student who wants only to care for his sick fellows becomes transmuted unawares into the embodiment of a biomedical problem-solver" (Nuland 1993, 247). Unfortunately, those who attain the most cognitive and social authority within medicine are usually those most closely identified with an 'objective,' 'scientific' point of view, not those who are most closely in touch with patients' perspectives.

The Role of Philosophers

Philosophers of biomedical ethics do not usually question or criticize the cognitive and social authority of medicine. Instead they focus on how medical authority can be exercised ethically, most often in relation to individual patients, but also in formulating and applying medical policies. They tend to take background social conditions and distributions of power and resources for granted (Weston 1991; Sherwin 1992). Biomedical ethics has also adopted medicine's preoccupation with life-and-death issues, such as abortion and euthanasia, and virtually ignored other issues of concern to people with disabilities, such as the low priority given to rehabilitative medicine.

However, the emerging field of feminist medical ethics is examining the powers and practices of medicine in their larger social contexts, expanding ethical concerns beyond the relationship between individual patients and health-care providers, and beyond life-and-death issues (Sherwin 1992). Susan Sherwin describes feminist bioethics as criticizing institutional structures, authoritarian patterns of controlling information and behaviour, differential treatment of male and female patients, obsessive focus on women's reproductive capacities at the expense of other aspects of their health, and medical authority to set social standards of mental and physical 'normality' for women and of 'normal' sexuality for both women and men.' Thus, feminist medical ethics is already committed to criticizing some aspects of the cognitive and social authority of medicine. This feminist critique will be greatly expanded and deepened by increasing consideration of the experiences of people with disabilities and unrecognized or incurable illnesses.

6 🅼

Disability and Feminist Ethics

The experiences and interests of both people with disabilities and those who care for people with disabilities are vitally relevant to central philosophical concerns of feminist ethics and to feminist ethical approaches to practical matters such as abortion, euthanasia, and health care reform. In this chapter I hope to demonstrate that relevance by discussing a few key concerns raised by people with disabilities, and caregivers to people with disabilities, in relation to questions currently under debate in feminist ethics. My purpose here is not to argue for certain positions on the questions or to express any conclusions I have reached about them, but to show how analyses by people who have some experience of disability, especially those with feminist perspectives, must be considered in any adequate treatment of these questions.

Feminist ethics is currently grappling with two central and related philosophical concerns that have important implications for the lives of people with disabilities. The first is the question of how to combine an ethic of care, which emphasizes relationships and responsibilities to care for others who need care, with the traditional morality of justice, which emphasizes individuals and their rights, duties, and freedoms. The second is the question of what to do about the traditional ethical ideals of autonomy and independence, which feminist ethicists have criticized for reflecting the lives of some men far better than the lives of most women; should these ideals be retained, revised or rejected?

The Ethics and Politics of Care

Most feminist discussions of an ethic of care and its relationship to the practices and politics of caregiving are conducted from the perspective of the caregiver, most discuss caregiving as though the caregiver were not also in need of care, and most assume that the receivers of care are not equals with whom the nature of the care and the conditions of its being provided are negotiable. In discussions of an ethic of care, the paradigm caring situation is usually a non-disabled adult caring for non-disabled children (Tronto 1993, 103). Yet many children who need care have disabilities, and providing care for children with disabilities is significantly different from providing care for non-disabled children. Moreover, many people who give care also need it. People with disabilities who need care are also parents providing care to children (Shaul, Dowling, and Laden 1985), and friends and relatives providing care to others with disabilities (Morris 1991, 166–67). This means that an adequate ethic of care must address the needs of caregivers and the possibilities of reciprocal care. In addition many people who need care are adults with disabilities. One major survey in the United States found that the average woman spent seventeen years caring for children and an additional eighteen years caring for ill or disabled adult relatives (not including spouses) (Ms. 1989, 73). Whereas the vast majority of children are not ready or competent to make a lot of decisions about their lives, most people with disabilities are both competent and eager to make most of the decisions about their lives. This means that an adequate ethic of care must deal with the problems that arise for the caregiver and the receiver of care when they are both competent adults and yet one needs more physical help than the other. It must also address the more ambiguous, complex relationships where one person's competence is partial, intermittent, or deteriorating (i.e., when one person has mental disabilities). Thus, it is essential to consult the experiences, thoughts, and feelings of people with disabilities and caregivers to people with disabilities when formulating an ethics that gives importance to care.

Barbara Hillyer (1993) offers many insights on caregiving from her relationship with her multiply-disabled daughter and her experience as a feminist and an advocate for people with disabilities. She points out that mothers who care for children with disabilities face significantly different demands than mothers of non-disabled children, and that the circumstances of their caregiving have profound effects on their relationships with their disabled children. For example, they have many more interactions with medical professionals and institutions, where they are frequently in the position of trying to get appropriate treatment and services for their children. In these interactions, the status of mothers is frequently so reduced that their knowledge of their own children is ignored or discounted.[1] Medical professionals and institutions assume that mothers of children with disabilities will be completely self-sacrificing in their caregiving. Moreover, they often blame parents (especially mothers) for their children's disabilities, for the failure of treatment programmes, and for the children's inabilities to become 'independent.' In short, mothers of children with disabilities are subjected to more institutionalized control, more bureaucratic monitoring, and more social judgements of the quality of their caregiving than mothers of children without disabilities.

Relationships between mothers and children with disabilities may also be subjected to greater stresses. Caregiving often requires that mothers force their children with disabilities to take unwanted medications, perform unpleasant and/or painful therapeutic procedures on them at home, and turn them over to doctors and hospitals for frightening and painful treatments (Hillyer 1993, 97; Samuelson 1986). As Hillyer points out, these requirements of caregiving, which may in fact be lifesaving or life-improving for the children, are likely to be experienced or remembered by them as abuse or failures of love and care. Mothers of children without disabilities may also have to do these things to their children, but relatively rarely; rare incidents are not as likely to become major struggles in their relationships and major themes of resentment and guilt between children and mothers.

Moreover, Hillyer argues that mothers of adults with disabilities are often blamed by their children and by disability activists if the children do not attain the degree of 'independence' considered desirable for them. Parents who care for a disabled young adult at home because the only available alternatives are overcrowded, poor-quality institutions may be seen as stifling the young adult's efforts to become independent of the parents' care. Although Hillyer does not deny that parents sometimes have trouble letting go of a disabled child, and that they may become dependent emotionally on being needed by the child, she emphasizes that parents, especially mothers, are often the scapegoats of a society that fails to provide adequate resources for people with disabilities but increasingly holds them to a high ideal of 'independence.' Such a society exploits mothers' caregiving, demands unlimited sacrifice from them, and then blames them for giving too much care.

Hillyer also points out that, of the people employed as caregivers to peo-ple with disabilities, those who provide the most immediate care, and have the most daily contact with the receivers of care, are the attendants, nurses' aides, and homeworkers who are paid the least. Often recruited from ethnic minority groups, these low-income caregivers have a low status in the bureaucratic hierarchies of institutions providing services for people with disabilities. Their intimate knowledge of the needs and capabilities of their clients, like the knowledge of their clients' mothers, is rarely sought and carries little weight. The social conditions of their caregiving mean that they have responsibility without authority. Hillyer emphasizes the need to under-stand experiences of caregiving from the perspectives of all the caregivers. She believes that this understanding would lead to better care for people with disabilities and more realistic beliefs about the needs of caregivers.

Hillyer has made a major contribution to feminist discussions of ethics of care by insisting that we acknowledge the needs of caregivers to people with disabilities and the social and political context in which their care is given. In my opinion, there has been too little concern in our philosophical discussions for the welfare of caregivers and the practical limits of caregiv-ing; an ethic of care which assumed that a person could give care without receiving it would be useless in practice. On the other hand, the social and political context of caregiving has been a major theme in disputes about how to balance an ethic of care with justice-based ethics; feminist ethicists recognize that women's caregiving is exploited, that many women do not provide care by choice but because they are socialized and pressured into it and have no viable alternative, and that an ethic of care is in danger of lend-ing support to the continued subordination and exploitation of women (See Sherwin 1992, 42–57). On this subject, Hillyer has enriched our pic-ture of the social and political context of caregiving by adding many facets of the context of caring for people with disabilities.

In sharp contrast to Hillyer, Jenny Morris (Morris 1991), a disabled British feminist writer and researcher, argues that feminist political analysis of women's caregiving has been done almost exclusively from the perspec-tive of the caregivers, and it has tended to assume both that the "cared for" are dependent, passive recipients of care, and that the categories "women" and "feminists" do not include women who need care. She shows that one major consequence of these limitations of the analysis has been feminist opposition (in Britain) to the push for increasing "community care" for people with disabilities. Feminists have emphasized the danger that increased community care will increase the exploitation of women's unpaid work, since, in reality, "community care" usually means home care. Although Morris does not minimize that danger, she points out that failure to integrate the subjective experiences of people with disabilities into the analysis leads non-disabled feminists too readily to support forms of institutional care that many people with disabilities, including disabled feminists, oppose. Moreover, she points out that disability activists recognize the home and family as sites of oppression for people with disabilities and seek the right to purchase services instead of depending upon family members to provide them; thus, there is the potential for alliance between non-disabled feminists and people with disabilities in opposing existing family structures that exploit women and oppress people with disabilities. However, such an alliance cannot take place unless the 'us' (women caregivers) versus 'them' (dependent people) dichotomy is abandoned by non-disabled feminists and the perspective of receivers of care is brought centrally into feminist analyses of caregiving (Morris 1991, 167–68).

Although Morris emphasizes the perspective of people receiving care, and Hillyer emphasizes the perspective of people giving care, they share one major concern: that the assumption that women who give care do not need care and vice versa obscures the real needs of many caregivers and the often reciprocal nature of actual caregiving situations. Hillyer suggests that reciprocity worked out between women with disabilities and their caregivers could serve as a model of reciprocity for everyone else, but only if "we attend thoughtfully to what they have learned and believe them when they tell us about it" (Hillyer 1993, 18). I will return to the subject of reciprocity, which seems to me important to the development of an ethic of care, when I discuss dependency and independence.

Anita Silvers (1995), a leader for the inclusion of people with disabilities in higher education, assesses the ethics of care in comparison to the ethics of equality by considering their respective effects on the lives of people with disabilities.[2] She argues that institutionalizing the ethics of care obliges people with disabilities to present themselves as incompetent and in need of care by placing them in the social role of dependent recipients of care:

> far from vanquishing patriarchal systems, substituting the ethics of caring for the ethics of equality threatens an even more oppressive paternalism. We can grasp this by noting that helping relationships are voluntary, but asymmetrically so. Help-givers choose how they are willing to help, but help-takers cannot choose how they will be helped, for in choosing to reject proffered help one withdraws oneself from being helped as well as

from being in a helping relationship. To relate to others primarily by being helped by them, then, implies subordinating one's choices to one's caretakers, at least insofar as one remains in the state of being helped. Of course, helping need not be repressive, for bonds of affection encourage mutual helping, and bonds of respect support reciprocal helping. This suggests that if being cared for is to advance those previously subservient, helping cannot itself be institutionalized but must instead be permitted to transpire within a frame of sharing or collectivizing or equalizing practice which corrects its fundamental asymmetry. (Silvers 1995, 41)

I am more optimistic than Silvers about the possibility of an ethics of care, even an institutionalized ethics of care, that does not cast those who receive care in subordinate social roles of permanent dependency. Teaching, for example, presents many of the same pitfalls as Silvers describes for caring. It is a necessarily asymmetrical relationship that can place the student in a permanent social position of subordination and dependency, but it need not do so. An adequate ethics of teaching, even when the teaching and the ethics are practised in an institution, requires that both teacher and student foster a changing relationship that progresses beyond subordination and dependency, and I think it can be put into practice. Perhaps Silvers and I are not so far apart on this issue, since she envisions arrangements that might overcome the repressive possibilities of caring relationships. Nevertheless, even if she is overly pessimistic about an ethics of care, Silvers's warnings of the dangers of giving it priority over concerns about social equality in creating institutions are timely and important. She has shown that some of the pitfalls of an ethics of care are much more apparent when we imagine the recipients of care as adults with disabilities, because people with disabilities are struggling with a heavy historical burden of being wrongly cast in a role of helpless dependency. And she has shown that the consequences for adults with disabilities must be considered carefully when we are thinking about institutionalizing any ethical ideals.

Dependency, Independence, and Reciprocity

Non-disabled feminist ethicists have criticized autonomy and independence as ethical ideals on the grounds that they fail to represent and value women's life experiences, which are typically more connected than autonomous, more interdependent than independent (Gilligan 1982;

Sherwin 1984, 1987, 1992; Kittay and Meyers 1987). They have asked: What ideals should replace autonomy and independence? What would be a good alternative concept of virtue with respect to our reliance on others and their reliance on us? People with disabilities and people who provide care for people with disabilities are also questioning, on different grounds, the acceptance of autonomy and independence as unequivocal ideals. "Independent living" has long been a rallying cry and a major goal of organizations of people with disabilities. Although this has many advantages, especially in societies that regard independence as a central virtue, it tends to diminish the esteem of people who cannot live without a great deal of help from others, and to ignore or undervalue relationships of dependency or interdependence. Moreover, ideals of independence can be turned against people with disabilities as unrealistic demands that they achieve goals deemed appropriate by others or as excuses for refusing to provide necessary services. Thus the problem of formulating alternative ideals that would recognize, value, and guide relationships of dependency and interdependence is shared by those who want ethics to be sensitive to non-disabled women's lives and those who want ethics to be sensitive to the lives of both women and men with disabilities.

Jenny Morris points out some of the illusions fostered by the non-disabled world's understanding of 'independence.'[3] While most non-disabled people in industrialized societies believe that being able to perform the so-called "activities of daily living" (a term used in assessment of disability), such as washing, dressing, cooking, shopping, cleaning, and writing, by and for oneself is a necessary condition of independence, and therefore regard people with disabilities as dependent if they cannot perform them, they do not recognize their own dependence on services, such as the provision of the water that comes out of the tap, as obstacles to their own 'independence.' Yet, "[j]ust as it is possible to create the technology and the infrastructure which means that we can depend on the water industry to produce water out of a tap, rather than being dependent on our own efforts for gathering water from a river, so the technology and services can be developed which can change the nature of disabled people's dependency" (Morris 1991, 140).

Clearly, "independence," like "disability," is defined according to a society's expectations about what people 'normally' do for themselves and how they do it. Few people in my city would consider me a 'dependent' person because I rely on others to provide me with water out of the tap, electricity to heat and light my home, run my computer, and wash my clothes, and food and clothing in markets where I can buy them instead of producing them myself. Perhaps some would consider me 'dependent' because I rely on a gardener to do the heavy work in my yard and a cleaner to clean my house, but these services are also widely used by people who are considered 'independent,' even when they cannot perform the tasks themselves.[4] Yet if I needed to rely on someone else to help me out of bed, help me use the toilet, bathe me, dress me, feed me, and brush my teeth, most people would consider me very 'dependent' indeed. The philosophical arbitrariness of our ideas concerning which of us is 'independent' seems obvious. Psychologically, they may not be as arbitrary; many of us seem to be priding ourselves on not needing the same kinds of physical help as infants. Perhaps if we could feel and show more respect for children, it would not be as important to distinguish ourselves from them. In any case, it is instructive to remember that, to people who meet their own needs for water, food, shelter, and clothing more directly, all of us who live in industrialized societies may seem as helpless as infants.

Nevertheless, dependence on others to meet some of the basic physical needs is humiliating in a society that so clearly prizes independence from that particular kind of help. Moreover, the help is too often provided on the condition that those providing it control the lives of those who receive it. Small wonder that many people with disabilities who see the possibility of living as independently as any non-disabled person, or who have achieved this goal after long struggle, value their independence very highly. Far from questionning the high social value placed on 'independence,' early disability-rights movements sought more of it for their members, demanding access to public places and events, education and training, and jobs. Yet the emphasis the disability-rights movements placed on 'independence' had a price for some people with disabilities. As Cheryl Marie Wade points out (Wade 1994a and 1994b), it created a new image of people with disabilities, "the able-disabled," along with a reluctance to admit to weakness, vulnerability, and the importance of physical limitations in shaping some people's lives; it reinforced, rather than undermined, the sense of shame attached to some people's needs.

> To put it bluntly—because this need is blunt as it gets—we must have our asses cleaned after we shit and pee. Or we have others' fingers inserted in our rectums to assist shitting. Or we have tubes of plastic inserted inside us to assist peeing or we have re-routed anuses and pissers so we do it all into bags attached to our bodies. . . .

The difference between those of us who need attendants and those who don't is the difference between those who know privacy and those who don't. We rarely talk about these things, and when we do the realities are usually disguised in generic language or gimp humor. Because, let's face it: we have great shame about this need. This need that only babies and the "broken" have.

And because this shame is so deep, and because it is perpetuated even by our own movement when we emphasize only the able-ness of our beings, we buy into that language that lies about us and becomes part of our movement, and our movement dances over the surface of our real lives by spending all its precious energy on bus access while millions of us don't get out of bed or get by with inadequate personal care. Because we don't want to say this need that shames us out loud in front of people who have no understanding of the unprivate universe we live in, even if that person is a disabled sister or brother. We don't want to say out loud a basic truth: that we have no place in our bodies (other than our imagination) that is private.

And yes, this makes us different from you who have privacy of body. Yes, this is a profound difference. And as long as we allow our shame to silence us, it will remain a profound difference.

If we are ever to be really at home in the world and in ourselves, then we must say these things out loud. And we must say them with real language. So they are understood as the everyday necessity and struggle they are. How can we assert a right (for personal care) if we are too ashamed of the need to state it openly? (Wade 1994a, 89; originally published in 1991)

In "Identity" (Wade 1994b) Wade discusses the fact that her identity as a disability activist made it difficult for her to acknowledge her physical limitations until her body broke down, which was bad not only for her health but for her self-image and self-esteem. She says, "What was missing in the political, able-disabled crip identity was a true esteeming of the Cripple body" (Wade 1994b, 35).

There are people who will always need a lot of help from other individuals just to survive (those who have very little control of movement, for example), and there are people who sometimes need a lot of help to survive (those who get very sick from time to time). To the extent that everyone continues to consider 'independence' necessary to respect and self-esteem, all those people will be devalued. Moreover, some people will expend tremendous energy being 'independent' in ways that might be considered trivial in a culture less insistent on certain forms of self-reliance; in a culture that valued interdependence more highly, they could use that energy for more satisfying activities.

To be fair, disability rights organizations do not always accept the definitions of 'independence' used by non-disabled people. Especially now that there is greater awareness of the need to include more people of varying abilities in their goals, organizations of people with disabilities usually define the 'independence' they are seeking as: First, not living in an institution; second, not being dependent on the good will of family members to meet basic needs; third, being able to make all the most important decisions about your daily life and knowing that they will be carried out; and fourth (this one is usually, but not always, part of the meaning of 'independence' for disability activists), being able to do meaningful work, preferably for an income sufficient to be self-supporting and to buy necessary services.[5] But even these more limited criteria of 'independence' may be burdensome to some people with disabilities and exclude others. Hugh Gallagher says:

> this self-reliance model places a new burden upon the severely disabled— a burden which some are simply unable to bear in any consistent manner. These people are fighting chronic infection, weakness, fatigue and depression.
>
> They struggle to find, keep and pay for adequate attendant care. Although in disability-rights circles it may not be fashionable to say so, these people are displaying extraordinary courage just staying alive. The last thing they need is to be told that they are failures as handicapped people if they do not hold down a full-time job. (Gallagher 1993)

Demands for their 'independence' can also be used in ways that are harmful to people with disabilities by the authorities who have power over them. In her study of the life of Diane DeVries, Gelya Frank (Frank 1988) shows how the goal of 'independence' was defined by doctors and rehabilitation specialists to their own stereotypes and to Diane DeVries's disadvantage. (They demanded that she use prostheses when she judged that she could function better without them.) Consequently, Ms. DeVries had to fight their influence in order to build the life she knew she wanted. On the other hand, when governments want to make cutbacks in social services, they may 'release' people from institutions without adequate support to enable them to live on their own in the community, describing the changes they make as creating more 'independence.' This kind of 'independence' can lead not only to loneliness and isolation but to sickness and death from neglect.

Barbara Hillyer describes how mothers and other caregivers to people with mental disabilities are expected to work constantly toward the goal of making them 'independent,' regardless of whether this goal is realistic. One consequence is "that programs that adopt unrealistic goals are forced constantly to fabricate illusory progress toward those goals, to blame the 'client' for failing to progress, or to invent such euphemisms as 'independent living' for inadequately supervised care or 'capable of managing her own medication' for someone who can take a pill when it is placed in her hand by someone else" (Hillyer 1993, 204–205). Another consequence is the sacrifice of warmth and friendliness in a relationship when one person's overriding goal is to get another person to do things for her/himself.[6]

The realization that 'autonomy' and 'independence' are unattainable goals for some people, even when they are defined in ways that take some kinds of disability into account, calls into question the value of these in any scheme of virtues and moral goals. Should a society have ethical ideals that are universally applied but which some people are precluded from attaining because they have certain kinds of bodies?

Some feminist ethicists, who are not necessarily theorizing from the perspective of people with disabilities, are also asking whether ethical ideals should not reflect better the realities of most people's needs for each others' care. Joan Tronto puts it this way:

> The simple fact that care is a fundamental aspect of human life has profound implications. It means, in the first instance, that humans are not fully autonomous, but must always be understood in a condition of interdependence. While not all people need others' assistance at all times, it is a part of the human condition that our autonomy occurs only after a long period of dependence, and that in many regards, we remain dependent on others throughout our lives. At the same time, we are often called upon to help others, and to care, as well. Since people are sometimes autonomous, sometimes dependent, sometimes providing care for those who are dependent, humans are best described as interdependent. Thinking of people as interdependent allows us to understand both autonomous and involved elements of human life. (Tronto 1993, 162)

As many disability activists have pointed out, the tendency to pretend that only some people need care and to lump together those whose need for care is publicly recognized, seeing them all as 'dependent' people, makes it difficult to keep in mind important differences among people who need care. For example, many people who need care can and should make all the major decisions about their lives and negotiate the nature of the care they receive and the conditions under which it is delivered, some of them (such as infants, or adults with advanced Alzheimer's disease) definitely cannot and should not, and many others have degrees of competency to make decisions that lie between those two extremes. Moreover, some people who need care give as much or more care than they receive and others need more care than they could ever give. When we think of all people as interdependent, these differences, previously concealed by dualistic assumptions, become apparent and significant.

In addition, when we think of all people as interdependent, we are less likely to imagine that those who give care do not also need it, more likely to ask what forms of care caregivers need. We are also less likely to overlook the forms of care, including emotional care (Morris 1991, 167), that people who receive a lot of care give to others.[7] The reciprocity Morris and Hillyer emphasize in describing relationships between people with disabilities and those who give them care can be seen to be morally important; it may turn out to be an ethical ideal or guide for relationships among people who are capable of giving care. Hillyer says of reciprocity:

> Reciprocity involves the difficulty of recognizing each other's needs, relying on the other, asking and receiving help, delegating responsibility, giving and receiving empathy, and respecting boundaries. It also involves, as Eleanor Roosevelt pointed out, the ability to accept what we are unable to give and what others are unable to give, a much harder doctrine. (Hillyer 1993, 18)

Relationships of reciprocity are not necessarily equal, as Hillyer points out, in that one person may give more care, or have more responsibility for providing care, than another. Nevertheless, they involve moral obligations on both sides; they are ethical challenges and ethical achievements. I suspect that they are far more common than negotiations over justice between autonomous equals, and may therefore be more useful models not only for women, who in my society give more care than men, but for men as well, especially since disability is likely to play a significant role at some time in everyone's life.

Women and men thinking about ethical ideals from a disability perspective, and feminist ethicists who are not using a disability perspective, seem to be converging in their concerns about overestimating and overvaluing 'autonomy' and 'independence.' I find this an exciting development in ethical theorizing. I believe that if everyone with a disability is to be integrated fully into my society, without being 'the Other' who symbolizes moral failure, then social ideals must change in the direction of acknowledging the realities of our interdependence and the value of depending on others and being depended upon. Perhaps such a change would also improve the status of children and/or reduce the fear and shame associated with dependency in old age.

Abortion, Euthanasia, and Health Care Reform

"The widespread assumption that disabled people's lives are not worth living" (Morris 1991, 12) lies at the heart of much theorizing about abortion, euthanasia, and health care reform, putting the welfare and security, and the social acceptance, of people with disabilities in jeopardy. On the other hand, people with disabilities who have extensive experiences of medical treatment and its limitations are unlikely to support an ethic of life at any cost, or a reduction of individuals' rights to choose death. While wanting to increase disabled people's choices and control of their lives, disability activists are concerned that individual 'choices' and 'options' (such as those to abort, to die, or to choose a treatment) can quickly become social imperatives, especially when combined with such powerful social prejudices as fear of disability. Any feminist ethics that includes the perspectives of women with disabilities must consider which positions on abortion, euthanasia, and health care reform are compatible with valuing and protecting the lives of people with disabilities.

Abortion

In "Shared Dreams: A Left Perspective on Disability Rights and Reproductive Rights," Adrienne Asch and Michelle Fine argue that women have "the right to abortion for any reason they deem appropriate," and that newborns with disabilities have "the right to medical treatment whether or not their parent(s) wishes them to be treated" (Fine and Asch 1988, 297). They affirm the value of the lives of people with disabilities, while defending women's "unequivocal" right to choose abortion, by drawing the moral line between the fetus residing inside and the infant living outside the mother's body. They say this about aborting fetuses with potential disabilities:

> When a woman decides that she wants to abort, rather than carry to term, a fetus with Down's syndrome, this represents a statement about how she perceives such a child would affect her life and what she wants from rearing a child. Every woman has the right to make this decision in whatever way she needs, but the more information she has, the better her decision can be. Genetic counsellors, physicians, and all others involved with assisting women during amniocentesis should gain and provide far more and very different information about life with disabilities than is customarily available. Given proper information about how disabled children and adults live, many women might not choose to abort. And many will still choose to abort. While a fetus resides within her, a woman has the right to decide about her body and her life and to terminate a pregnancy for this or any other reason. (Fine and Asch 1988, 302)

In contrast, Jenny Morris says that women with disabilities who support non-disabled women's right to choose abortion while wishing that they would not choose to "deny existence to a disabled child" (Morris 1991, 81) are avoiding the issue.

> There is no absolute right to choose whether to have a disabled child or not. An acceptance of such an absolute right belongs within an individualistic tradition which, in the last analysis, gives all rights and responsibilities to individuals with no recognition of the collective rights and responsibilities of society. It is not in the interests of either women or disabled people [sic] to rely on liberal individualism for the furtherance of our rights. (Morris 1991, 81)

Morris believes that the extensive use of genetic screening for the purpose of aborting potentially disabled fetuses questions the right of all people with disabilities to exist. It devalues people with disabilities; it implies that people who were born with disabilities should never have been born and that the existence of others like them should be prevented. It is also likely, Morris predicts, that genetic screening will increase the pressure on women with genetic disabilities not to have children.[8]

Ultimately Morris supports a woman's "having some power" (82) to abort a potentially disabled fetus, but she insists that this power must be balanced against "the extent to which the fetus has rights as a human being" (82). Her solution is to say that a fetus which is viable outside the mother's body has a greater right to live than the mother's right to refuse to give birth to it. Given the fact that much prenatal diagnosis takes place near or after fetal viability, this solution, which Morris chooses on moral grounds, would in fact allow many infants with disabilities to be born. But if the rapid development of technology for genetic screening and prenatal diagnosis makes it possible to detect most potentially disabling physical conditions before viability, the conflicts between women's rights to choose abortion and the harms threatened to people with disabilities by selective abortion of potentially disabled fetuses will not be easily resolved.

Positions on abortion among people with disabilities, even among feminists with disabilities, vary widely, from Asch and Fine's pro-choice-with-better-information position to alliance with anti-choice activists. The issues that people who do not devalue disability have raised have deepened the debates on the morality and politics of abortion by questionning the consequences of reproductive technologies and abortion policies for everyone with a disability. Rather than attempting to cover the extensive literature on the subject, I shall try here to summarize some major points, with references that the reader can pursue further:

1. The development of increasingly sophisticated genetic screening and prenatal diagnostic techniques holds out the 'hope' of eliminating many inherited and prenatal potentially disabling conditions by selective abortion. Nevertheless, there will always be diseases and accidents. Therefore, unless medicine becomes so powerful that it can cure anything, in which case it could cure any neonatal disability, there will always be adults and children with disabilities. It turns out that the promise of prenatal medicine is not to eliminate disability, but to reduce the number of people with disabilities by reducing the number of people born with disabilities[9] (Blumberg 1994).

2. The widespread use of selective abortion to reduce the number of people born with disabilities has potential effects that have not been considered by people who have little knowledge of disability and/or take its disvalue for granted, including these:

a. It sends a message to children and adults with disabilities, especially people who have genetic or prenatal disabilities, that "We do not want any more like you." Knowing that your society is doing everything possible to prevent people with bodies like yours from being born is bound to make you feel as though you are not valued and do not really belong, especially when there are so many attitudes and conditions in the society that derogate and/or exclude you. Laura Hershey, who was born with a rare disabling neuromuscular condition, says, "I believe the choice to abort a disabled fetus represents a rejection of children who have disabilities" (Hershey 1994, 30).

b. It strengthens the widely-held belief that life with a disability is not worth living. This belief is usually arrived at in ignorance of the lives of people with disabilities. Remember Anita Silvers's remark (discussed in chapter 2) that the suicide rate among people with disabilities would be much greater if it reflected the frequency with which non-disabled people report that they would rather be dead than disabled (Silvers 1994, 159). Moreover, the judgement that life with a disability is not worth living usually assumes that the person with a disability will have to live with the present level of prejudice and social exclusion, rather than recognizing that social improvements could make life with a disability much more worth living than it is now.

Many people with disabilities, even those with the strongest social-constructionist perspective, admit that there are often heavy personal burdens associated with the physical and mental consequences of disabling physical conditions—such as pain, illness, frustration, and unwanted limitation— that no amount of accessibility and social justice could eliminate (Finger 1990; Morris 1991). But there is a crucial difference between not wanting others to suffer from the burdens of a disability and not wanting those who will suffer from them to exist, between wanting to prevent or cure disabilities and wanting to prevent people with those disabilities from being born. For example, I would be terribly sorry to learn that a friend's fetus was very likely to be born with ME, but I would not urge her to abort it. In other words, many people with disabilities, while we understand quite well the personal burdens of disability, are not willing to make the judgement that lives like ours are not worth living. Every life has burdens, some of them far worse than disability.

c. It might weaken efforts to increase accessibility and opportunities for people with disabilities, because it appears to reduce the social problems of people with disabilities by reducing the number of people with disabilities. Thus, Laura Hershey wonders: "Are expensive, government-funded genetic research projects initiated primarily for the benefit of a society unwilling to support disability-related needs?" (Hershey 1994, 31). If so, we have to ask what will be the social fate of people who already have disabilities and those who, in the future, will become disabled by accident or disease.

d. It might lead to even greater reluctance to commit resources to medical treatment of people with incurable conditions—treatment that makes their lives more comfortable and rewarding. As Mary Johnson says, "treatments that don't lead to cure are boring to a society whose interest is not in making the lives of cripples comfortable but in ridding society of them altogether" (Johnson 1990, 34).

3. Feminists with disabilities recognize that, under present conditions in most societies, individual parents, especially mothers (who do most of the care-giving work), must provide the extra resources, especially the time and energy, required for raising children with disabilities. Thus many feminists with disabilities support women's right to choose not to give birth to a baby with a disability. Yet we are also aware that most women faced with the knowledge of their fetuses' potential disability are not given adequate information.

For example, as Lisa Blumberg points out, prospective parents may not be informed that most prenatal tests can only place a diagnostic label on a fetus; they cannot predict the degree of functional disability that the fetus would experience as a child or adult:

> A diagnosis of spina bifida, for example, will not indicate whether a child would walk with just some degree of difficulty or use a wheelchair, or whether he [sic] would be intellectually gifted, have average intelligence or be slightly retarded. Neither would a finding of cystic fibrosis provide guidance on whether a person's lifespan would be eight years or 58 years or somewhere in between. (Blumberg 1994, 220)[10]

Moreover, prospective parents of a fetus with a potential disability may not be given information about the quality of life that people with those disabilities can and do have, or the services and support available to parents should they choose to have the babies (Morris 1991; Hershey 1994). Too often, potential disability is treated as an 'objective' medical matter on which physicians can advise parents without reference to values or the social context. "Rarely are clients encouraged to discuss disability related concerns with people who are disabled or are parents of disabled children" (Blumberg 1994, 221).

4. Screening of fetuses and selective abortion are likely to begin as voluntary medical procedures but become socially mandatory fairly quickly. Given that so many people believe that being born with a disability is a tragedy, they are likely to blame women for creating a tragedy if they do not

undergo all the available medical procedures. Moreover, since most non-disabled people regard people with disabilities as noncontributing burdens on society, women who give birth to babies with disabilities are liable to be blamed for creating drains on social resources. The more women 'choose' to screen and selectively abort fetuses, the more blame will be placed on those who give birth to babies with disabilities, the fewer resources will be made available for raising babies with disabilities, and the more the element of choice will diminish (Morris 1991).

5. Genetic screening and selective abortion of potentially disabled fetuses might lead to increased tolerance of eugenic policies in general and expansion of eugenic efforts into other areas (Degener 1990; Hershey 1994). This is a particular danger in societies already caught up in myths of control and perfection of the body. Nor is it a baseless fear when there is strong governmental and scientific support for the multibillion dollar Human Genome Project in the United States, a long-term scientific effort to map all the genetic material inside the nuclei of human cells. This project is now conceived of primarily as having medical benefits in prediction and prevention of disease and disability (*The Women's Review of Books*, July 1994). Scientific research into genetic contributions to disvalued characteristics is proceeding quickly and with some success. It seems that every month we hear about the discovery of a 'gene' for some disease or disability, or for some unwanted propensity of character or personality.

The desire for perfection and control of the body, or for the elimination of differences that are feared, poorly understood, and widely considered to be marks of inferiority, easily masquerades as the compassionate desire to prevent or stop suffering. It is not only a matter of being deceived by others, but all too often a matter of deceiving ourselves. It is easy to make the leaps from imagining that I would not want to live in certain circumstances to believing that no one would want to live in those circumstances, to deciding to prevent people from being born into those circumstances, to supporting proposals 'mercifully' to kill people living in those circumstances—all without ever consulting anyone who knows life in those circumstances from experience.

Nor is it reassuring to insist that genetic screening, prenatal diagnosis, and selective abortion are voluntary, individual choices, unlike previous eugenic efforts, which were often coercive. We know how quickly the possibilities offered by medical technology become social necessities in complex consumer cultures (Sherwin 1992).

Euthanasia

Perhaps it is an indication of reluctance in feminist theory to confront the rejected, suffering body[11] that feminist medical ethics has dealt little with the ethics of euthanasia. Since euthanasia is an issue of personal importance to many women with disabilities, and to non-disabled women growing old enough to think practically about their own deaths, it should be an issue for feminist ethics. Moreover, like the abortion issue and debates over medical procedures such as in vitro fertilization, it involves concerns about the rights of individuals to control what happens in and to their own bodies but also concerns about the cumulative social effects of individual choices.

Discussion of euthanasia in the writings of disability activists has tended to focus upon two major issues: medical killing of newborns with disabilities, or allowing them to die by withholding food, water, or necessary medical treatment; and assisted suicide of adults with disabilities who are physically unable to end their own lives.

Killing newborns with disabilities or letting them die of neglect has been widely condemned by disability activists as unjustified killing—killing that seems to be euthanasia only because it is socially acceptable to assume that life with a disability is not worth living. There is considerable agreement among disability activists that people who do not have the same disabilities as the newborns are in no moral position to judge whether their lives will be worth living.[12] Yet, in my experience, it is still not unusual for non-disabled women (including feminists) to assume that birth mothers should have the power to demand medical killing of disabled newborns. Clearly, this issue needs the attention of feminist ethicists who do not devalue disability in considering whether killing newborns is ever morally justified.[13]

Assisted suicide has been much more controversial among disability activists. Support for euthanasia among people with disabilities has tended to focus upon assisted suicide, because although people with disabilities have many of the same concerns as non-disabled people about the quality of their deaths, they are more likely to see suicide as a right to which they do not, or may not in the future, have equal access with non-disabled people. In Canada, where suicide is not illegal, some people with disabilities have tried to bring about changes in the Criminal Code to allow assisted suicide for people who are physically unable to end their lives themselves, arguing that this is an equal rights issue. A submission by the B.C. Coalition of People with Disabilities to the Canadian Senate Committee on Assisted Suicide and Euthanasia stated that, "People with disabilities who are physically unable to end their lives without assistance must have the same rights and choices as able-bodied people, including the right to end their lives when they choose" (B.C. Coalition of People with Disabilities 1995, 2). Of course the Coalition recommended safeguards to ensure that the person requesting assistance in fact desires suicide, that the person is fully informed about all possibilities of treatment and community support that might improve her/his quality of life, that the person understands all the alternatives, and that the request is not coerced. The submission warned against a misplaced paternalism that might deprive people with disabilities of their choices:

> If an able-bodied person chooses to end their life, we will most likely never know if that person was coerced or encouraged to do so. However, if a person with a severe physical disability considers suicide, they become subject to the assumption in public opinion and in law that coercion may exist and their choices must therefore be controlled in a way that those of able-bodied people are not. Our Western society's fear of death—and the desire to control it—should not be used to rationalize controlling the choices of people who by virtue of their physical condition can be controlled (B.C. Coalition of People with Disabilities 1995, 5).

Ironically, the illegality of assisted suicide coerces some people into shortening their lives. People with progressive debilitating diseases, such as ALS, can risk living longer and having a greater degree of disability if they know that their wishes will be carried out even if they can no longer act for themselves. If they cannot count on assisted suicide, they must end their own lives while they still can; those with unpredictable illnesses must constantly weigh their desire to live a little longer against the risk of losing the power to commit suicide before their lives become unbearable (Hofsess 1993).

Opponents of assisted suicide express two major objections to it: That the assumption that life with a disability is not worth living will be made too easily by both the people with disabilities and their caregivers; and that the 'choice' or 'option' to commit suicide will become a social imperative, perhaps not directly coerced, but assumed to be the only acceptable thing to do when one has become a 'burden' to one's family, caregivers, and society.

Mary Johnson (1994; originally published in 1990) and Jenny Morris (1991, chapter 2), discussing some celebrated cases of people with disabilities who sought the legal right to assisted suicide, point out that both the person with the disability and others are liable to assume that the main reason for wanting to die is the disabled person's physical condition, when in fact it may be that inadequate support services and poor opportunities are rendering the person's life miserable and meaningless. If no one around the person who wants to die is aware of the possibilities for a better life that would emerge from different circumstances, the relevant questions about whether the situation is really hopeless may never be asked. The fact that most non-disabled people might assume that they would want to die if they were in the same physical condition also contributes to neglecting the social construction of the person's disability. Here, as in the case of selective abortion, ignorance of the lives of people with disabilities can make an individual's situation seem hopeless when it is not; people with the same physical condition may be living and feeling much better.

Legal safeguards to ensure that the person who requests suicide really wants it will not solve this problem unless they include offering her/him better services and opportunities, as well as informing her/him of possible ways to live better. Unfortunately, as Morris points out, "[i]t is non-disabled society which has control over financial resources, over residential establishments, over housing, personal care services, transport and all the other resources essential to achieve a good quality of life" (Morris 1991, 46). Non-disabled society is still quick to assume that a person's physical condition is the source of despair. Moreover, holding on to this assumption may be in non-disabled people's financial interest; non-disabled people may be reluctant to pay for the means of deconstructing a person's social disability. As Morris points out, if people accept that a person's physical condition inevitably renders her/his life intolerable, why would they devote resources to services and access? "If to lose your eyesight means that your life is a write-off, what's the point in developing the technology which turns the printed word into speech?" (Morris 1991, 60).

Legal safeguards may also be relatively powerless against a disabled person's internalized feelings of worthlessness. Morris says, "The prejudices against disabled people do not just exist out there in the public world, they also reside within our own heads, particularly for those of us who become disabled in adult life" (1991, 43). She points out that people with disabilities often declare that if their disabilities got worse in some particular way—for example, if they had to use a wheelchair—they would not want to live. The assumption that more disability than one's own would render life not worth living devalues the lives of people who are already living with that greater degree of disability. No one is immune to the rash assumptions that are supported by a culture which fears and devalues 'imperfect' bodies.

Opponents of assisted suicide for people with disabilities fear that the worse the economic and social conditions of people with disabilities are, the more people will 'choose' to die; the more people 'choose' to die, the more refusal to provide services and access will seem to be justified by the 'inevitable' unbearability of life with a disability. Eventually, assisted suicide will be the socially expected 'solution' to severe disability.[14] This expectation will be reinforced if, because of inadequate provision of services, the greater part of supporting and giving care to people with severe disabilities falls upon friends and family members, causing feelings of guilt in the people with disabilities and strained relationships with those who care for them.

Is there some way to meet the demand for assisted suicide as a human right of people who are not physically able to kill themselves, without threatening the social value of other disabled people's lives or undermining political efforts to gain services and access? Morris (1991, 60–61) describes the British Medical Association's position, which limits euthanasia to the terminally ill. It states specifically that doctors should not comply with requests for assisted suicide from physically disabled people. Although this seems to be a promising line of compromise, it raises considerable difficulties of interpretation, as Morris recognizes. Many physical disabilities are consequences of illnesses that will eventually be fatal, so for many people requesting assistance, doctors or others would have to weigh their suffering, probable closeness to death, and chances of a better life in order to determine whether assisted suicide was justified.

Health Care Reform

On questions of health care reform, people with disabilities and those who care for them have a great deal of knowledge of both the flaws and the potentialities of health care systems. Moreover, trends in medical care have a profound impact on the lives of people with disabilities. For example, heroic, lifesaving medical procedures often save people to live with long-term disabilities; yet, ironically, medical emphasis on such procedures is usually bought at the expense of the long-term care and rehabilitation that would improve the lives of people with disabilities.

In a review of medical ethicist Daniel Callahan's *What Kind of Life: The Limits of Medical Progress*, Barrett Shaw, the editor of *The Disability Rag and ReSource*, notes the attractiveness, especially to people with disabilities, of Callahan's call for giving higher priority to care and lower priority to cure (Shaw 1994). But Shaw also notes one of the implications of giving higher priority to long-term care and lower priority to acute, high technology care (an implication Callahan himself draws attention to): If fewer lives are saved, there will be fewer people with disabilities needing long-term care. This is liable to be regarded as an obvious good by non-disabled people who devalue life with a disability, and also by politicians who want to save money on health care. De-emphasize acute lifesaving care and there will be fewer people needing expensive long-term care and rehabilitation. Money could be saved on both kinds of care; it seems like the answer to a budget cutter's dream. Looked at from the point of view of a disability activist, it also seems dangerous.

Nevertheless, there are reasons for disability activists to be critical of medicine's emphasis on discovering cures at the expense of providing care for the incurable, some of which I discussed in chapter 4. Moreover, expensive high-technology cures, or the prospect of such cures, can be offered to a few people who can afford them as substitutes for a more healthful environment or for better services and accessibility. Few of us would criticize someone who sought a lung transplant for emphysema caused by air pollution, or spinal cord regeneration (a long-promised development) for paraplegia caused by an automobile accident, but the fact remains that such 'cures' function not only as benefits to individuals, but also as ways of depoliticizing health, safety, and ability for those who are privileged enough to have access to high-technology medicine. The very existence of 'cures' which are available to a few people places some onus on individuals to buy solutions to problems that have social causes and could have social solutions.

Increased discussion among bioethicists of health care "rationing" (Rothman 1992), by which they usually mean rationing of expensive, life-saving medical procedures, raises questions about whether such rationing would be done by attempting to compare the value and worthiness of the lives that might be saved. This sort of comparison was done in the early 1960s, by a committee of middle-class citizens in Seattle, to ration access to kidney dialysis when dialysis machines first became available at the University of Washington Medical School. (Rothman 1992, 32) Britain currently practices rationing of kidney dialysis, which is not available to

National Health Service patients over sixty-five, presumably on the grounds that most of them do not have much life left to save (Rothman 1992, 33).[15] In societies where life with a disability is widely assumed to be not worth living, the prospect of health care rationing raises concerns among people with disabilities that they will be denied lifesaving medical procedures that are made available to non-disabled citizens.

When Oregon designed its health care plan to extend medical coverage to more poor people by rationing the care available to public beneficiaries, its Health Services Commission sought public opinion through community meetings, public hearings, and a thousand-person survey, about the values that should guide health care policies, including rationing. The commission used this input to develop and prioritize categories of medical care (Korda 1994). Public opinion predictably reflected the belief that life with a disability is not worth living. Consequently, in the original Oregon Health Plan, an incurable impairment reduced a person's eligibility for various kinds of health care (Silvers 1994). Although the United States federal government forced Oregon to change this aspect of its plan, the ease with which it was introduced and approved in Oregon illustrates the danger to people with disabilities.

In assessments of existing and proposed health care systems, their effectiveness for people with disabilities is too often neglected.[16] John R. Woodward (1994b) describes his Herculean effort to get authorization for necessary surgery for a disabled client whose Medicaid benefits were controlled by a health maintenance organization (HMO). The HMO's "gatekeeper," an administrator (not a physician) who decides which medical procedures will be authorized for patients, had decided not to authorize the surgery, which was recommended by the patient's doctor to close a bedsore. In the end, Woodward's client had to disenroll from the HMO to get the surgery. Woodward came to believe that the economic structure of HMOs works against their serving the health care needs of people with disabilities. But he discovered that, although there are over a thousand books and articles on the economics of HMOs, he could not find a single study of their effectiveness at serving members/patients with disabilities (Woodward 1994b, 22). Yet HMOs are becoming widespread in the United States (they now provide basic health insurance coverage for over sixteen percent of residents) and are looked to for potential solutions to problems of health care cost and delivery.

In closing this chapter, I do not want to leave the reader with the impression that abortion, euthanasia, and health care reform are the only matters of practical ethics on which people with disabilities might contribute essential perspectives from their experiences of disability. It seems to me that we have only begun to explore how experiences of disability affect our values and our ethical thinking. Feminists with disabilities will have to contribute to the development of all aspects of feminist ethics (and not just feminist medical ethics) if feminist ethics is to reflect the diversity of women's lives and to offer moral visions that are meaningful from birth to death.

Feminist ethics needs the insights of people with disabilities, but do people with disabilities need feminist ethics? Yes, I think so, not only because feminist ethics is already involved in developing an ethic of care and questioning the value of autonomy and independence as moral ideals, but also because the methodological approaches of feminist ethics are particularly conducive to addressing the concerns of people with disabilities. In her list of basic constituents of a feminist ethics, Susan Sherwin includes: "rejecting the picture . . . of a world organized around purely self-interested agents;" recognizing the moral value of caring work, while realizing that caring is not always the morally or politically appropriate response; respecting the importance of personal feelings while pursuing social justice; attending to the details of experiences when evaluating practices; rejecting "the paradigm of moral subjects as autonomous, rational, independent, and virtually indistinguishable from one another;" examining persons and their behaviour in the context of political relations and experiences; giving central importance to the insight that oppression is morally wrong; uncovering oppressive practices; and exploring ways of creating egalitarian relationships and nonoppressive social structures (Sherwin 1992, 49–57). As I read over this list, it seems to be a pretty good description of the ethical approach of many contemporary books, journals, and magazines of disability movements. People (especially the feminists, of course) who are involved in disability ethics and politics are already practicing feminist ethics; it's time that more feminist ethicists also practised disability ethics.

7

Feminism, Disability, and Transcendence of the Body

Ideas of transcending the body have generally been rejected by feminists, including feminist theologians, because they are seen to originate from philosophies and/or religions that devalue the body (especially women's bodies) and bodily experience. For example, Naomi Goldenberg describes the notion of transcendence in traditional theology as "a wish for something beyond body, beyond time, and beyond specific relationships to life" and "a notion of perfect safety . . . probably motivated by a characteristically (but not exclusively) male fear of being merged with matter" (Goldenberg 1990, 211).

Feminist theorists have criticized the mind-body dichotomy and the intellectual derogation of the body, both of which make important contributions to motivations for transcending the body, and both of which are prevalent in the history of Western thought. We can see their philosophical roots in such ancient ideas as those of Plato and Aristotle, that abstract forms are superior to material things, and that reason is superior to the appetites that originate in the body. Feminists have also argued that the dominant forms of Christian theology strengthened these ancient views by representing the body as a major source of the desires and weaknesses that lead to sin, and overcoming the body as an essential ingredient in moral perfection.

Yet feminist theory has so far failed to appreciate the strength of another motive for wanting to transcend the body. We need to recognize that much of the appeal of philosophies of life that recommend some form of transcendence of the body lies, not in elevation of the mind and derogation of the body, but in the rational (as opposed to pathological) desire to make one's happiness, or at least one's sense of self, independent of illness, pain, weakness, exhaustion, and accident. We have not recognized this because feminist writing about the body has not fully confronted experience of the negative body. This is partly because feminism's primary concern has always been to identify and change social arrangements that cause preventable suffering, and we have applied this approach to the body. But it is also because we have focussed the rest of our attention to the body on alienation from the body and on women's bodily differences from men, and these directions of focus have not been conducive to developing a feminist understanding of bodily suffering.

Feminist Theory and the Body

One of the central concerns of feminism has been men's control of women's bodies, especially women's sexuality and reproductive processes, through violence and coercion, law, economic relations, religion, custom, and institutionalized medicine. Outrage over the injustice of this control and the many ways it hurts women led to the long-established movements to increase women's own control of their sexuality, reproductive lives, and health care. Because these movements have sought to increase women's power to make decisions about their own bodies and to prevent or reduce their bodily suffering, and because there is still so much that needs to be done toward both these goals, they do not foster discussion of experiences of bodily suffering that cannot be controlled or prevented.

Another direction of feminist discussion of the body has been particularly concerned with how men's and women's alienation from their bodies contributes to women's oppression, and how women are alienated from their bodies by male-dominated society. Understandably, alienation from the body is a very negative concept in these discussions; it is something to be overcome by reuniting culture and people with bodily experience.

Dorothy Dinnerstein (Dinnerstein 1976) and Susan Griffin (Griffin 1981) are the major developers of the view that alienation from the body contributes to women's oppression. Both focus upon the desire to escape the vulnerability of the body, especially its vulnerability to unfulfilled need, which is experienced by infants in relation to their mothers. They argue that this desire is a primary motive for creating/maintaining cultures and ideologies that objectify, rage against, and attempt to control women. Because Dinnerstein and Griffin want us to see the pathology of cultures that are pitted against the bodily experiences of men and women, it makes sense that both discuss only the experiences of healthy bodies in relatively favourable physical circumstances. However, for those of us who find their theories persuasive (as I do), there is a potential difficulty that arises from ignoring negative adult experiences of the body: We may come to believe that all will be well between us and our bodies if we can overcome cultural alienation from them.

Other feminist discussions of the body have explicitly focussed on overcoming women's social and cultural alienation from our bodies. A major concern of feminists has been the redescription, by women, of bodily experiences unique to women. Because the Western tradition particularly devalued women's bodies and appropriated the authority to describe bodily experiences unique to women, feminist writings about experience of the body tend to focus on sexuality (heterosexual, lesbian, and bisexual), the changes of monthly cycles, pregnancy, birth, and mothering. Also in reaction to this tradition and its consequences, feminists have celebrated the body, emphasizing aspects of bodily experience that are sources of pleasure, satisfaction, and feelings of connection. These two understandable and valuable reactions, however, have led feminists to overlook or underestimate the fact that the body is also a source of frustration, suffering, and even torment. One consequence is that women with disabilities may feel that feminists have an ideal of the female body or of female bodily experience in which they cannot participate any more than they can in the idealized images of sexist society, and that their experiences cannot be included in feminist understandings of the body.

Nevertheless, although feminists have often ignored the suffering body in their theorizing, they have not ignored other aspects of the negative or rejected body. They have always drawn attention to and criticized body image ideals that alienate women from our own bodies and function as instruments of social control. There have been feminist critiques of fashions in body type and clothing, of the cult of youth, of the tyranny of slimness, of standards of femininity that require restricted movement, extensive grooming and use of makeup, and of growing cultural pressures on women in wealthy countries to alter their bodies by 'cosmetic' surgery, to name but a few. (For more discussion of these issues, see Bartky 1990 and Bordo 1993.) These critiques have usually encouraged women to cultivate more positive and realistic body images in resistance to the idealizations with which they are pressured, and to reduce their alienation from their bodies by focussing on bodily experience and competence rather than appearance. These are important aims for women with disabilities as well as for women without them. But, as in the other feminist treatments of alienation, there is little room to examine bodily suffering when the goal is to restore women's appreciation of embodiment. Recent work along these lines has taken another direction, urging women to adopt a playful, mocking stance toward standards of beauty and femininity, using their own bodies to resist and comment upon these standards. (See, for example, Wolf 1990 and Morgan 1991.) Here the emphasis moves away from subjectivity altogether and toward a kind of taking control of how one is objectified. I believe the latter line of thought is influenced by feminist postmodernist treatments of the body, which are a development of feminist inquiries into the significance of women's bodily differences from men.

Western feminist attention to women's bodily differences from men began with arguments that, contrary to long scientific and popular traditions, these differences do not by themselves determine women's social and psychological gender (or the more limited "sex roles" we used to talk about). These arguments still go on, especially among biologists, anthropologists, and psychologists; understandably, they have little or nothing to say about bodily suffering. But the view that gender is not biologically determined has taken a much more radical turn in feminist poststructuralist and postmodernist criticism, where the symbolic and cultural significance of women's bodily differences from men are examined closely. Here "the body" is often discussed as a cultural construction, and the body or body parts are taken to be symbolic forms in a culture. In this latter development, experience of the body is at best left out of the discussion, and at worst precluded by the theory; here feminist theory itself is alienated from the body. As Carol Bigwood says, "A body and nature formed solely by social and political significations, discourses, and inscriptions are cultural products, disemboweled of their full existential content. The poststructuralist body . . . is so fluid it can take on almost limitless embodiments. It has no real terrestrial *weight*" (Bigwood 1991, 59). A body experienced has both limitations and weight.[1]

I was particularly struck by the alienation from bodily experience of some recent forms of feminist theorizing about the body when I read

Donna Haraway's exciting and witty essay, "A Manifesto for Cyborgs" (Haraway 1990).[2] The view she presents there, of the body as cultural and technological construct, seems to preclude the sort of experience I have had. When I became ill, I felt taken over and betrayed by a profound bodily vulnerability. I was forced by my body to reconceptualize my relationship to it. This experience was not the result of any change of cultural "reading" of the body or of technological incursions into the body. I was infected by a virus, with debilitating physical and psychological consequences. Of course, my illness occurred in a social and cultural context, which profoundly affected my experience of it, but a major aspect of my experience was precisely that of being forced to acknowledge and learn to live with bodily, not cultural, limitation. In its radical movement away from the view that every facet of women's lives is determined by biology, feminist theory is in danger of idealizing "the body" and erasing much of the reality of lived bodies.[3] As Susan Bordo says: "The deconstructionist erasure of the body is not effected, as in the Cartesian version, by a trip to 'nowhere,' but in a resistance to the recognition that one is always *somewhere*, and limited." (Bordo 1990, 145)

Feminism's continuing efforts on behalf of increasing women's control of our bodies and preventing unnecessary suffering tend to make us think of bodily suffering as a socially curable phenomenon. Moreover, its focus on alienation from the body and women's bodily differences from men has created in feminist theory an unrealistic picture of our relationship to our bodies. On the one hand, there is the implicit belief that, if we can only create social justice and overcome our cultural alienation from the body, our experience of it will be mostly pleasant and rewarding. On the other hand, there is a concept of the body which is limited only by the imagination and ignores bodily experience altogether. In neither case does feminist thought confront the experience of bodily suffering. One important consequence is that feminist theory has not taken account of a very strong reason for wanting to transcend the body. Unless we do take account of it, I suspect that we may not only underestimate the subjective appeal of mind-body dualism but also fail to offer an adequate alternative conception of the relationship of consciousness to the body.

The Suffering and Limited Body

In *The Absent Body*, philosophical phenomenologist Drew Leder argues that the Western tradition of mind-body dualism and devaluation of the body is encouraged and supported by the phenomenology of bodily experience. He describes how the body tends to be absent to consciousness except in times of suffering, disruption, rapid change (as in puberty or pregnancy), or the acquisition of new skills (Leder 1990, 92). Our experiences of bodily absence, he says, "seem to support the doctrine of an immaterial mind trapped inside an alien body" (1990, 3). Leder does not like or subscribe to Cartesian dualism and claims that it contributes to the oppression of women, animals, nature, and other 'Others.' However, he argues that we must reclaim the experiential truths that have lent it support even as we "break its conceptual hegemony" (1990, 3).

Other writers comment upon the phenomenon that the body seems to come to conscious awareness with the onset of illness or disability. Robert Murphy said that "illness negates this lack of awareness of the body in guiding our thoughts and actions. The body no longer can be taken for granted, implicit and axiomatic, for it has become a problem" (Murphy 1990, 12). May Sarton, in her journal *After the Stroke*, writes, "Youth, it occurs to me, has to do with not being aware of one's body, whereas old age is often a matter of consciously *overcoming* some misery or other inside the body. One is acutely aware of it" (quoted in Woodward 1991, 19).

At the very least, we must recognize that awareness of the body is often awareness of pain, discomfort, or physical difficulty. Since people with disabilities collectively have a great deal of knowledge about these aspects of bodily experience, they should be major contributors to our cultural understanding of the body. I propose to demonstrate this, in a modest way, by discussing some interesting aspects of pain and some of the effects that bodily suffering has on our desire to identify with our bodies. I hope to open a new feminist discussion of transcendence of the body, one that will eventually take full account of the phenomenology of bodily suffering.

Pain

Virtually everyone has some experience of physical pain. Drew Leder gives a good phenomenological account of acute or nonchronic pain. He points out that our experience of it is episodic, that it always demands our attention, that it constricts our perception of space to the body and of time to the here-and-now, that the goal of getting rid of it becomes the focus of our intentions and actions, that it often renders us alone psychologically by cutting us off from other people's reality, and that it causes some degree of alienation of the self from the painful body (Leder 1990, 70–79). All this seems true to me. Nevertheless, I believe our understanding of pain can be greatly enriched by experiences of chronic pain. By chronic pain I mean pain that is not endured for some purpose or goal (unlike the pain of intense athletic training, for instance), pain that promises to go on indefinitely (although sometimes intermittently and sometimes unpredictably), pain that demands no action because as far as we know, no action can get rid of it.

From my own and other people's experiences of chronic pain, I have learned that pain is an interpreted experience. By this I mean not only that we interpret the experience of pain to mean this or that (we do, as Leder points out, and I shall discuss the meaning of pain later), but also that the experience of pain itself is sometimes and in part a product of the interpretation of sensations. For example, it is a fascinating paradox that a major aspect of the painfulness of pain, or I might say the suffering caused by pain, is the desire to get rid of it, to escape from it, to make it stop. A cultivated attitude of acceptance toward it, giving in to it, or just watching/observing it as an experience like others, can reduce the suffering it usually causes. People with chronic pain sometimes describe this as making friends with their pain; I suspect they have achieved a degree of acceptance that still eludes me, but I think I know what they mean. (See, for example, Albert Kreinheder's description of his relationship to the severe pain of rheumatoid arthritis in Kreinheder 1991, chapter 6.)

I want to make it clear before I continue that my descriptions of living with chronic pain do not apply to everyone and are certainly not prescriptions for anyone else. Living with pain is a very complex and individual negotiation; successful strategies depend on such factors as how intense the pain is, where it is in the body (for instance, I find pain in my head or my abdomen much more demanding than pain in my back, arms, or legs), how much energy a person has, whether her/his energy and attention are drained into worries about money, family, medical treatment, or other things, what kind of work s/he does, whether her/his physicians and friends encourage and help her/him, how much pleasure s/he has, what s/he feels passionate about, and many other factors. (For a sample of strategies, see Register 1987.) In other words, it is important to remember that pain occurs in a complex physical, psychological, and social context that forms and transforms our experience of it.

For me, pain is no longer the phenomenon described by Leder. I have found that when focussed upon and accepted without resistance, it is often transformed into something I would not describe as pain or even discomfort. For example, my disease causes virtually constant aching in the muscles of my arms, upper chest, and upper back. I know this, because any time I turn my attention to those parts of my body, I experience pain; I think of this pain as similar to a radio that is always playing, but whose volume varies a great deal. When the volume is low, or when I am doing something that absorbs my attention very fully, I can ignore it; but when the volume is turned up high, it demands my attention, and I cannot ignore it for long. If I focus my attention fully on the pain, in which case I must stop doing everything else, I am usually able to relax 'into it,' which is a state of mind difficult to describe except by saying that I concentrate on remaining aware of the pain and not resisting it. Then the experience of being in pain is transformed into something else—sometimes a mental image, sometimes a train of thought, sometimes an emotion, sometimes a desire to do something, such as lying down or getting warmer, sometimes sleep. Perhaps if I remained focussed upon it in this way, I would rarely suffer from pain, but I do not want to devote much conscious attention to this process. Other things interest me more, and this, for me, is the problem of pain.

I must balance the frequency of attention to how my body feels that is required by the constant presence of pain with whatever attention is required by something else I am doing. It surprised me to find that I could learn to do this, and that I got better at it with practice. (Of course, it requires structuring my life so that I can rest and withdraw my attention into my body much more than healthy people my age normally do.) But the most surprising thing about it is that my ability to think, my attitudes, and feelings seem to me less, not more, dependent on the state of my body than they were before I became ill. Thus, before I had ME, I would never have considered setting to work at a difficult piece of writing if I woke up feeling quite sick, not only because I knew that I should rest in order to recover, but because I thought I could not possibly write well, or even think well, unless my body felt fairly good. Now I do it often, not because I 'have to,' but because I know how to do it and I want to. This outcome is the opposite of my expectation that paying much more attention to my bodily experience would make every aspect of myself more dependent on its fluctuating states. In a sense I discovered that experiences of the body can teach consciousness a certain freedom from the sufferings and limitations of the body. I shall return to this subject later, after discussing some strategies of disengagement from the body.

Some Strategies of Disengagement

Attempting to transcend or disengage oneself from the body by ignoring or discounting its needs and sensations is generally a luxury of the healthy and able-bodied. For people who are ill or disabled, a fairly high degree of attention to the body is necessary for survival, or at least for preventing significant (and sometimes irreversible) deterioration of their physical conditions. Yet illness and disability often render bodily experiences whose meanings we once took for granted difficult to interpret, and even deceptive. Barbara Rosenblum described how a "crisis of meaning" was created by the radical unpredictability of her body with cancer:

> In our culture it is very common to rely on the body as the ultimate arbiter of truth. . . . By noticing the body's responses to situations, we have an idea of how we "really feel about things." For example, if you get knots in your stomach every time a certain person walks into the room, you have an important body clue to investigate. . . . Interpretations of bodily signals are premised on the uninterrupted stability and continuity of the body. . . . When the body, like my body, is no longer consistent over time . . . when something that meant one thing in April may have an entirely different meaning in May, then it is hard to rely on the stability—and therefore the truth—of the body. (Butler and Rosenblum 1991, 136–37)

Chronic pain creates a similar (but more limited) crisis of meaning, since, to a healthy person, pain means that something is wrong that should be acted upon. With chronic pain, I must remind myself over and over again that the pain is meaningless, that there is nothing to fear or resist, that resistance only creates tension, which makes it worse. When I simply notice and accept the pain, my mind is often freed to pay attention to something else. This is not the same as ignoring my body, which would be dangerous, since not resting when I need to rest can cause extreme symptoms or a relapse into illness that would require several days' bed rest. I think of it as a reinterpretation of bodily sensations so as not to be overwhelmed or victimized by them. This process has affected profoundly my whole relationship to my body, since fatigue, nausea, dizziness, lack of appetite, and even depression are all caused by my disease from time to time, and thus all have changed their meanings. It is usually, though not always, inappropriate now to interpret them as indications of my relationship to the external world or of the need to take action. Unfortunately, it is often much easier to recognize that something is inappropriate than to refrain from doing it.

For this reason, I have found it important to cultivate an 'observer's' attitude to many bodily sensations and even depressive moods caused by my illness. With this attitude, I observe what is happening as a phenomenon, attend to it, tolerate the cognitive dissonance that results from, for example, feeling depressed or nauseated when there is nothing obviously depressing or disgusting going on, accommodate to it as best I can, and wait for it to pass. This is very different from the reactions that come most easily to me, which have to do with finding the causes of these feelings and acting on them. I find it hardest to adopt an observer's attitude toward depression, since although in the past I had brief illnesses that caused the other symptoms, I had never experienced severe depression without something to be depressed about. Thus, my first, easiest response to depression was to search my life for something that might be depressing me. Since my world (like virtually everyone's) is full of things that, if focussed upon, might cause depression, I increased and prolonged my depressions with this habitual response. Learning to regard severe depression (by this I mean, not the lows of everyday living, but the sorts of feelings that make you wish you were dead) as a physical phenomenon to be endured until it is over and not taken seriously has greatly reduced my suffering from it and may have saved my life. Register describes a similar strategy used by a man who suffers from recurring depressive illness (Register 1987, 280).

In general, being able to say (usually to myself): "My body is painful (or nauseated, exhausted, etc.), but I'm happy," can be very encouraging and lift my spirits, because it asserts that the way my body feels is not the totality of my experience, that my mind and feelings can wander beyond the painful messages of my body, and that my state of mind is not completely dependent on the state of my body. Even being able to say, "My brain is badly affected right now, so I'm depressed, but I'm fine and my life is going well," is a way of asserting that the quality of my life is not completely dependent on the state of my body, that projects can still be imagined and accomplished, and that the present is not all there is. In short, I am learning not to identify myself with my body, and this helps me to live a good life with a debilitating chronic illness.

I know that many people will suspect this attitude of being psychologically or spiritually naive. They will insist that the sufferings of the body have psychological and/or spiritual meanings, and that I should be searching for them in order to heal myself (Wilber 1988). This is a widespread belief, not only in North America but in many parts of the world, and I have discussed some of its consequences for people with disabilities and/or life-threatening illnesses earlier in this book. I do not reject it entirely. I too believe that, if my stomach tightens every time a particular person enters the room, it is an important sign of how I feel about her/him, and I may feel better physically if I avoid or change my relationship to that person. But, having experienced a crisis of meaning in my body, I can no longer assume that even powerful bodily experiences are psychologically or spiritually meaningful. To do so seems to me to give the body too little importance as a cause in psychological and spiritual life. It reduces the body to a mere reflector of other processes and implicitly rejects the idea that the body may have a complex life of its own, much of which we cannot interpret.

When I look back on the beginning of my illness, I still think of it, as I did then, as an involuntary violation of my body. But now I feel that such violations are sometimes the beginnings of a better life, in that they force the self to expand or be destroyed. Illness has forced me to change in ways that I am grateful for, and so, although I would joyfully accept a cure if it were offered me, I do not regret having become ill. Yet I do not believe that I became ill *because* I needed to learn what illness has taught me, nor that I will get well when I have learned everything I need to know from it. We learn from many things that do not happen to us because we need to learn from them (to regard the death of a loved one, for example, as primarily a lesson for oneself, is hideously narcissistic), and many people who could benefit from learning the same things never have the experiences that would teach them.

When I began to accept and give in to my symptoms, when I stopped searching for medical, psychological, or spiritual cures, when I began to develop the ability to observe my symptoms and reduced my identification with the transient miseries of my body, I was able to reconstruct my life. The state of my body limited the possibilities in new ways, but it also presented new kinds of understanding, new interests, new passions, and projects. In this sense, my experience of illness has been profoundly meaningful, but only because I accepted my body as a cause. If I had insisted on seeing it primarily as reflecting psychological or spiritual problems and devoted my energy to uncovering the 'meanings' of my symptoms, I would still be completely absorbed in being ill. As it is, my body has led me to a changed identity, to a very different sense of myself, even as I have come to identify myself less with what is occurring in my body.

People with disabilities often describe advantages of not identifying the self with the body. For those who are ill, the difficulty of living moment to moment with unpredictable, debilitating symptoms can be alleviated by having a strong sense of self that negotiates its ability to carry out its projects with the sick body (Register 1987, chapter 9). This sense of self and its projects provides continuity in lives that would be chaotic if those who led them were highly identified with their bodies. The anthropologist Robert Murphy, who was quadriplegic and studied the lives of people with paralysis, described another motive for disembodying the self: "The paralytic becomes accustomed to being lifted, rolled, pushed, pulled, and twisted, and he survives this treatment by putting emotional distance between himself and his body" (Murphy 1990, 100–101).

In addition, people with disabilities often express a strong desire not to be identified with their bodily weaknesses, inabilities, or illnesses. This is why the phrase "people with disabilities" has come to be preferred over "disabled people." When the world sees a whole person as disabled, the person's abilities are overlooked or discounted. It is easy to slip into believing other people's perceptions of oneself, and this can take a great toll on the self-esteem of a person with a disability. Those people with disabilities who still have impressive and reliable physical abilities can counteract people's misperceptions by asserting those abilities. For those of us whose remaining physical abilities are unimpressive or unreliable, not to identify ourselves with our bodies may be the best defense. It is good psychological strategy to base our sense of ourselves, and therefore our self-esteem, on our intellectual and/or emotional experiences, activities, and connections to others.

Robert Murphy, whose paralysis increased steadily as a tumor in his spinal column grew, wrote eloquently about the consequences of losing the ability to move. He said of himself: "My thoughts and sense of being alive have been driven back into my brain, where I now reside," (1990, 102) and: "Like all quadriplegics, I have a great fear of being left stranded and helpless, but my sense of self is otherwise shrunken to the confines of my head" (1990, 193). Although Murphy did not shrink from recognizing what he had lost by this, he described vividly what he had gained:

> I have become a receptor in physical things, and I must continually fight the tendency for this growing passivity to overcome my thoughts. But there is a certain security and comfort in returning to my little cocoon every night, enswathed in a warm electric blanket, settled into a microen-

vironment consisting of one's essentials. It is a breach of communication with the toils of social ties and obligations, a retreat into a private cerebral world. And it is at these times that my mind wanders furthest afield. In such deep quietude, one indeed finds a perverse freedom. (Murphy 1990, 193–94)

I do not want to give an exaggerated impression of the degree to which people with disabilities rely upon strategies of disembodiment. For all the advantages that some degree of disembodying the self may have in coping with illness or disability, the process of coming to identify with a sick or disabled body can play an important part in adjusting to it. For many of us who became ill or disabled as adults, reconstructing our lives depended upon forging a new identity. An important aspect of this process is what Register calls "acceptance: ability to regard the illness [or, I would add, disability] as your normal state of being" (Register 1987, 31). This could also be described as learning to identify with a new body, as well as, for most of us, a new social role. For me, this had many advantages: I stopped expecting to recover and postponing my life until I was well, I sought help and invented strategies for living with my sick body, I changed my projects and my working life to accommodate my physical limitations, and, perhaps most important, I began to identify with other people with disabilities and to learn from them. Thus, I do identify with my sick body to a significant degree, but I also believe that my thoughts and feelings are more independent from my experiences of it than they ever were from my experiences of my well body.

Transcendence

What has all this to do with transcendence of the body? That, of course, depends on what we have in mind when we speak of transcendence. The forms of independence from the body's sufferings that I have described are partial and mundane. They are strategies of daily living, not grand spiritual victories. Some people might even regard them as forms of alienation from physical experience. I think that would be a mistake. Alienation, as we usually understand it, reduces freedom, because it constricts the possibilities of experience. If we spoke of being alienated from suffering, I think we would mean being unable to face up to and undergo some necessary, perhaps purposeful, pain. To choose to exercise some habits of mind that distance oneself from chronic, often meaningless physical suffering increases freedom, because it expands the possibilities of experience beyond the miseries and limitations of the body.

It is because they increase the freedom of consciousness that I am drawn to calling these strategies forms of transcendence. It is because we are led to adopt them by the body's pain, discomfort, or difficulty, and because they are ways of interpreting and dealing with bodily experience, that I call them transcendence of the body. I do not think that we need to subscribe to some kind of mind-body dualism to recognize that there are degrees to which consciousness and the sense of self may be tied to bodily sensations and limitations, or to see the value of practices, available to some people in some circumstances, that loosen the connection. Nor do I think we need to devalue the body or bodily experience to value the ability to gain some emotional and cognitive distance from them. On the contrary, to devalue the body for this reason would be foolish, since it is bodily changes and conditions that lead us to discover these strategies. The onset of illness, disability, or pain destroys the "absence" of the body to consciousness, described by Leder and others, and forces us to find conscious responses to new, often acute, awareness of our bodies. Thus, the body itself takes us into and then beyond its sufferings and limitations.

As an alternative to the traditional theological concept of transcendence, Naomi Goldenberg calls for a new concept of transcendence "with body," which would involve feeling and knowing our connection to other lives, human history, and society (Goldenberg 1990, 211–12). Drew Leder offers an understanding of transcendence that rejects Cartesian dualism and distrust of the body in favour of the realization that the lived body is transpersonal, that we form one body with the world, and that we can experience this one-body relation in compassion, aesthetic absorption, and spiritual communion (Leder 1990, chapter 6). I like both of their conceptions, but I also think they are both talking about transcendence of the *ego*, which they see as an ideal to replace transcendence of the body. The ability at least sometimes to transcend the demands of the ego seems to me central to spiritual life and probably to human happiness. So perhaps it is a more important form of transcendence than transcendence of the body. Nevertheless, I suspect that the idea of transcendence of the body may be too easily rejected in an attempt to throw out mind-body dualism, derogation of the body, and all the sins that have been committed in their names.

By defending some notion of transcendence of the body I do not mean to suggest that strategies of disembodying the self should be adopted by people without disabilities. Instead, I want to demonstrate how important it is to consider the experiences of people with disabilities when theorizing about the relationship of consciousness to the body. One thing is clear: We cannot speak only of reducing our alienation from our bodies, becoming more aware of them, and celebrating their strengths and pleasures; we must also talk about how to live with the suffering body, with that which cannot be noticed without pain, and that which cannot be celebrated without ambivalence. We may find then that there is a place in our discussion of the body for some concept of transcendence.

Notes

Introduction

1. There is a grim joke among people who have lived a long time with ME: The good news is that it doesn't kill you, and the bad news is that it doesn't kill you.

1. Who Is Disabled? Defining Disability

1. The most often cited work on stigma is Erving Goffman's 1963 book on the subject, *Stigma: Notes on the Management of Spoiled Identity*, which I find painfully patronizing of people with disabilities. I will discuss Goffman's views in chapter 3.

2. For an account of African women's efforts to end genital mutilation and a detailed description of some of the disabling consequences of genital mutilation for Nigerian women, see Edemikpong 1992. For an excellent discussion of genital mutilation as a challenge to feminist moral relativism, see Sherwin 1992.

3. Here Young is not using "handicapped" as defined by the UN definitions. She is using it to include anatomical structure (e.g., muscle development), function (e.g., strength), and a range of physical abilities, as well as the disadvantages that are associated with them (Young 1990, 153).

4. Jenny Morris (1991, 128) points out that, in England, there is a strong assumption that disabled old people should live in institutions.

5. Amundson suggests that societies are constructed with the biomedical norm of humanity in mind. Since my social and physical environment is clearly not constructed for the convenience of children, women, elderly people, ill people or people with disabilities, and since these collectively form the vast majority of people living in that environment, I am unwilling to believe that it was constructed for any norm. I think it was constructed for the young non-disabled male paradigm of humanity. I will discuss this more in the next chapter.

6. I do recognize that, for some purposes, it may be appropriate to distinguish old people with disabilities from young and middle-aged people with disabilities. For example, it would make sense for a society with very limited resources to give higher priority to providing expensive medical procedures to those who have more time left to benefit from them, or costly occupational retraining to those who will use it longer.

7. There is a conceptual distinction between the two, as Amundson insisted to me in a personal communication. People may be disabled without being ill, or ill without being disabled. The same illness may cause different disabilities, and different illnesses may cause the same disability. I am not disputing the conceptual distinction here, but I am discussing the politics of emphasizing the practical distinction, as Amundson does in his article.

8. Statistics on causes of disability vary among countries and among age groups within a country, and, of course, according to how disability is defined. Here I am relying on statistics on disability in Canada and the United States, when disability is defined as long-term major activity limitation. (Health and Welfare Canada and Statistics Canada 1981; Statistics Canada 1986 and 1991; Pope and Tarlov 1991; LaPlante 1991.) Worldwide, we would see considerable variation in patterns of disability, with malaria, leprosy, and disease consequences of malnutrition playing major roles in some countries.

9. I say *may* because some opportunities are not appropriate for children, and some opportunities cannot be given to certain groups by a society, such as the opportunity for men to bear children (not yet, anyway).

10. On the other hand, it is in the financial interest of those who provide health care and therapies for profit to define "health" narrowly so that as many people as possible will see themselves as needing their services. This is apparent in the advertising and operation of 'fitness' centres but also in the attitudes promoted in some of the nonallopathic or alternative medical practices. Here "health" is often a perpetually distant goal. People who consult such providers about a specific problem may come away believing themselves to be much sicker (by their newly acquired standards) than they ever imagined or felt themselves to be before. Nevertheless, I do not think this significantly increases the number of people who are identified by practitioners or identi-

fy themselves as *disabled*, because the stigma of disability is great enough to make most patients strongly resistant to this identification.

11. One striking example of this was reported by *Newsweek* (3 February 1992, 57). There is considerable variation, from one school district in the United States to another, in how learning disability is defined, depending partly on the resources that are available for helping children with learning disabilities.

12. The stigma of being ill is very complex, and for the sake of continuity I will not attempt to describe it here. I will describe it at length in chapter 3.

13. The people whose writings I am discussing here refer to themselves as the Deaf.

14. For superb examples of the contextuality of disability, see Sacks 1987 and 1992a.

15. This question is discussed extensively in feminist literature. For an introduction to it, I recommend Spelman 1988, Bordo 1990, and Higginbotham 1992.

16. This is an indication of the strength of the stigma of disability, at least in the minds of social scientists.

17. Linda Alcoff suggests that we should define "woman" thus: "[W]oman is a position from which a feminist politics can emerge rather than a set of attributes that are 'objectively identifiable'" (Alcoff 1988, 435). My approach to defining "people with disabilities" is influenced by Alcoff's suggestion.

2. The Social Construction of Disability

1. Nanette Sutherland pointed out to me that some disabilities may be entirely social. In some instances of psychiatric disability, there may be no relevant biological condition, only a psychiatric label that was originally misapplied and is still disabling to the person who is stuck with it. Nevertheless, the vast majority of disabilities are created by the interaction of biological and social factors.

2. The idea that disability is socially constructed is of such importance in identifying approaches to disability that a recent definition of Disability Studies by Linton, Mello, and O'Neill (quoted in Linton 1994, 46) says that it "reframes the study of disability by focusing on it as a social phenomenon, *social construct*, metaphor and culture . . ." (my emphasis).

3. For example, a friend who recently spent time on the spinal cord ward of a hospital in a major U.S. city discovered that many people on the ward had been shot.

4. For a discussion of the interactions of race, age, income, education, and marital status in the rates of work disability among women in the United States, see Russo and Jansen 1988.

5. For a discussion of how people with disabilities and those who care for them are affected by social expectations of pace, see Hillyer 1993, chapter 4, "Productivity and Pace."

6. I do not mean to imply that increasing the pace of professors' work would be bad (although it would be bad for me), only to show how expectations of pace have a role in constructing work disability.

7. Here I am speaking about people who do not receive private disability insurance benefits, settlements from accident claims, veterans' disability benefits, or workers' compensation benefits, any of which may be high enough to keep them out of poverty. In Canada, the majority of people with disabilities are not eligible for these more adequate forms of support.

8. An acquaintance of mine who uses a wheelchair and lives on a disability pension discovered recently, when her wheelchair wore out beyond repair, that her insurance company's policy is to pay for only one wheelchair in a lifetime. Wheelchairs are expensive items, and they do wear out. Not only is such a policy stupidly unrealistic, but it reinforces the message (which people who are ill or disabled encounter everywhere) that society expects her to get well or die.

9. For more on the cultural meanings of disabilities and illnesses, see Sontag 1977 and 1988; Fine and Asch 1988; Kleinman 1988; Morris 1991.

10. For a first-person account of living with facial scarring, see Grealy 1994.

11. I like much of Maxine Sheets-Johnstone's criticism of feminist theory of 'the body' and 'embodiment' that does not take account of the body or bodily experience, and in which "the body is simply the place one puts one's epistemology" (Sheets-Johnstone 1992, 43). Nevertheless, I do not accept her notion of the "body simpliciter," which I think takes too little account of the cultural meanings of bodily capabilities and possibilities, and of the cultural relativity of their importance to an individual.

12. For a fuller discussion of the limitations, for understanding disability, of feminist postmodern and other feminist theorizing about the body, see chapter 7.

13. Ellen Frank pointed this out to me.

14. For an interesting discussion of these questions as they apply to designing products, see Vanderheiden 1990.

15. For example, the Canadian-based group, Tetra Development Society, modifies existing equipment and creates new equipment to enable people with

severe disabilities to participate in all aspects of life. Volunteers provide the engineering skills, and the capital cost of most projects is minimal.

16. For example, in Isabel Dyck's study of Canadian women with multiple sclerosis who left the paid labour force, several women mentioned the need for flexible, part-time hours, but only one woman had been able to find such a work arrangement (and that only temporarily) (Dyck 1995, 310).

17. I put this expression in quotation marks because, in my view, most people who are disabled are 'partially disabled,' that is, able to do some work under the right conditions.

18. This despite the fact that the new policy did not propose to reimburse us fully for our wage loss, but only at the same rate as wage loss replacement for workers on full disability leave.

19. Kavka explicitly did not describe employment for everyone in advantaged societies or employment for people with disabilities in other societies as a 'right,' since he did not regard these social goals as feasible at the time.

20. Stephen Hawking is one of the world's most influential theoretical physicists. He has had ALS for many years, which has reduced his voluntary muscle movement to the point that he needs a great deal of attendant care and the use of computers to communicate.

21. Moreover, we might consider her deserving of compensation for lost opportunities if someone else's actions deprived her of her ability. Still, we would not, I think, regard her as a person with a disability, if this was the only ability she had lost.

22. I say "wherever possible," because sometimes it is not possible. Not everyone can be given the ability to participate in all the major aspects of life in a society. For example, some people with mental disabilities cannot be given the ability to understand political issues or the voting process.

23. For a good overview of the current state of the debates and many references, see *Disability Studies Quarterly*, Spring 1994.

24. I do not mean to suggest that everything is fully accessible to people with disabilities in Sweden. Bill Bolt reports, based on a visit to Sweden to study conditions for people with disabilities there, that the benefits and practical help are very generous (by US and Canadian standards), but, in his opinion, "they have gained little physical, financial, or psychic mainstreaming, freedom, or productivity" (Bolt 1994, 18).

25. This statistic is from the survey conducted by Louis Harris and Associates for the National Organization on Disability, reported in *Disability Studies Quarterly*, Summer 1994: 13–14.

26. It is ironic that the belief in good luck which seems to underlie people's unwillingness to provide for their possible disablement is not fully balanced by belief in the bad luck of people with disabilities, who are often blamed for their conditions. Perhaps people without disabilities do not really believe it is a matter of luck at all, but a matter of their own control, effort, and moral worthiness. Or perhaps their beliefs are a confused, unexamined mixture of the two. I will discuss the myths of control and their consequences in chapter 4.

27. Gregory Kavka believed that the unpleasantness of thinking about the contingency of disability interferred with people's willingness to plan for long-term disability (Kavka 1992, 277). We find thinking of accident or sudden illness unpleasant too, but we do plan for acute medical care, so I suspect a stronger psychological force—fear so substantial as to prevent identification—is at work in relation to disability.

28. Anita Silvers points out that the suicide rate among people with disabilities is remarkably low considering how often non-disabled people declare that they would rather be dead than "confined to a wheelchair" (Silvers 1994, 159).

29. I realize that this statement violates what Hugh Gallagher calls "the new stereotype" of people with disabilities as basically non-disabled people who just happen to ride around in wheelchairs (Gallagher 1993), but the fact is that many severely disabled people cannot live without frequent daily help from others. For example, imagine telling Stephen Hawking that his goal should be to live independently. I discuss the issue of independence at length in chapter 6.

3. Disability as Difference

1. Fortunately, this is changing. As disability rights organizations and people with disability rights perspectives gain more cultural representation, they create a proud subculture in which one can participate even at a distance.

2. Phyllis Mueller, who was interviewed by Cheri Register, recalled: "The first day I ever realized you could be happy and still sick was a real red-letter day" (Register 1987, 315). Nancy Mairs, seconding Mueller's insight, says, "it is possible to be both sick and happy. This good news, once discovered, demands to be shared" (Mairs 1994, 127).

3. For example, see Driedger and Gray 1992, an international anthology in which women with disabilities describe their lives.

4. An important exception to these generalizations is that attitudes in some societies differentiate between disability in the elderly and disability in the

nonelderly, with disability being unlikely to affect the respect accorded to the elderly or the recognition of their remaining abilities.

5. I will return to the topic of control and idealization in chapter 4.

6. Sobsey estimates, based on studies in the United States and Canada, that people with disabilities are abused sexually 50 percent more often than people without disabilities.

7. Other 'Others' may also be less inclined to treat people with disabilities as 'the Other.' Robert Murphy, a professor of anthropology at Columbia University who became paralyzed in middle age, reported that students, most women, and black men ("fellow Outsiders,") became more open, relaxed, and friendly to him when he started using a wheelchair (Murphy 1990, 126–28).

8. For an interesting discussion of this issue, see Gill 1994.

9. For a different view of acute illness, see Arthur W. Frank (1991). Frank says, "(t)he healthy can begin to value illness by doubting the standard of productivity by which they measure their lives" (118).

10. I discuss cultural myths of control of the body in chapter 4. In chapter 7 I discuss at length some insights of people with disabilities concerning the value of transcending the body and strategies for doing so.

11. I will take up the theme of dependency and interdependence again in chapter 6.

12. I cannot even begin here to credit everyone I have read on these subjects over the years, much less everyone who has made a major contribution to the debates on universalization and essentialism. I refer in this discussion to only a few feminist intellectuals whose work has been important to my own recent thinking about how these debates apply to issues of disability.

13. It is important to note that most of the original feminist standpoint epistemologists qualified their claims about epistemic advantages in similar ways, that is, they did not claim that social positions by themselves conferred epistemic standpoints on those who occupied them.

14. Women with disabilities are also organizing separately, having found that early organizations of people with disabilities tended to ignore both significant differences between men's and women's experiences and issues of particular importance to women with disabilities. In Canada, women have become leaders in organizations of people with disabilities, which now reflect somewhat better women's experiences and issues, but women with disabilities still organize separately.

15. In a sense, the extreme form of emphasizing similarities is 'passing.' For good discussions of passing as non-disabled, see Todoroff and Lewis 1992; Hillyer 1993, chapter 8.

16. Of course organizing separately does not preclude forming alliances with people without disabilities.

17. The value of independence from the help of others is being questioned in feminist ethics and in the writings of people with disabilities. So far there has not been much interaction between these two literatures. See chapter 6 for further discussion of this issue.

18. See Butler and Rosenblum 1991, 136–38, on the inadequacy of English to express an experience of illness with cancer.

19. Zola's article gives a political perspective on the history of struggles over labels among people with disabilities, which I will not recapitulate here. Hillyer's book offers a more thorough discussion than mine of current problems of language and political acceptability among feminists and people with disabilities.

20. Hillyer (1993, 29) asserts that the use of sight metaphors hurts or offends blind people. I have never heard or read this from a blind person, but I bow to Hillyer's experience.

21. One notable exception is Deaf children born into a Deaf family or community.

22. For an excellent discussion of these issues in relation to the Human Genome Project, see *The Women's Review of Books*, July 1994b, 17–20.

4. The Flight from the Rejected Body

1. I refer to the "commercial-media-soaked societies of North America" to distinguish them from social groups who inhabit the North American continent while maintaining (or struggling to maintain) their own cultures and social forms. Prominent among the latter are native societies in Canada and the United States that, although they are inevitably influenced by the cultures imported and developed here by invading Europeans, have values and practices which are radically different from them and based in independent traditions. It is not accurate to refer to a single "European-based culture," because groups such as the Hasidic Jews and the Amish also came from Europe and yet maintain a way of life as separate from the commercial cultures created by Europeans as that of many native people. Nor is there only one, homogeneous commercial-media-soaked society in North America; there are sufficient differences in values and practice between Canada and the United States to make them different societies (as well as different nation states), and there are equally significant differences among regions within Canada and the United States. In this discussion, I try to stick to cultural trends and influences that I observe in media which reach all regions of the

United States and Canada and that are discussed by observers of both Canadian and American societies.

2. For a discussion of some psychological aspects of the reactions of 'normals' to 'abnormality,' see Fiedler 1984.

3. Ironically, Kathy Davis defends the reasonableness of choosing cosmetic surgery on the basis that there is no clear distinction (even within the standards of a particular society) between the normal and the abnormal: "Where is the line between the 'normal' deficiency, to be dealt with within the usual routines of body maintenance and improvement, and the abnormally ugly, that which can no longer be endured?" (Davis 1991, 37).

4. Disabled women suffer more than disabled men from the demand that people have ideal, or at least 'normal,' bodies, because in most male-dominated cultures women are judged more by their bodies than are men (Campling 1981; Matthews 1983; Hannaford 1985; Fine and Asch 1988; Driedger and Gray 1992).

5. For news about disability culture, see Cheryl Marie Wade's column, "Culture Rap," in *The Disability Rag and ReSource*. I also look for change to grow from contradictions, such as that of an aging population adhering to a death-denying culture of youth, health, and physical perfection.

6. In chapter 7 I will examine feminist discussion of the body at more length.

7. When I first read *Of Woman Born*, I found this passage moving and inspiring, so I do not mean to imply that Rich should have known then what I realized only with great reluctance ten years later (when I was forced to accept disability). Rather I mean to illustrate what I believe emerged as a widespread feminist attitude to the body.

8. Thanks to Joyce Frazee for pointing this out to me years ago.

9. Fear of losing control of the body has, I believe, contributed to the medicalization of both death and birth. I will say more about the medicalization of birth in chapter 5.

10. I have heard reports of alternative practices curing some patients deemed incurable by Western scientific medicine, but I have no personal experience of this.

11. Patients who have tried many 'natural' healing methods without being cured can begin to feel alienated from nature itself, like nature's outcasts or failures. Thanks to Barbara Secker for drawing my attention to these pitfalls of alternative treatments.

12. Zola also pointed out that this medical re-introduction of individual moral responsibility for illness fit well with "the beliefs of the man in the street" (Zola 1972, 491).

13. There is more evidence along the same lines. Jeffreys (1982, 177–78) reports: "A recent study showed that of twenty-six patients with proven myasthenia gravis, a disease causing seriously impaired muscle functioning, nine had been given initial diagnoses of hypochondriasis, depression or hysteria (T. Sneddon, 'Myasthenia Gravis—the Difficult Diagnosis,' British Journal of Psychiatry, 136: 92–93, 1980.)"

14. In an in-depth interview study of 8 women who had eventually been diagnosed with ME, Ingrid Deringer found that they had previously received a total of eight psychological diagnoses (some had received none, some more than one), including depression, stress, anorexia, psychosomatic disorder, and dementia (Deringer 1992, 56–59).

15. Although I agree with every other aspect of Jeffreys's description, I have encountered a significant number of people who were sent back to their original doctors by psychiatrists, with the message that there must be something wrong physically.

16. Clinical studies have now provided strong evidence confirming Dr. Marshall's hypothesis, and many ulcer patients have been cured with antibiotics (Monmaney 1993, 68).

17. Shelp (1984, 254) points out that first-person accounts of the experience of illness suggest that some interpretive metaphors can "assist patients in maintaining some sense of self and dignity at a time when both may be threatened."

18. I discuss the phenomenology of living with pain more fully in chapter 7.

19. Popular so-called "new age" belief systems, in particular various versions of the insistence that we 'create our own reality,' have contributed a great deal in recent years to the myth of control. One of the best discussions debunking these versions of the myth, while maintaining a spiritual perspective, was published in New Age Journal by Ken and Treya Wilber (1988).

20. For example, my rather sketchy understanding of what some aboriginal people in Canada call "bad medicine" is that it involves psychological action at a distance that can make a person sick.

21. I will say more about doctor-blaming in chapter 5.

22. Carol J. Gill also recognizes the harsher version. She says: "Are people with illnesses disabled? Only when they have the temerity to neither get well nor die" (Gill 1994, 6).

23. Zola pointed out that "the labels health and illness are remarkable 'depoliticizers' of an issue. By locating the source and the treatment of problems in an individual, other levels of intervention are effectively closed" (Zola 1972, 500).

24. For example, there are the Boston-based Women's Community Cancer Project, Breast Cancer Action in San Francisco, the Mautner Project in Washington, D.C., and One in Nine, on Long Island. The *Women's Review of Books* (July 1994a) reported that there were nearly one hundred such groups in the United States.

25. I will say more on the role of medical ethics in this issue in chapter 5.

5. The Cognitive and Social Authority of Medicine

1. For example, this is Woodward's approach in his critical review of the new fourth edition of *The Diagnostic and Statistical Manual of Mental Disorders* (Woodward 1995).

2. For a personal account of the pressures on a patient to objectify his own body and the costs of doing so, see Frank 1991, especially pages 10–11.

3. For a different exploration of the conflicts between patients' and physicians' perspectives, see Toombs 1992.

4. This explains why chronic pains are of relatively little interest to modern medicine. At best they are symptoms of diseases that medicine cannot cure or help. At worst, they are mere "complaints," unconnected to any known disease entity.

5. "I cannot find the cause of the problem," would be far less damaging to a patient's self-confidence. Moreover, it would encourage continuing the search for a cause, which sometimes might save the patient's life. I have often read and heard of patients dying from failure to treat curable conditions that were diagnosed as "psychosomatic illness." Nevertheless, "There is nothing wrong with you," and "There is nothing wrong with you but . . . (here fill in some psychological speculation)," seem to be very common pronouncements by physicians.

6. There are many diseases that are quite rare. Some of them may never be seen (or recognized) by a primary-care physician over a lifetime of general practice. Information concerning rare diseases and patient-support for people suffering from them is provided in the United States by the National Organization for Rare Disorders in New Fairfield, Connecticut.

7. I have heard from several people with undiagnosed illnesses who were sent by their family doctors to psychiatrists, who could not help them and sent them back to their family doctors saying that they must be physically ill. This left the patients in a dangerous medical and social limbo, causing feelings of isolation and despair. Those who can afford it often seek out 'alternative' practitioners when this happens, because, whether or not these practitioners

can provide other kinds of help, at least they acknowledge the reality of the patients' suffering.

8. I find it suggestive that they based their verdict of "mass hysteria" on examination of only the female victims' records in an epidemic that included male and female victims. One cannot help wondering whether they anticipated that "mass hysteria" would be a more acceptable hypothesis if it were applied explicitly only to the women who fell ill. Ramsay does not discuss this feature of their work.

9. In contrast, Ramsay himself spent more than thirty years fighting for medical recognition of the Royal Free disease as an infectious disease and supporting patients who were disabled by it. The fact that Ramsay, who had considerable medical prestige as an infectious diseases specialist, nevertheless had a hard fight, attests to the reluctance of other medical professionals to admit that there are significant gaps in their knowledge of the human body. Oliver Sacks comments on how both sleepy sickness (*encephalitis lethargica*) and Tourette's syndrome "virtually disappeared" (to doctors, not to patients) during the period when they could not be accommodated in the conventional frameworks of medicine (Sacks 1987, 92–94).

10. I sometimes wonder whether most physicians and those who train physicians know that patients value a doctor's willingness to admit ignorance. When my friends and acquaintances describe what they like about their doctors, they usually put the fact that their doctors sometimes say, "I don't know," high on their list.

11. One highly educated Chinese immigrant to Canada who is fluent in English told me that she and her friends always consulted one another about how to describe their symptoms before visiting a Western doctor. They were afraid that if they did not use exactly the right words, they would not be believed, especially since the doctors always seemed to be in a hurry. See also Toombs 1992.

12. Dallery points out that self-help groups for people with chronic illnesses promote "the overcoming of the alienation and self-interpretation foisted by medical practice and other social, cultural structures" (Dallery 1983, 169).

13. I regret that I have lost the source for this, which I believe I read some years ago in a patients' newsletter.

14. I describe some strategies for living with chronic pain in chapter 7.

6. Disability and Feminist Ethics

1. Hillyer tells of one situation in which she, who is normally accorded the status of a professional among other professionals, was so reduced in status by

being in the role of mother of a disabled child that her statements about her daughter were ignored at conferences about her daughter's treatment. It was only when she brought another professional with her to repeat everything she said about her daughter that it was heard (Hillyer 1993, 180).

2. Silvers does not take this to be a question of 'justice versus care,' but rather a question of "whether justice is best assessed against a standard of equality (understood as neutrality) or against a standard of difference (understood as corrective partiality)" (Silvers 1995, 53). Nevertheless, her discussion is highly relevant to debates about the relative merits of a care-based ethics and an ethics based on ideals traditionally associated with justice, such as equality.

3. Other feminists writing about disability have made similar criticisms of 'independence,' notably Debra Connors (1985).

4. It is worth noting that non-disabled married men who have never shopped, cooked, cleaned their homes, or gardened and do not know how to do these things are not considered as 'dependent' as non-disabled married women who do these things but do not work for wages. Meredith Kimball points out that the care that privileged, high-status people receive is seen as contributing to their independence rather than making them dependent (Kimball 1995).

5. This definition comes from my own impressions, gleaned from many sources, including personal correspondence about autonomy with Ron Amundson.

6. Hillyer's views about what forms of independence are appropriate for people with certain kinds of mental disabilities, including her daughter, have been controversial. See Anne Finger's review of Hillyer's book (Finger 1994).

7. My concerns here are focussed on adults, but I feel that the subject of children giving care is important and neglected. My impression is that the care that children, even young children, give to their caregivers is rarely recognized, except to be considered pathogenic. Surely some of the care that children give their caregivers strengthens their egos and develops their capacities for reciprocity.

8. Genetic screening also raises the spectre of sterilization. There is a long and shameful history of involuntary sterilization of women with disabilities throughout the Western world.

9. Meanwhile, advanced medical lifesaving techniques increase the number of people who survive with severe acquired disabilities, but that is a different matter, which will be discussed later in this chapter.

10. On this subject, see also Council for Responsible Genetics 1990 and McDonough 1990.

11. See chapter 7 for a discussion of feminist theory of the body.

12. See, for example, Asch and Fine 1988; Morris 1991; Woodward 1994a.

13. I consider this an open moral question, because babies might be born with conditions which are extremely painful and either inevitably fatal within a short time or so debilitating that there is no reasonable hope of their having lives that anyone would choose over death. However, I am inclined to stipulate that adults with severely debilitating, painful disabilities should be at least consulted in all such cases and perhaps asked to take responsibility for deciding whether a baby in such circumstances should be killed.

14. Of course, similar concerns can be raised about unassisted suicide by people with disabilities who are able to end their own lives. It is assumed that the risk of suicide is greater among people with more severe physical disabilities, at least in part because they usually receive a smaller proportion of the services and opportunities they need to live well, so the likelihood of their lives becoming unbearable is greater.

15. In many countries, expensive lifesaving procedures are 'rationed' by being made available only to those who can afford to pay for them (or afford the kind of private insurance that pays for them); bioethicists are usually looking for some way of distributing health care based on principles of justice or utility.

16. For example, a major health care issue for people with disabilities in the United States is the "pre-existing conditions" exclusion of health insurance companies, which means that many people with disabilities cannot get health insurance, and that those who have health insurance often cannot change jobs for fear of losing their insurance.

7. Feminism, Disability, and Transcendence of the Body

1. In 1984, Adrienne Rich wrote: "Perhaps we need a moratorium on saying 'the body.' For it's also possible to abstract 'the' body. When I write 'the body,' I see nothing in particular. To write 'my body' plunges me into lived experience, particularity. . . ." (Rich 1986, 215). Clearly, Rich saw the problems coming, and I like her suggestion, but so much has been written about "the body" both before and since 1984 that I find I must use the term to discuss this work and to locate my own position in relation to it. I try to use more specific references to bodies when speaking outside the context of the literature on "the body."

2. I seem to pick on Donna Haraway's work in this book, despite the fact that I enjoy and learn a great deal from her writings. It is because Haraway is one

of the postmodernist feminist theorists who talks most explicitly about the body that her work tends to focus my concerns about the limitations of postmodernist feminist theories for understanding disability.

3. Maxine Sheets-Johnstone also criticizes Haraway and other feminist theorists for talking about the body and "embodiment" while failing to take the body and bodily experience into account (Sheets-Johnstone 1992, esp. 43–44).

References

Addelson, Kathryn Pyne. 1983. "The Man of Professional Wisdom." In *Discovering Reality*, eds. Sandra Harding and Merrill B. Hintikka, 165–86. Boston: D. Reidel.

Alcoff, Linda. 1988. "Cultural Feminism versus Poststructuralism: The Identity Crisis in Feminist Theory." *Signs: Journal of Women in Culture and Society* 13 (3): 405–36.

Amundson, Ron. 1992. "Disability, Handicap, and the Environment." *Journal of Social Philosophy* 23 (1): 105–18.

Arsenault, Francine. 1994. "Stakeholder Speech—Chairperson of the Council of Canadians with Disabilities." *Transition* April/May: 6.

Asch, Adrienne, and Michelle Fine. 1988. "Shared Dreams: A Left Perspective on Disability Rights and Reproductive Rights." In *Women with Disabilities: Essays in Psychology, Culture and Politics*, eds. Michelle Fine and Adrienne Asch, 297–305. Philadelphia: Temple University Press.

B.C. Coalition of People with Disabilities. 1995. "Submission to the Special Senate Committee on Assisted Suicide and Euthanasia."

Bartky, Sandra Lee. 1990. *Femininity and Domination: Studies in the Phenomenology of Oppression*. New York: Routledge.

Beauvoir, Simone de. 1952. *The Second Sex*. New York: Alfred A. Knopf.

Bigwood, Carol. 1991. "Renaturalizing the Body (With a Little Help from Merleau-Ponty)." *Hypatia: A Journal of Feminist Philosophy* 6 (3): 54–73.

Blumberg, Lisa. 1994. "Eugenics and Reproductive Choice." In *The Ragged Edge: The*

Disability Experience from the Pages of The First Fifteen Years of The Disability Rag, ed. Barrett Shaw, 218–27. Louisville, Kentucky: Advocado Press.

Bolt, Bill. 1994. "Sweden: Not All It's Cracked Up To Be." *The Disability Rag and ReSource* September/October: 15–19, 43.

Bordo, Susan. 1990. "Feminism, Postmodernism, and Gender-Scepticism." In *Feminism/Postmodernism*, ed. Linda J. Nicholson, 133–56. New York: Routledge.

Bordo, Susan. 1993. *Unbearable Weight: Feminism, Western Culture, and the Body*. Berkeley: University of California Press.

Brison, Susan J. 1993. "Surviving Sexual Violence: A Philosophical Perspective." *Journal of Social Philosophy* 24 (1): 5–22.

Browne, Susan E., Debra Connors, and Nanci Stern, eds. 1985. *With The Power of Each Breath: A Disabled Women's Anthology*. San Francisco: Cleis Press.

Bullard, David G., and Susan E. Knight, eds. 1981. *Sexuality and Physical Disability*. St. Louis: C. V. Mosby.

Bury, Michael R. 1978. "Disablement in Society: Towards an Integrated Perspective." *International Journal of Rehabilitation Research* 2 (1): 33–40.

Butler, Sandra, and Barbara Rosenblum. 1991. *Cancer in Two Voices*. San Francisco: Spinsters Book Company.

Callahan, Daniel. 1990. *What Kind of Life: The Limits of Medical Progress*. New York: Simon and Schuster.

Campling, Jo, ed. 1981. *Images of Ourselves—Women with Disabilities Talking*. London: Routledge and Kegan Paul.

Canadian Woman Studies: Women and Disability. Summer 1993. 13 (4). North York, Ontario: York University.

Carver, Roger J. 1992. "Deaf Culture or Disability?" *Transition* December 92/January 93: 6–7, 24–25.

Collins, Patricia Hill. 1989. "The Social Construction of Black Feminist Thought." *Signs: Journal of Women in Culture and Society* 14 (4): 745–73.

Collins, Patricia Hill. 1991. *Black Feminist Thought*. New York: Routledge.

Connors, Debra. 1985. "Disability, Sexism and the Social Order." In *With the Power of Each Breath: A Disabled Women's Anthology*, eds. Susan E. Browne, Debra Connors, and Nanci Stern, 92–107. San Francisco: Cleis Press.

Council for Responsible Genetics. 1990. "Documents: Position Papers." *Issues in Reproductive and Genetic Engineering* 3 (3): 287–95.

Dahl, Marilyn. 1993. "The Role of the Media in Promoting Images of Disability—Disability as Metaphor: The Evil Crip." *Canadian Journal of Communication* 18: 75–80.

Dallery, Arleen B. 1983. "Illness and Health: Alternatives to Medicine." In

Phenomenology in a Pluralistic Context, eds. William L. McBride and Calvin O. Schrag, 139–54. Albany: State University of New York Press.

Davis, Kathy. 1991. "Remaking the She-Devil: A Critical Look at Feminist Approaches to Beauty." *Hypatia: A Journal of Feminist Philosophy* 6 (2): 21–43.

Degener, Theresia. 1990. "Female Self-Determination between Feminist Claims and 'Voluntary' Eugenics, between 'Rights' and Ethics." *Issues in Reproductive and Genetic Engineering* 3 (2): 87–99.

Deringer, Ingrid C. 1992. "Women's Experiences of Myalgic Encephalomyelitis/ Chronic Fatigue Syndrome." Unpublished MA Thesis in the Department of Women's Studies, Simon Fraser University.

Dinnerstein, Dorothy. 1976. *The Mermaid and the Minotaur: Sexual Arrangements and Human Malaise*. New York: Harper.

Disability Studies Quarterly 14 (2). Spring 1994. Irving Kenneth Zola, ed. Waltham, Massachusetts: Department of Sociology, Brandeis University.

Disability Studies Quarterly 14 (3). Summer 1994. Irving Kenneth Zola, ed. "Persons with Disabilities Lag Behind Other Americans in Employment, Education, Income." Waltham, Massachusetts: Department of Sociology, Brandeis University.

Driedger, Diane, and Susan Gray, eds. 1992. *Imprinting Our Image: An International Anthology by Women with Disabilities*. Canada: Gynergy Books.

Duden, Barbara. 1991. Translated by Thomas Dunlap. *The Woman beneath the Skin: A Doctor's Patients in Eighteeth-Century Germany*. Cambridge, Massachusetts: Harvard University Press.

Dyck, Isabel. 1995. "Human Geographies: The Changing Lifeworlds of Women with Multiple Sclerosis." *Social Science and Medicine* 40 (3): 307–20.

Edemikpong, Ntiense Ben. 1992. "We Shall Not Fold Our Arms and Wait: Female Genital Mutilation." In *Imprinting Our Image: An International Anthology by Women with Disabilities*, eds. Diane Dreiger and Susan Gray, 124–33. Canada: Gynergy Books.

Englehardt, H. Tristram Jr. 1986. *The Foundations of Bioethics*. Oxford: Oxford University Press.

Fellows, Mary Louise, and Sherene Razack. 1994. "Seeking Relations: Law and Feminism Roundtables." *Signs: Journal of Women in Culture and Society* 19 (4): 1048–83.

Fiedler, Leslie A. 1984. "The Tyranny of the Normal." *The Hastings Center Report* April: 40–42.

Fine, Michelle, and Adrienne Asch, eds. 1988. *Women with Disabilities: Essays in Psychology, Culture and Politics*. Philadelphia: Temple University Press.

Finger, Anne. 1983. "Disability and Reproductive Rights." *Off Our Backs* 13 (9): 18–19.

Finger, Anne. 1990. *Past Due: A Story of Disability, Pregnancy and Birth.* Seattle: Seal Press.

Finger, Anne. 1994. "Feminism and Disability: Mother Knows Best?" *The Disability Rag and ReSource* September/October: 38–40.

Fisher, Bernice, and Roberta Galler. 1988. "Friendship and Fairness: How Disability Affects Friendship Between Women." In *Women with Disabilities: Essays in Psychology, Culture, and Politics,* eds. Michelle Fine and Adrienne Asch, 172–94. Philadelphia: Temple University Press.

Foucault, Michel. 1979. *Discipline and Punish.* New York: Vintage Books.

Fox, Meg. 1989. "Unreliable Allies: Subjective and Objective Time in Childbirth." In *Taking Our Time: Feminist Perspectives on Temporality,* eds. Frieda Johles Forman and Caoran Sowton, 123–34. Toronto: Pergamon Press.

Frank, Arthur W. 1991. *At the Will of the Body: Reflections on Illness.* Boston: Houghton Mifflin.

Frank, Gelya. 1988. "On Embodiment: A Case Study of Congenital Limb Deficiency in American Culture." In *Women with Disabilities: Essays in Psychology, Culture and Politics,* eds. Michelle Fine and Adrienne Asch, 41–71. Philadelphia: Temple University Press.

Gallagher, Hugh. 1993. "The New Stereotype." *Polio Society Update* August: 2–5.

Gill, Carol J. 1994. "Continuum Retort—Part II." *The Disability Rag and ReSource* March/April: 3–7.

Gilligan, Carol. 1982. In *A Different Voice: Psychological Theory and Women's Development.* Cambridge: Harvard University Press.

Goffman, Erving. 1963. *Stigma: Notes on the Management of Spoiled Identity.* New York: Simon and Schuster.

Goldenberg, Naomi R. 1990. *Returning Words to Flesh: Feminism, Psychoanalysis, and the Resurrection of the Body.* Boston: Beacon Press.

Grealy, Lucy. 1994. *Autobiography of a Face.* New York: HarperCollins.

Griffin, Susan. 1981. *Pornography and Silence: Culture's Revenge Against Nature.* New York: Harper.

Griffin, Susan. 1982. "The Way of All Ideology." *Signs: Journal of Women in Culture and Society* 8 (3): 641–60.

Hannaford, Susan. 1985. *Living Outside Inside. A Disabled Woman's Experience. Towards A Social and Political Perspective.* Berkeley: Canterbury Press.

Haraway, Donna. 1990. "A Manifesto for Cyborgs: Science, Technology, and Socialist Feminism in the 1980s." In *Feminism/Postmodernism,* ed. Linda J. Nicholson, 190–233. New York: Routledge.

Haraway, Donna J. 1991. *Simians, Cyborgs, and Women: The Reinvention of Nature.* New York: Routledge.

Harding, Sandra. 1986. *The Science Question in Feminism*. Ithaca, New York: Cornell University Press.

Health and Welfare Canada and Statistics Canada. 1981. *The Health of Canadians: Report of the Canada Health Survey*. Ottawa: Supply and Services Canada.

Hershey, Laura. 1994. "Choosing Disability." *Ms.* July/August: 26–32.

Higginbotham, Evelyn Brooks. 1992. "African-American Women's History and the Metalanguage of Race." *Signs: Journal of Women in Culture and Society* 17 (2): 251–74.

Hillyer, Barbara. 1993. *Feminism and Disability*. Norman and London: University of Oklahoma Press.

Hofsess, John. 1993. "Sue Rodriguez." *Transition* February: 6.

James, Janet Lee. 1993. *One Particular Harbor*. Chicago: The Noble Press.

Jeffreys, Toni. 1982. *The Mile-High Staircase*. Sydney: Hodder and Stoughton.

Johnson, Mary. 1990. "Defective Fetuses and Us." *The Disability Rag* March/April: 34.

Johnson, Mary. 1994. "Unanswered Questions." In *The Ragged Edge: The Disability Experience from the Pages of The First Fifteen Years of The Disability Rag*, ed. Barrett Shaw, 186–201. Louisville, Kentucky: The Advocado Press. (Article originally published in 1990.)

Jongbloed, Lyn, and Anne Crichton. 1990. "A New Definition of Disability: Implications for Rehabilitation Practice and Social Policy." *Canadian Journal of Occupational Therapy* 57 (1): 32–38.

Kahn, Robbie Pfeufer. 1989. "Women and Time in Childbirth and During Lactation." In *Taking Our Time: Feminist Perspectives on Temporality*, eds. Frieda Johles Forman and Caoran Sowton, 20–36. Toronto: Pergamon Press.

Kavka, Gregory S. 1992. "Disability and the Right to Work." *Social Philosophy and Policy* 9 (1): 262–90.

Kent, Deborah. 1988. "In Search of a Heroine: Images of Women with Disabilities in Fiction and Drama." In *Women with Disabilities: Essays in Psychology, Culture, and Politics*, eds. Michelle Fine and Adrienne Asch, 229–44. Philadelphia: Temple University Press.

Kimball, Meredith M. 1995. *Feminist Visions of Gender Similarities and Differences*. Binghamton, NY: The Haworth Press.

Kittay, Eva Feder, and Diana T. Meyers, eds. 1987. *Women and Moral Theory*. Totowa: Rowman and Littlefield.

Klein, Bonnie Sherr. 1992. "'We Are Who You Are:' Feminism and Disability." *Ms.* 3 (3): 70–74.

Kleinman, Arthur, MD. 1988. *The Illness Narratives: Suffering, Healing, and the Human Condition*. New York: Basic Books.

Korda, Holly. 1994. "Review of *Rationing America's Medical Care: The Oregon Plan and Beyond.*" *Disability Studies Quarterly* 14 (3): 54–56.

Kreinheder, Albert. 1991. *Body and Soul: The Other Side of Illness.* Toronto: Inner City Books.

LaPlante, Mitchell P. 1991. *Disability Statistics Report (2): Disability Risks of Chronic Illnesses and Impairments.* Washington, DC: National Institute on Disability and Rehabilitation Research, U.S. Department of Education.

Leder, Drew. 1990. *The Absent Body.* Chicago: University of Chicago Press.

Lessing, Jill. 1981. "Denial and Disability." *Off Our Backs* 11 (5): 21.

Linton, Simi. 1994. "Teaching Disability Studies." *Disability Studies Quarterly* 14 (2): 44–46.

Lorde, Audre. 1984. *Sister Outsider: Essays and Speeches.* Freedom, CA: The Crossing Press.

Macauley, David. 1991. "Interview with Susan Griffin." *American Philosophical Association Newsletter on Feminism and Philosophy,* Fall.

Madruga, Lenor. 1979. *One Step at a Time.* Toronto: McGraw-Hill.

Mairs, Nancy. 1994. *Voice Lessons: On Becoming a (Woman) Writer.* Boston: Beacon Press.

Martin, Jane Roland. 1994. "Methodological Essentialism, False Difference, and Other Dangerous Traps." *Signs: Journal of Women in Culture and Society* 19 (3): 630–57.

Mason, Micheline. 1987. "'The Courage of Crippled Clara'—the Media and Disability." In *Out of Focus: Writings on Women and the Media,* eds. Kath Davies, Julienne Dickey, and Teresa Stratford, 63–66. London: The Women's Press.

Matthews, Gwyneth Ferguson. 1983. *Voices from the Shadows: Women with Disabilities Speak Out.* Toronto: The Women's Press.

McDonough, Peggy. 1990. "Congenital Disability and Medical Research: The Development of Amniocentesis." *Women and Health* 16 (3/4): 137–53.

Milner, Henry. 1989. *Sweden: Social Democracy in Practice.* New York: Oxford University Press.

Monmaney, Terence. 1993. "Marshall's Hunch." *The New Yorker,* 20 September: 64–72.

Moore, Maureen. 1985. "Coping with Pelvic Inflammatory Disease." In *Women and Disability,* eds. Frances Rooney and Pat Israel, 18–20. *Resources for Feminist Research* 14 (1).

Morgan, Kathryn. 1991. "Women and the Knife. Cosmetic Surgery and the Colonization of Women's Bodies." *Hypatia: A Journal of Feminist Philosophy* 6 (3): 25–53.

Morris, Jenny, ed. 1989. *Able Lives: Women's Experience of Paralysis*. London: The Women's Press.

Morris, Jenny. 1991. *Pride Against Prejudice: Transforming Attitudes to Disability*. Philadelphia, PA: New Society Publishers.

Ms., 1989. "Crisis of Elder Care." October: 73–79.

Muller, Charlotte. 1979. "Women and Health Statistics: Areas of Deficient Data Collection and Integration." *Women and Health* 4 (1): 37–59.

Murphy, Robert F. 1990. *The Body Silent*. New York: W.W. Norton.

Newsweek. 1992. "The Misreading of Dyslexia." 3 February: 57.

Nuland, Sherwin B. 1993. *How We Die: Reflections on Life's Final Chapter*. New York: Vintage Books.

Owen, Mary Jane. 1994. "Like Squabbling Cubs." In *The Ragged Edge: The Disability Experience from the Pages of The First Fifteen Years of The Disability Rag*, ed. Barrett Shaw, 7–10. Louisville, KY: Advocado Press.

Pope, Andrew M., and Alvin R. Tarlov, eds. 1991. *Disability in America: Toward a National Agenda for Prevention*. Washington, DC: National Academy Press.

Ramsay, A. Melvin. 1986. *Postviral Fatigue Syndrome: The Saga of Royal Free Disease*. London: Gower Medical Publishing.

Rawlinson, Mary C. 1983. "The Facticity of Illness and the Appropriation of Health." In *Phenomenology in a Pluralistic Context*, eds. William L. McBride and Calvin O. Schrag, 155–66. Albany: SUNY Press.

Register, Cheri. 1987. *Living with Chronic Illness: Days of Patience and Passion*. New York: Bantam.

Reisine, Susan T., and Judith Fifield. 1988. "Defining Disability for Women and the Problem of Unpaid Work." *Psychology of Women Quarterly* 12: 401–15.

Rich, Adrienne. 1976. *Of Woman Born: Motherhood as Experience and Institution*. New York: W.W. Norton.

Rich, Adrienne. 1986. "Notes toward a Politics of Location (1984)." In *Blood, Bread and Poetry*, 210–31. New York: W.W. Norton.

Ridington, Jillian. 1989. "Beating the 'Odds': Violence and Women with Disabilities." Vancouver, B.C.: DisAbled Women's Network Canada Position Paper 2.

Rooney, Frances, and Pat Israel, eds. 1985. *Women and Disability*. *Resources for Feminist Research* 14 (1).

Rothman, David J. 1992. "Rationing Life." *The New York Review of Books* 5 March: 32–37.

Rudner, Andrea. 1992. "Chronic Fatigue Syndrome: Searching for the Answers." *Ms.* May/June: 33–36.

Russell, Susan. 1985. "Social Dimensions of Disability: Women and M.S." In *Women and Disability. Resources for Feminist Research* 14 (1): 56–58.

Russo, Nancy Felipe, and Mary A. Jansen. 1988. "Women, Work, and Disability: Opportunities and Challenges." In *Women with Disabilities: Essays in Psychology, Culture, and Politics*, eds. Michelle Fine and Adrienne Asch, 229–44. Philadelphia: Temple University Press.

Sacks, Oliver. 1987. *The Man Who Mistook His Wife for a Hat and Other Clinical Tales.* New York: HarperCollins.

Sacks, Oliver. 1988. "The Revolution of the Deaf." *The New York Review of Books* 2 June: 23–28.

Sacks, Oliver. 1992a. "The Last Hippie." *The New York Review of Books* 26 March: 53–62.

Sacks, Oliver. 1992b. "Letters: Phantom Limbs—Oliver Sacks Replies." *The New York Review of Books* 30 January: 45–46.

Samuelson, Deborah. 1986. "A Letter to My Daughter/Myself on Facing the Collective Fear of Being Different." *Feminist Studies* 12 (1): 155–67.

Saxton, Marsha, and Florence Howe, eds. 1987. *With Wings: An Anthology of Literature by and about Women with Disabilities.* New York: The Feminist Press at the City University of New York.

Shaul, Susan, Pamela J. Dowling, and Bernice F. Laden. 1985. "Like Other Women: Perspectives of Mothers with Disabilities." In *Women and Disability: The Double Handicap*, eds. Mary Jo Deegan and Nancy A. Brooks, 133–42. New Brunswick, NJ: Transaction Books.

Shaw, Barrett. 1994. "Meet the Other Callahan." *The Disability Rag and ReSource* March/April: 32–33.

Sheets-Johnstone, Maxine. 1992a. "Corporeal Archetypes and Power: Preliminary Clarifications and Considerations of Sex." *Hypatia: A Journal of Feminist Philosophy* 7 (3): 38–76.

Sheets-Johnstone, Maxine, ed. 1992b. *Giving the Body Its Due.* Albany: State University of New York Press.

Shelp, Earl E. 1984. "The Experience of Illness: Integrating Metaphors and the Transcendence of Illness." *The Journal of Medicine and Philosophy* 9: 253–56.

Sherwin, Susan. 1984–85. "A Feminist Approach to Ethics." *Dalhousie Review* 64 (4): 704–13.

Sherwin, Susan. 1987. "Feminist Ethics and In Vitro Fertilization." In *Science, Morality and Feminist Theory*, eds. Marsha Hanen and Kai Nielsen, 265–84. Calgary: University of Calgary Press.

Sherwin, Susan. 1992. *No Longer Patient: Feminist Ethics and Health Care.* Philadelphia: Temple University Press.

Silvers, Anita. 1994. "'Defective' Agents: Equality, Difference and the Tyranny of the Normal." *Journal of Social Philosophy* 25 (June): 154–75.

Silvers, Anita. 1995. "Reconciling Equality to Difference: Caring (F)or Justice For People With Disabilities." *Hypatia: A Journal of Feminist Philosophy* 10 (1): 30–55.

Snitow, Ann. 1990. "A Gender Diary." In *Conflicts in Feminism*, eds. Marianne Hirsch and Evelyn Fox Keller. New York: Routledge.

Sobsey, Dick. 1989. "Sexual Offenses: Research and Implications." *Transition*, May: 17–18.

Sontag, Susan. 1977. "Illness as Metaphor." In *Illness as Metaphor and AIDS and Its Metaphors*. New York: Doubleday Anchor.

Sontag, Susan. 1988. "AIDS and Its Metaphors." In *Illness as Metaphor and AIDS and Its Metaphors*. New York: Doubleday Anchor.

Spelman, Elizabeth V. 1988. *Inessential Woman: Problems of Exclusion in Feminist Thought.* Boston: Beacon Press.

Statistics Canada. 1986 and 1991. *The Health and Activity Limitation Survey.* Ottawa: Minister of Supply and Services Canada.

Stewart, Houston, Beth Percival, and Elizabeth R. Epperly, eds. 1992. *The More We Get Together: Women and Disability.* Charlottetown, PEI: Gynergy Books.

Thorne, Sally E. 1993. *Negotiating Health Care: The Social Context of Chronic Illness.* Newbury Park, CA: Sage Publications.

Todoroff, Milana, and Tanya Lewis. 1992. "The Personal and Social Implications of 'Passing' in the Lives of Women Living with a Chronic Illness or Disability." In *The More We Get Together: Women and Disability*, eds. Houston Stewart, Beth Percival, and Elizabeth R. Epperly, 29–38. Charlottetown, PEI: Gynergy Books.

Toombs, Kay S. 1992. *The Meaning of Illness: A Phenomenological Account of the Different Perspectives of Physician and Patient* (Philosophy and Medicine, Vol. 42). Dordrecht: Kluwer.

Tronto, Joan C. 1993. *Moral Boundaries: A Political Argument for an Ethic of Care.* New York: Routledge.

U.N. Decade of Disabled Persons 1983–1992. 1983. *World Programme of Action Concerning Disabled Persons.* New York: United Nations.

Vanderheiden, Gregg C. 1990. "Thirty-Something Million: Should They Be Exceptions?" *Human Factors* 32 (4): 383–96.

Vargas, James W. 1989. "Enhancing Self-Esteem." Keynote Address to the 10th Annual Adult Special Education Conference, Vancouver, B.C. 22–23 February. Personal copy.

Vlug, Henry. 1992. "Deaf Culture or Disability?" *Transition* December 92/January 93: 6–7, 24–25.

Wade, Cheryl Marie. 1994a. "It Ain't Exactly Sexy." In *The Ragged Edge: The Disability Experience from the Pages of The First Fifteen Years of The Disability Rag*, ed. Barrett Shaw, 88–90. Louisville, KY: Advocado Press. (Article originally published in 1991.)

Wade, Cheryl Marie. 1994b. "Identity." *The Disability Rag and ReSource* September/October: 32–36.

Weston, Anthony. 1991. "Toward a Social Critique of Bioethics." *Journal of Social Philosophy* 22 (2): 109–118.

Wilber, Ken, and Treya Wilber. 1988. "Do We Make Ourselves Sick?" *New Age Journal* September/October: 50–54, 85–90.

Wolf, Naomi. 1990. *The Beauty Myth*. Toronto: Vintage Books.

The Women's Review of Books. July 1994a. "Biology is Not Destiny: An Interview with the Women's Community Cancer Project." 11 (10–11): 7–10. Wellesley, MA: The Women's Review.

The Women's Review of Books. July 1994b. "The Politics of Genetics: A conversation with Anne Fausto-Sterling and Diane Paul." 11 (10–11): 17–20. Wellesley, MA: The Women's Review.

Woodward, John R. 1994a. "It Can Happen Here." In *The Ragged Edge: The Disability Experience from the Pages of The First Fifteen Years of The Disability Rag*, ed. Barrett Shaw, 230–35. Louisville, KY: Advocado Press.

Woodward, John R. 1994b. "Mismanaged Care." *The Disability Rag and ReSource* July/August: 18–23.

Woodward, John R. 1995. "A Place for Everyone, and Everyone in Place: A History of the Diagnostic and Statistical Manual of Mental Disorders." *The Disability Rag and ReSource* March/April: 17–22.

Woodward, Kathleen. 1991. *Aging and Its Discontents: Freud and Other Fictions*. Bloomington: Indiana University Press.

Wright, Beatrice A. 1983. *Physical Disability—A Psychosocial Approach*, 2nd ed. New York: HarperCollins.

Young, Iris Marion. 1990. *Throwing Like a Girl and Other Essays in Feminist Philosophy and Social Theory*. Bloomington: Indiana University Press.

Zaner, Richard M. 1983. "Flirtations or Engagement? Prolegomenon to a Philosophy of Medicine." In *Phenomenology in a Pluralistic Context*, eds. William L. McBride and Calvin O. Schrag, 139–54. Albany: State University of New York Press.

Zola, Irving Kenneth. 1972. "Medicine as an Institution of Social Control." *Sociological Review* 20: 487–504.

Zola, Irving Kenneth. 1993. "Self, Identity, and the Naming Question: Reflections on the Language of Disability." *Social Science and Medicine* 36 (2): 167–73.